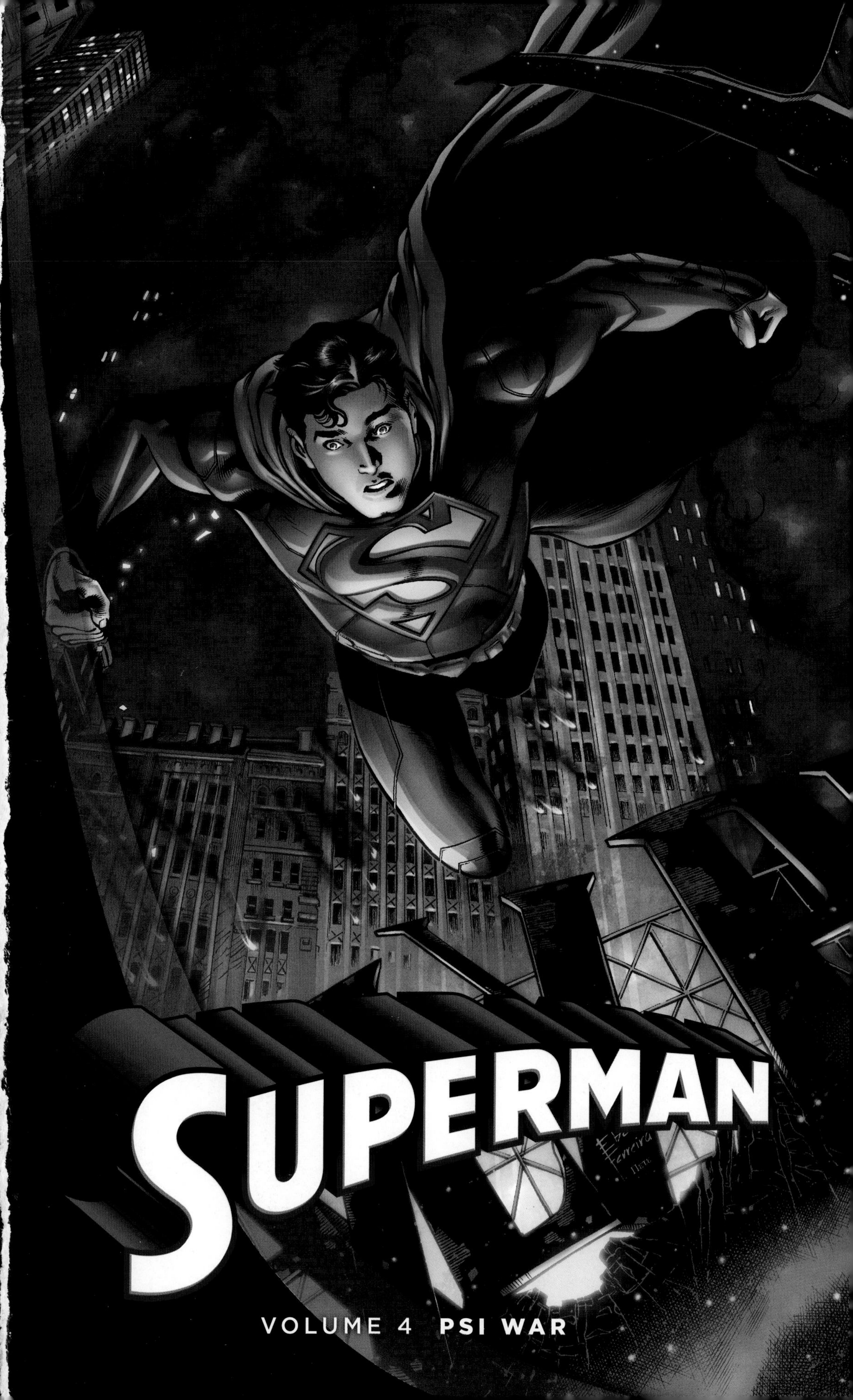

SUPERMAN

VOLUME 4 **PSI WAR**

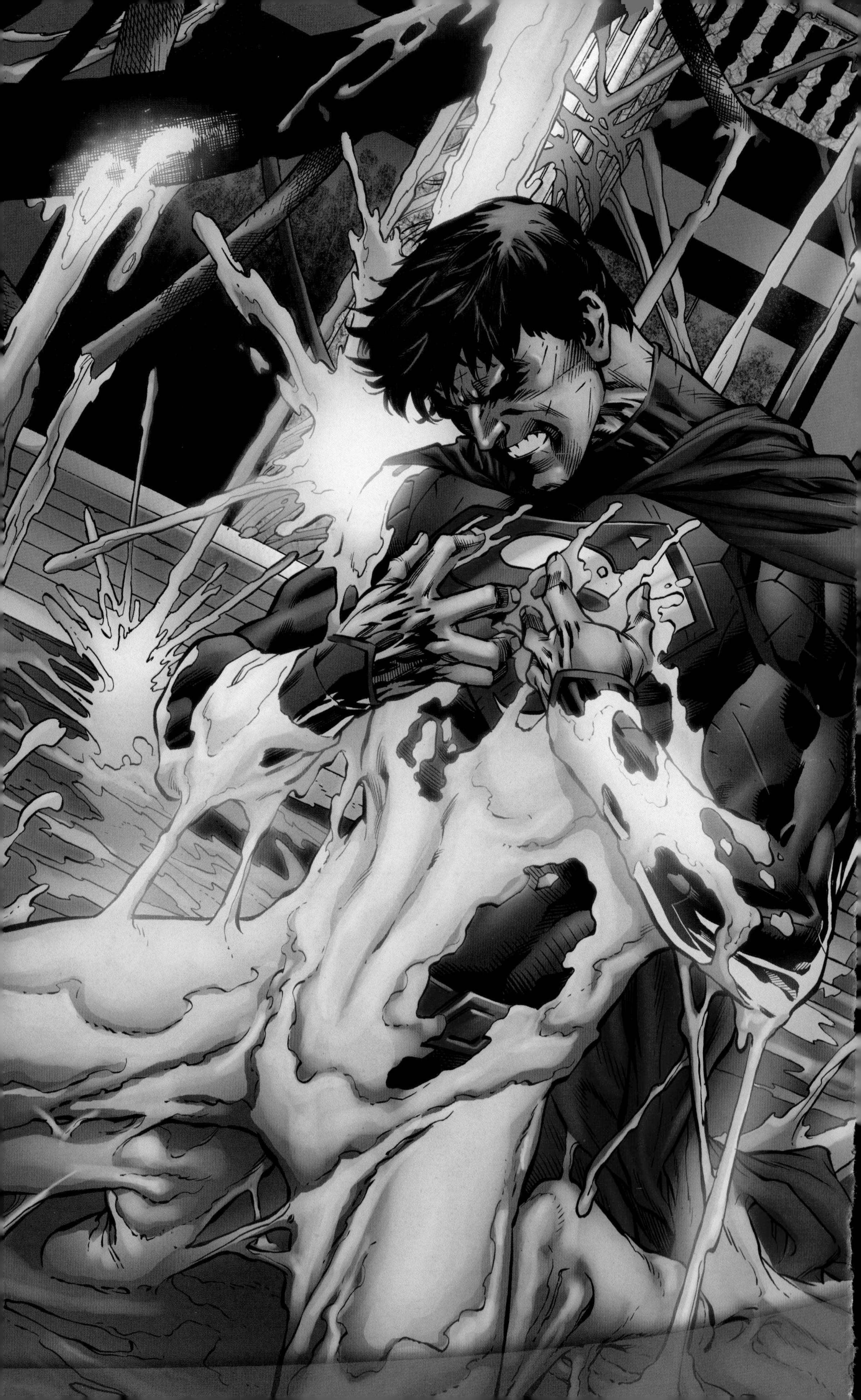

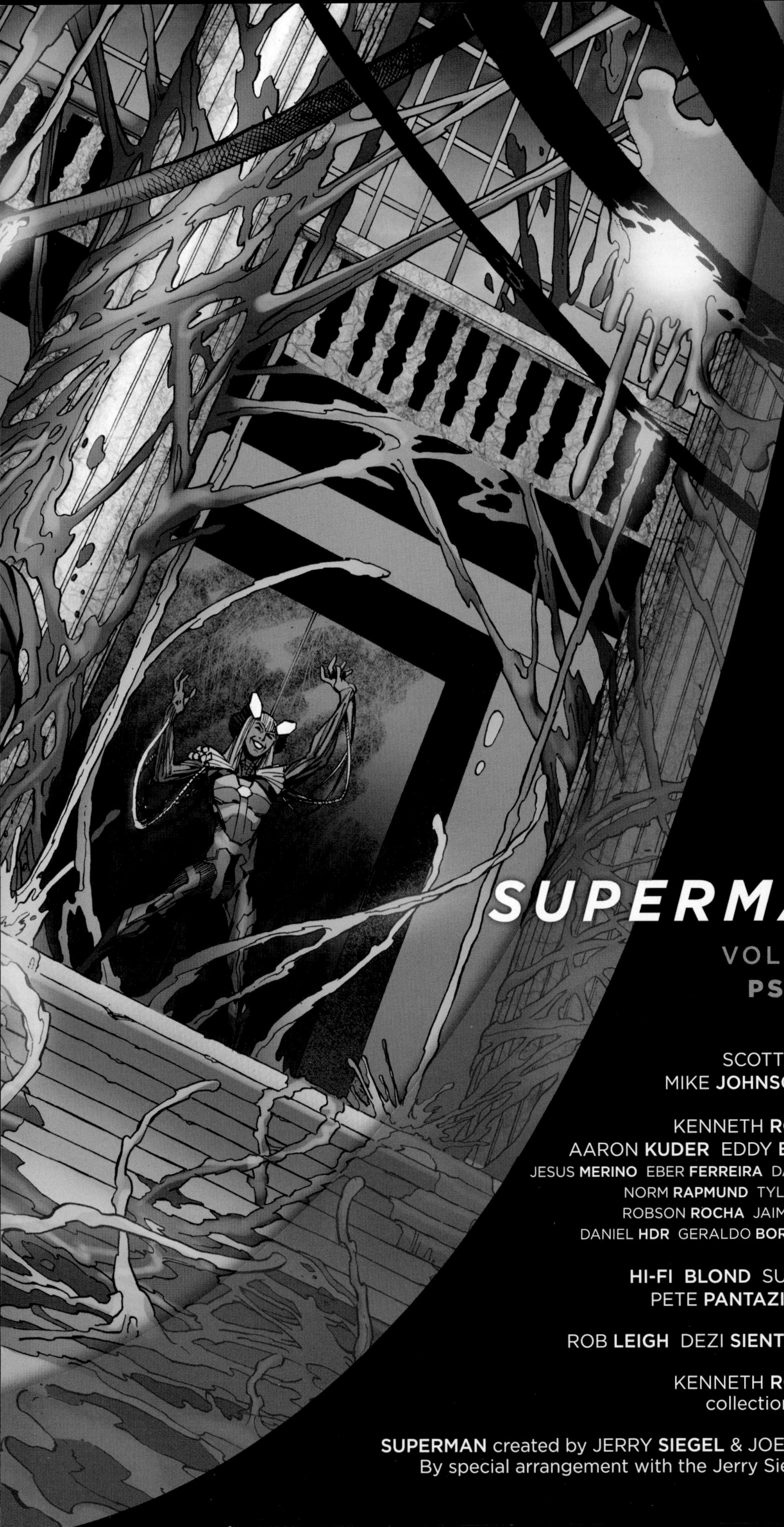

SUPERMAN

VOLUME 4
PSI WAR

SCOTT **LOBDELL**
MIKE **JOHNSON** writers

KENNETH **ROCAFORT**
AARON **KUDER** EDDY **BARROWS**
JESUS **MERINO** EBER **FERREIRA** DAN **JURGENS**
NORM **RAPMUND** TYLER **KIRKHAM**
ROBSON **ROCHA** JAIME **MENDOZA**
DANIEL **HDR** GERALDO **BORGES** artists

HI-FI BLOND SUNNY **GHO**
PETE **PANTAZIS** colorists

ROB **LEIGH** DEZI **SIENTY** letterers

KENNETH **ROCAFORT**
collection cover art

SUPERMAN created by JERRY **SIEGEL** & JOE **SHUSTER**
By special arrangement with the Jerry Siegel family

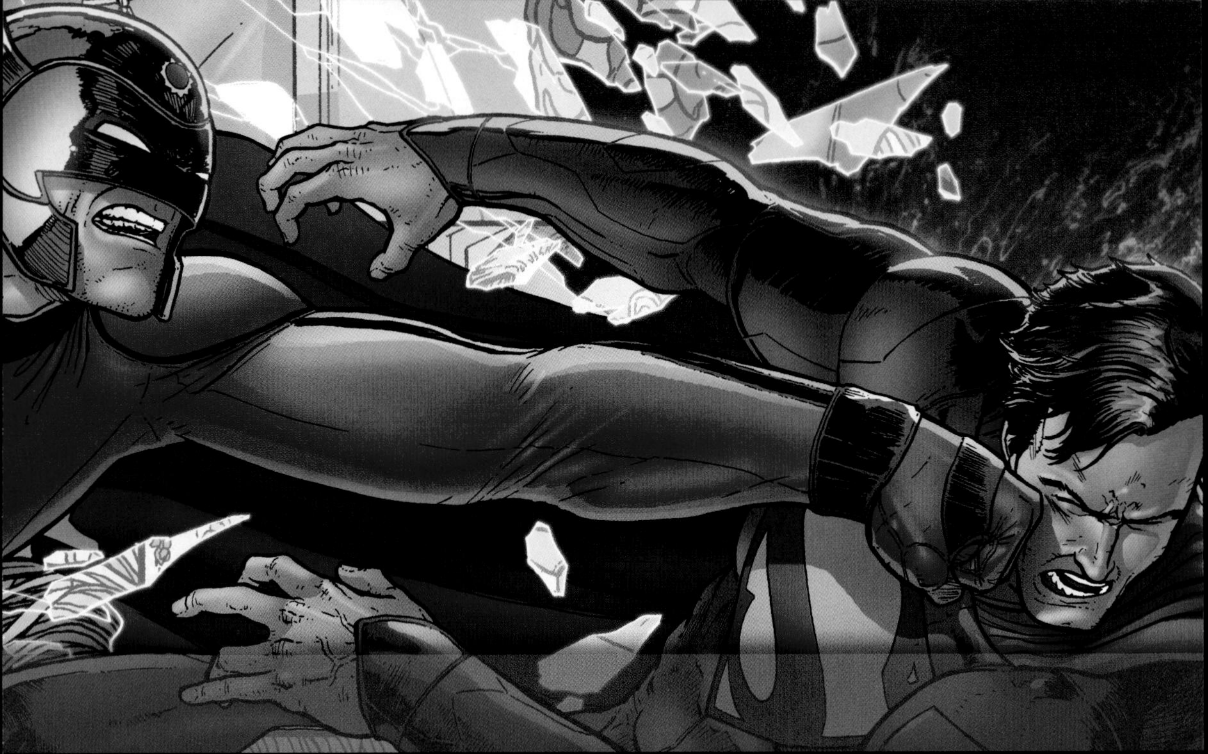

EDDIE BERGANZA Editor - Original Series ANTHONY MARQUES Assistant Editor - Original Series
ROWENA YOW Editor ROBBIN BROSTERMAN Design Director - Books ROBBIE BIEDERMAN Publication Design

BOB HARRAS Senior VP - Editor-in-Chief, DC Comics

DIANE NELSON President DAN DIDIO and JIM LEE Co-Publishers GEOFF JOHNS Chief Creative Officer
AMIT DESAI Senior VP - Marketing and Franchise Management AMY GENKINS Senior VP - Business and Legal Affairs
NAIRI GARDINER Senior VP - Finance JEFF BOISON VP - Publishing Planning
MARK CHIARELLO VP - Art Direction and Design JOHN CUNNINGHAM VP - Marketing
TERRI CUNNINGHAM VP - Editorial Administration LARRY GANEM VP - Talent Relations and Services
ALISON GILL Senior VP - Manufacturing and Operations HANK KANALZ Senior VP - Vertigo and Integrated Publishing
JAY KOGAN VP - Business and Legal Affairs, Publishing JACK MAHAN VP - Business Affairs, Talent
NICK NAPOLITANO VP - Manufacturing Administration SUE POHJA VP - Book Sales FRED RUIZ VP - Manufacturing Operations
COURTNEY SIMMONS Senior VP - Publicity BOB WAYNE Senior VP - Sales

SUPERMAN VOLUME 4: PSI WAR

DC Comics, 1700 Broadway, New York, NY 10019
A Warner Bros. Entertainment Company.
Printed by RR Donnelley, Salem, VA, USA. 7/4/14. First Printing.

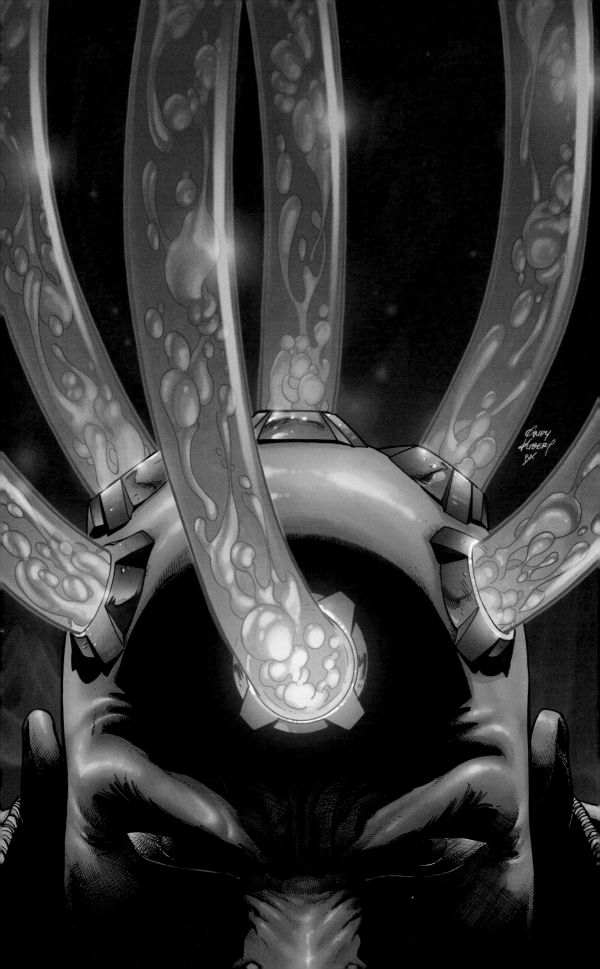

THE LAST BYLINE

SCOTT LOBDELL writer DAN JURGENS penciller NORM RAPMUND inker cover art by ANDY KUBERT & BRAD ANDERSON

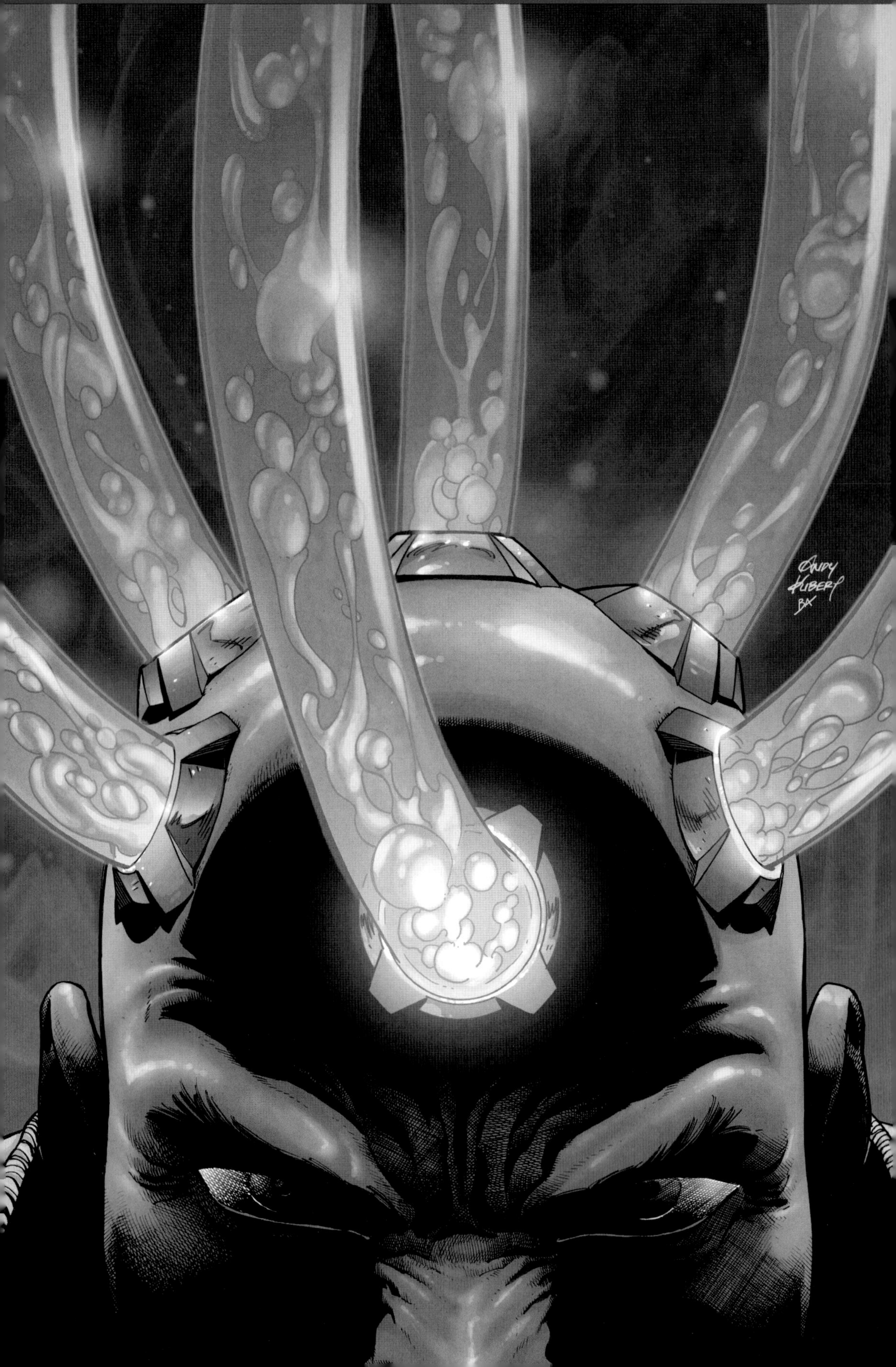

ANDY
KUBERT
BA

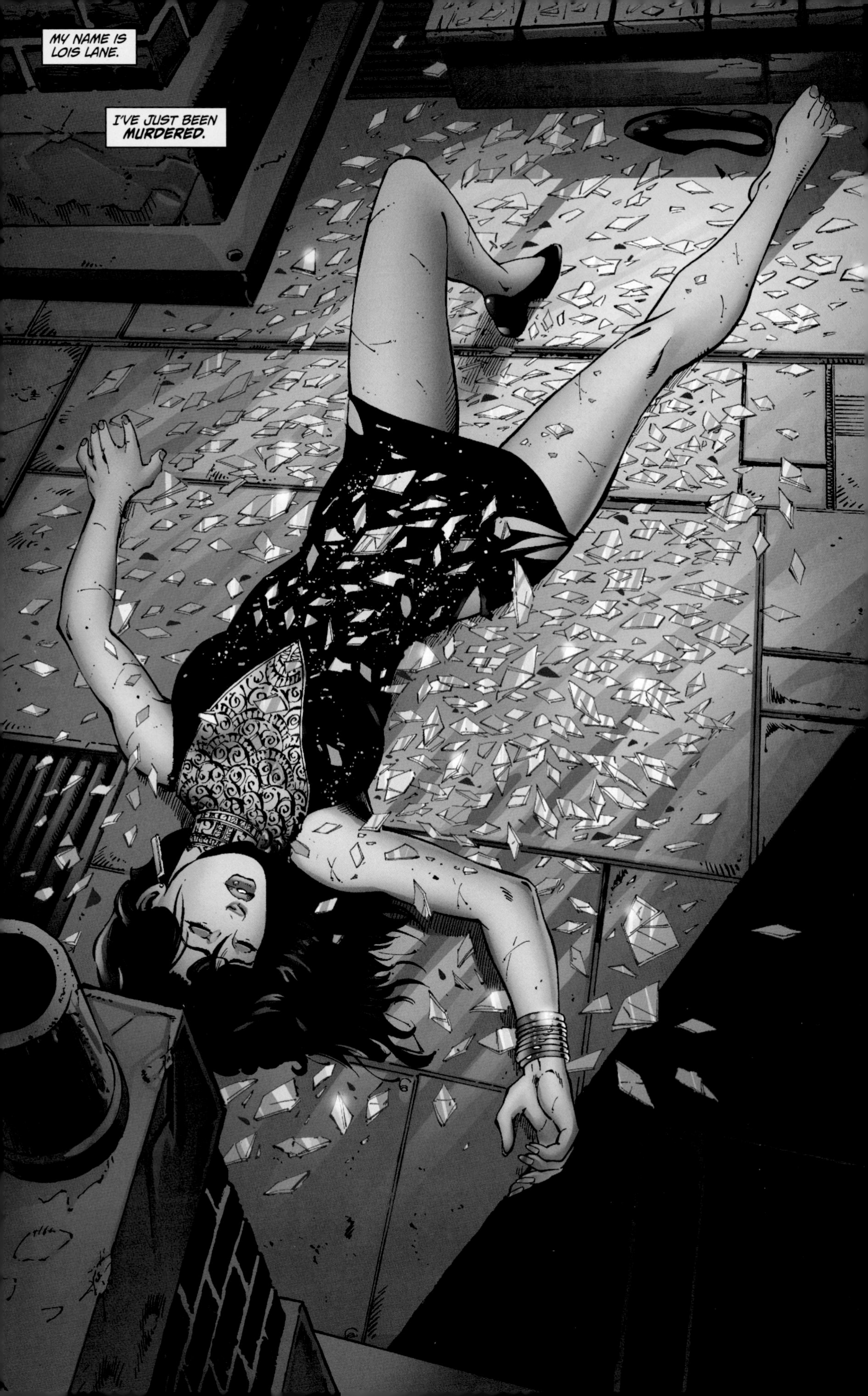
MY NAME IS LOIS LANE.
I'VE JUST BEEN MURDERED.

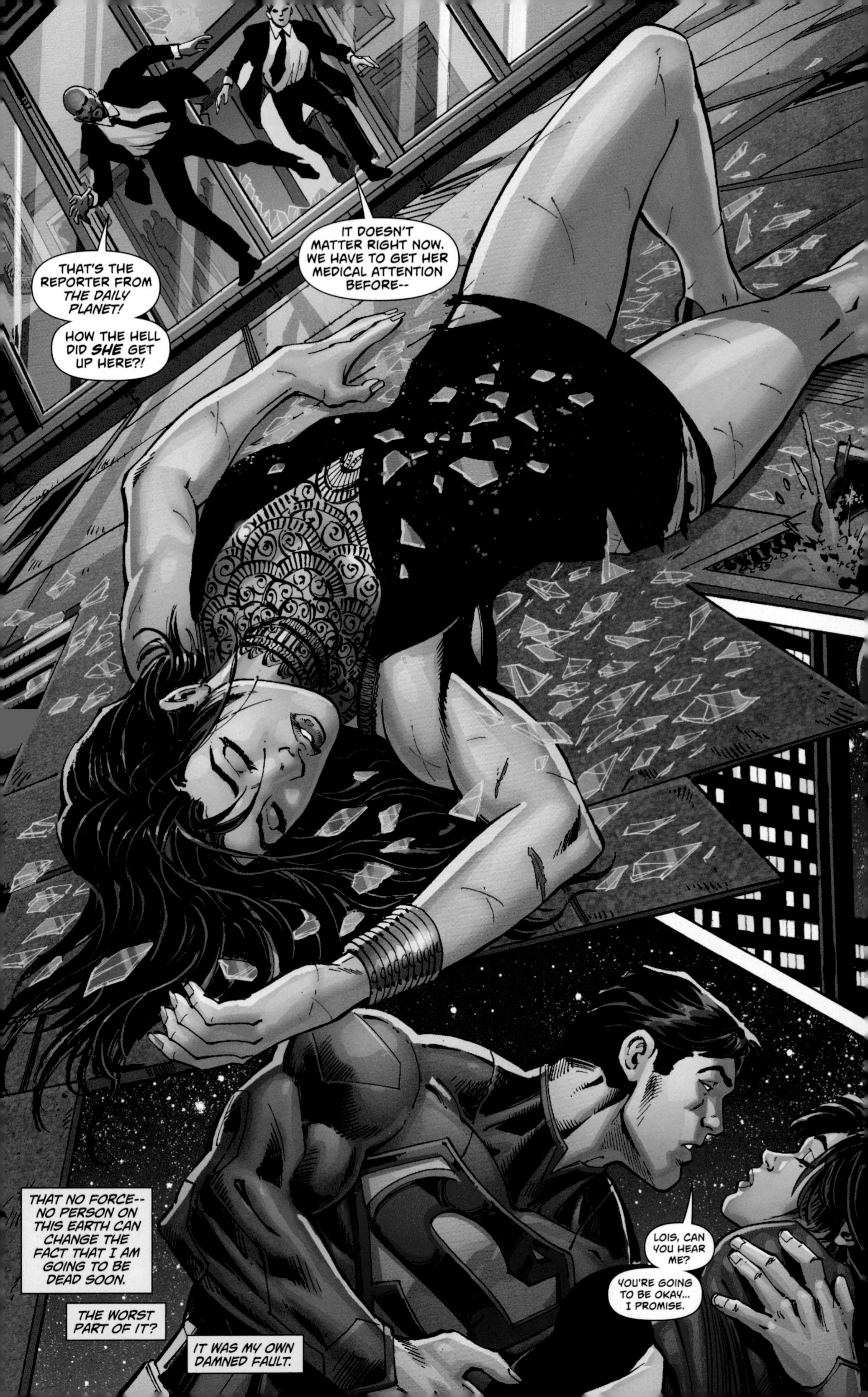
THAT'S THE REPORTER FROM THE DAILY PLANET!
HOW THE HELL DID SHE GET UP HERE?!
IT DOESN'T MATTER RIGHT NOW. WE HAVE TO GET HER MEDICAL ATTENTION BEFORE--
THAT NO FORCE-- NO PERSON ON THIS EARTH CAN CHANGE THE FACT THAT I AM GOING TO BE DEAD SOON.
THE WORST PART OF IT?
IT WAS MY OWN DAMNED FAULT.
LOIS, CAN YOU HEAR ME?
YOU'RE GOING TO BE OKAY... I PROMISE.

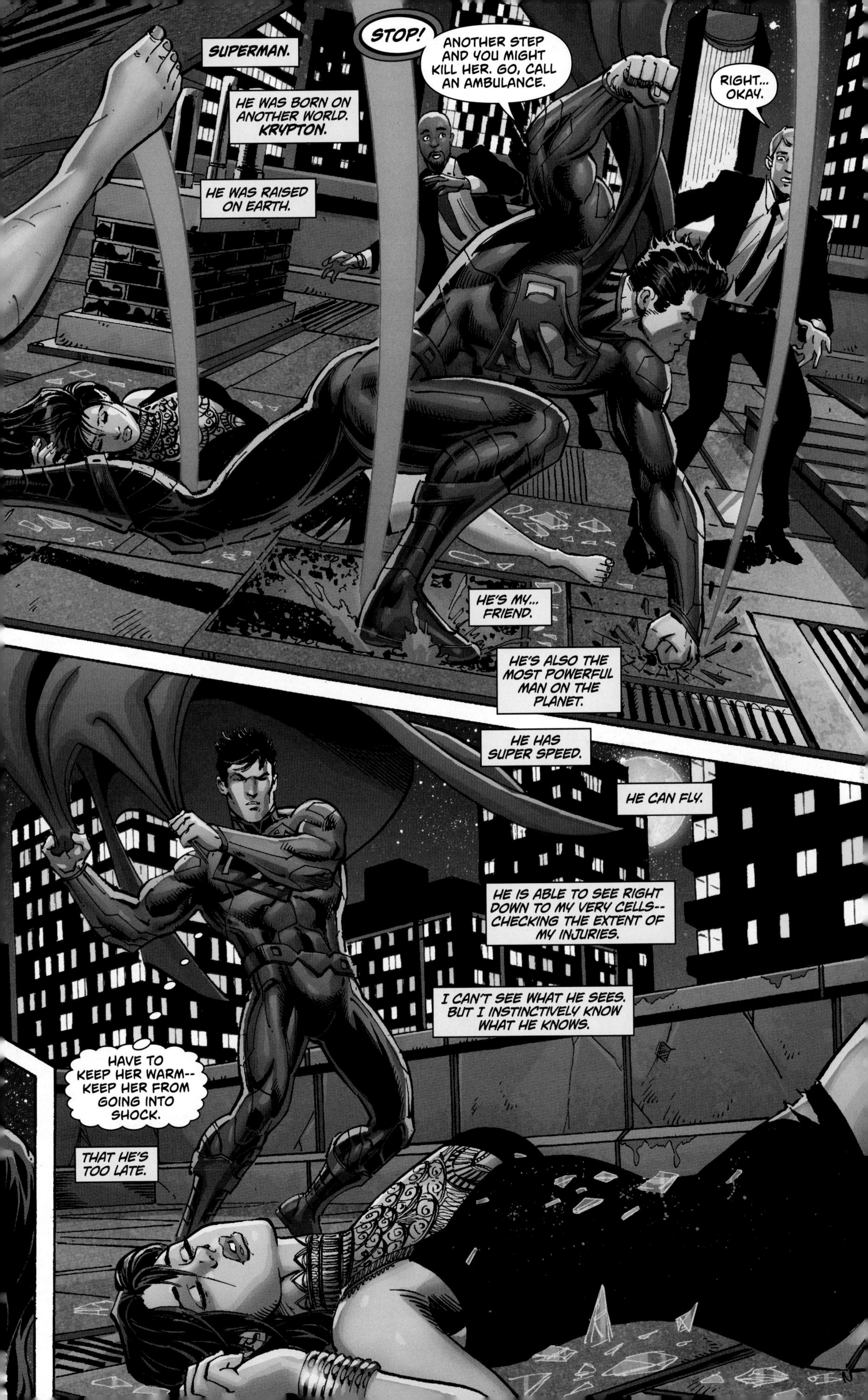
SUPERMAN.
HE WAS BORN ON ANOTHER WORLD. KRYPTON.
HE WAS RAISED ON EARTH.
STOP!
ANOTHER STEP AND YOU MIGHT KILL HER. GO, CALL AN AMBULANCE.
RIGHT... OKAY.
HE'S MY... FRIEND.
HE'S ALSO THE MOST POWERFUL MAN ON THE PLANET.
HE HAS SUPER SPEED.
HE CAN FLY.
HE IS ABLE TO SEE RIGHT DOWN TO MY VERY CELLS-- CHECKING THE EXTENT OF MY INJURIES.
I CAN'T SEE WHAT HE SEES. BUT I INSTINCTIVELY KNOW WHAT HE KNOWS.
HAVE TO KEEP HER WARM-- KEEP HER FROM GOING INTO SHOCK.
THAT HE'S TOO LATE.

Chapter One

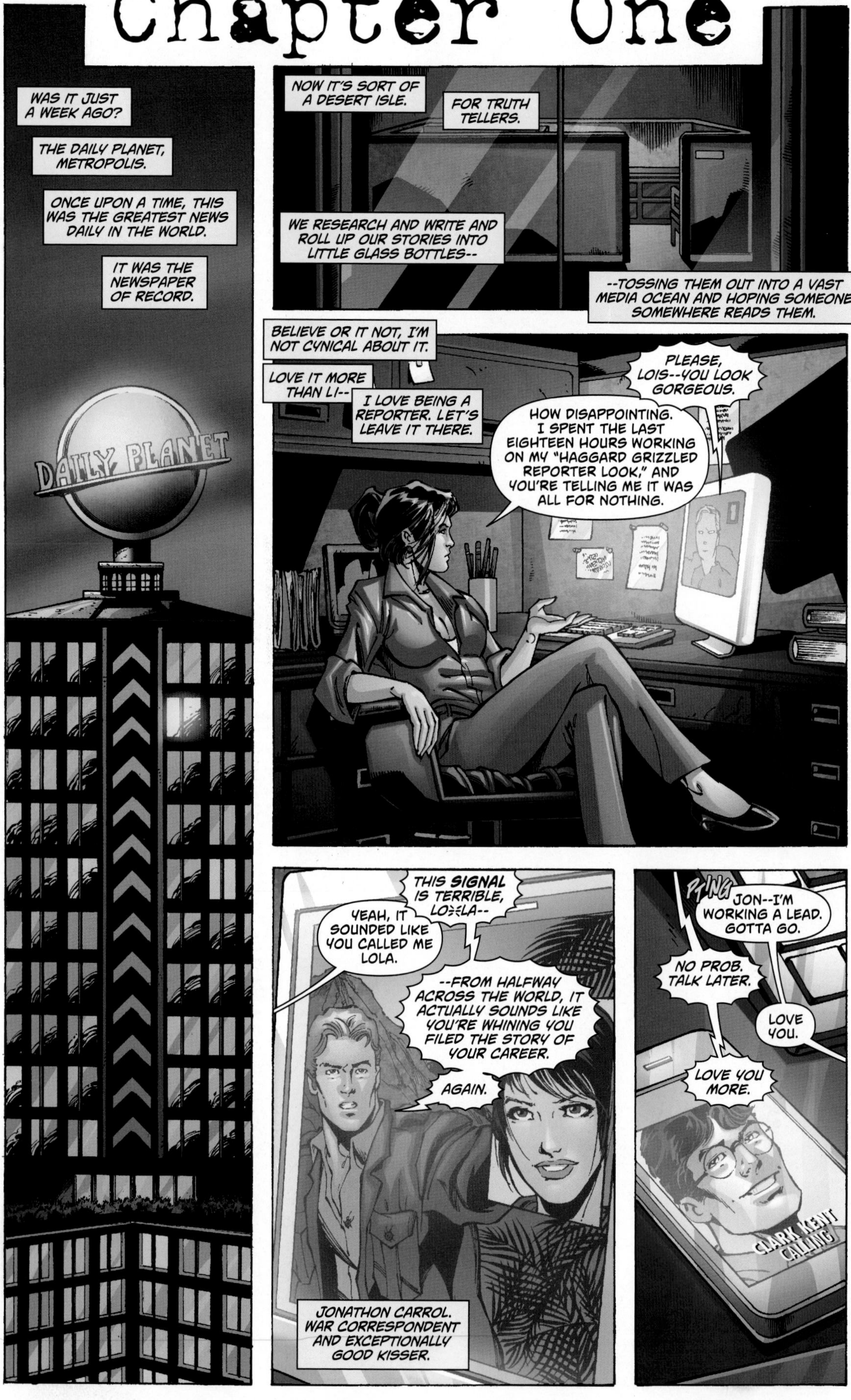

WAS IT JUST A WEEK AGO?
THE DAILY PLANET, METROPOLIS.
ONCE UPON A TIME, THIS WAS THE GREATEST NEWS DAILY IN THE WORLD.
IT WAS THE NEWSPAPER OF RECORD.
DAILY PLANET
NOW IT'S SORT OF A DESERT ISLE.
FOR TRUTH TELLERS.
WE RESEARCH AND WRITE AND ROLL UP OUR STORIES INTO LITTLE GLASS BOTTLES--
--TOSSING THEM OUT INTO A VAST MEDIA OCEAN AND HOPING SOMEONE SOMEWHERE READS THEM.
BELIEVE OR IT NOT, I'M NOT CYNICAL ABOUT IT.
LOVE IT MORE THAN LI--
I LOVE BEING A REPORTER. LET'S LEAVE IT THERE.
PLEASE, LOIS--YOU LOOK GORGEOUS.
HOW DISAPPOINTING. I SPENT THE LAST EIGHTEEN HOURS WORKING ON MY "HAGGARD GRIZZLED REPORTER LOOK," AND YOU'RE TELLING ME IT WAS ALL FOR NOTHING.
THIS SIGNAL IS TERRIBLE, LO--LA--
YEAH, IT SOUNDED LIKE YOU CALLED ME LOLA.
--FROM HALFWAY ACROSS THE WORLD, IT ACTUALLY SOUNDS LIKE YOU'RE WHINING YOU FILED THE STORY OF YOUR CAREER.
AGAIN.
JONATHON CARROL. WAR CORRESPONDENT AND EXCEPTIONALLY GOOD KISSER.
PING
JON--I'M WORKING A LEAD. GOTTA GO.
NO PROB. TALK LATER.
LOVE YOU.
LOVE YOU MORE.
CLARK KENT CALLING

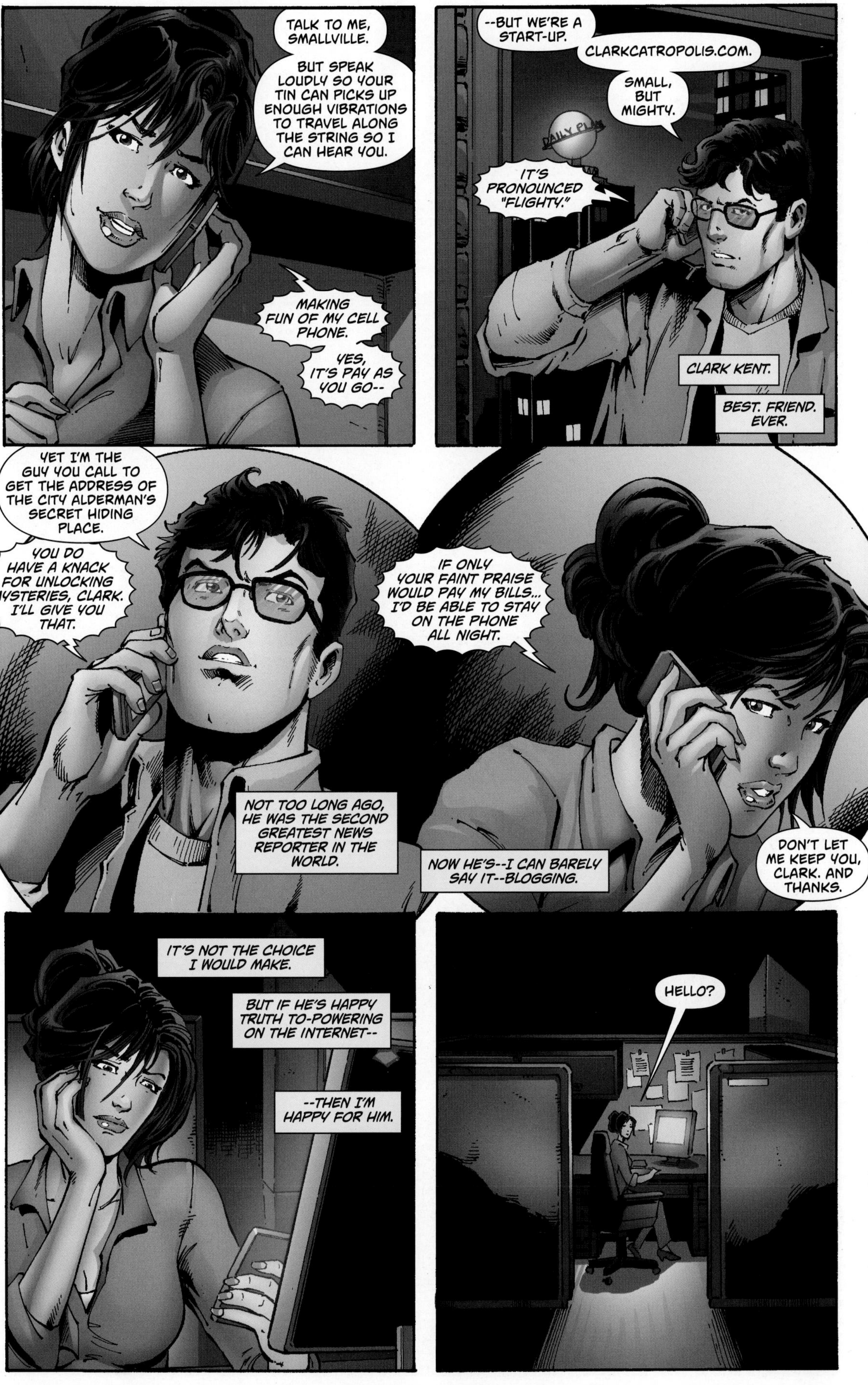
TALK TO ME, SMALLVILLE.
BUT SPEAK LOUDLY SO YOUR TIN CAN PICKS UP ENOUGH VIBRATIONS TO TRAVEL ALONG THE STRING SO I CAN HEAR YOU.
MAKING FUN OF MY CELL PHONE.
YES, IT'S PAY AS YOU GO--
--BUT WE'RE A START-UP.
CLARKCATROPOLIS.COM.
SMALL, BUT MIGHTY.
IT'S PRONOUNCED "FLIGHTY."
CLARK KENT.
BEST. FRIEND. EVER.
YET I'M THE GUY YOU CALL TO GET THE ADDRESS OF THE CITY ALDERMAN'S SECRET HIDING PLACE.
YOU DO HAVE A KNACK FOR UNLOCKING MYSTERIES, CLARK. I'LL GIVE YOU THAT.
IF ONLY YOUR FAINT PRAISE WOULD PAY MY BILLS... I'D BE ABLE TO STAY ON THE PHONE ALL NIGHT.
NOT TOO LONG AGO, HE WAS THE SECOND GREATEST NEWS REPORTER IN THE WORLD.
NOW HE'S--I CAN BARELY SAY IT--BLOGGING.
DON'T LET ME KEEP YOU, CLARK. AND THANKS.
IT'S NOT THE CHOICE I WOULD MAKE.
BUT IF HE'S HAPPY TRUTH TO-POWERING ON THE INTERNET--
--THEN I'M HAPPY FOR HIM.
HELLO?

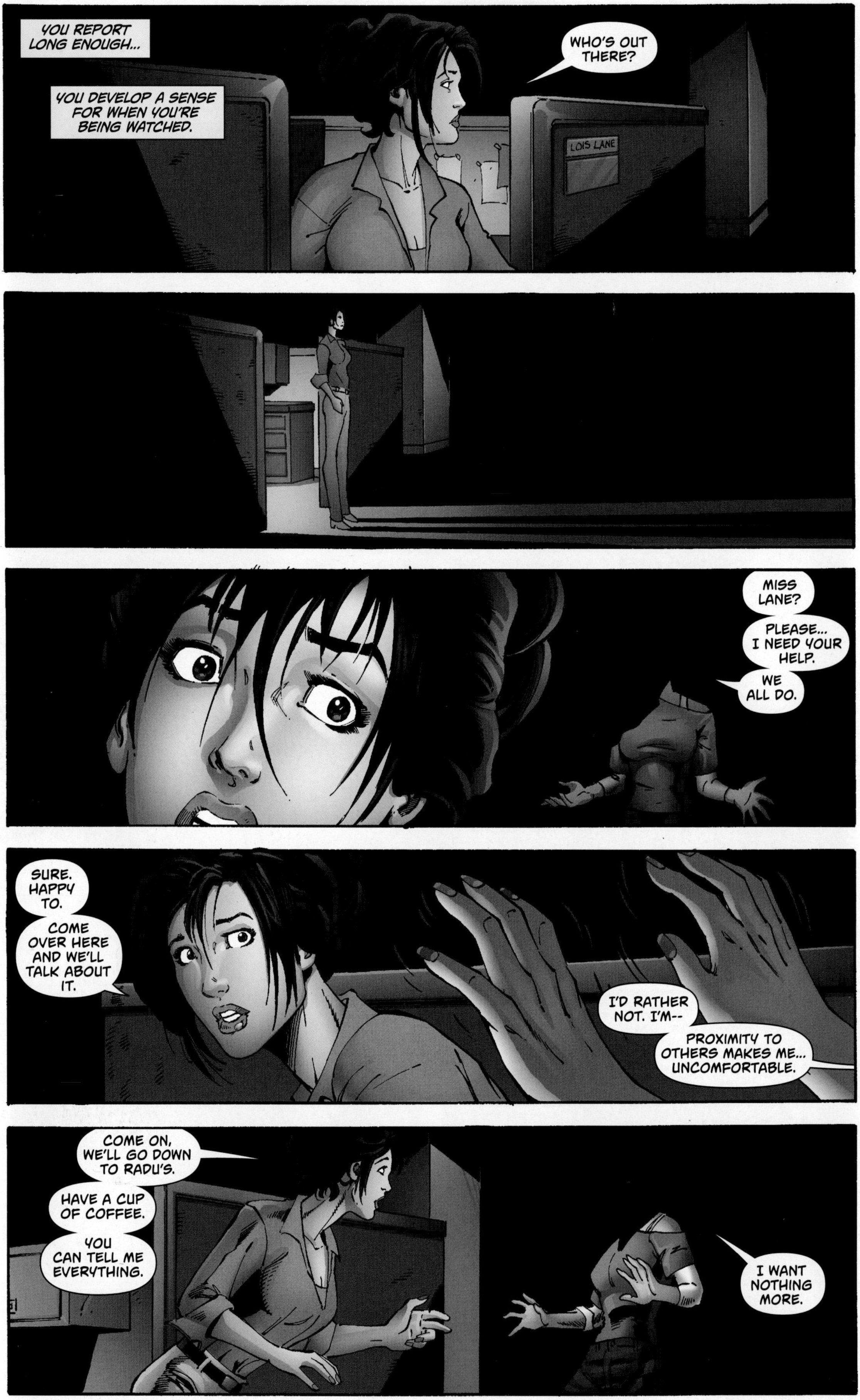
YOU REPORT LONG ENOUGH...
YOU DEVELOP A SENSE FOR WHEN YOU'RE BEING WATCHED.
WHO'S OUT THERE?
LOIS LANE
MISS LANE?
PLEASE... I NEED YOUR HELP.
WE ALL DO.
SURE. HAPPY TO.
COME OVER HERE AND WE'LL TALK ABOUT IT.
I'D RATHER NOT. I'M--
PROXIMITY TO OTHERS MAKES ME... UNCOMFORTABLE.
COME ON, WE'LL GO DOWN TO RADU'S.
HAVE A CUP OF COFFEE.
YOU CAN TELL ME EVERYTHING.
I WANT NOTHING MORE.

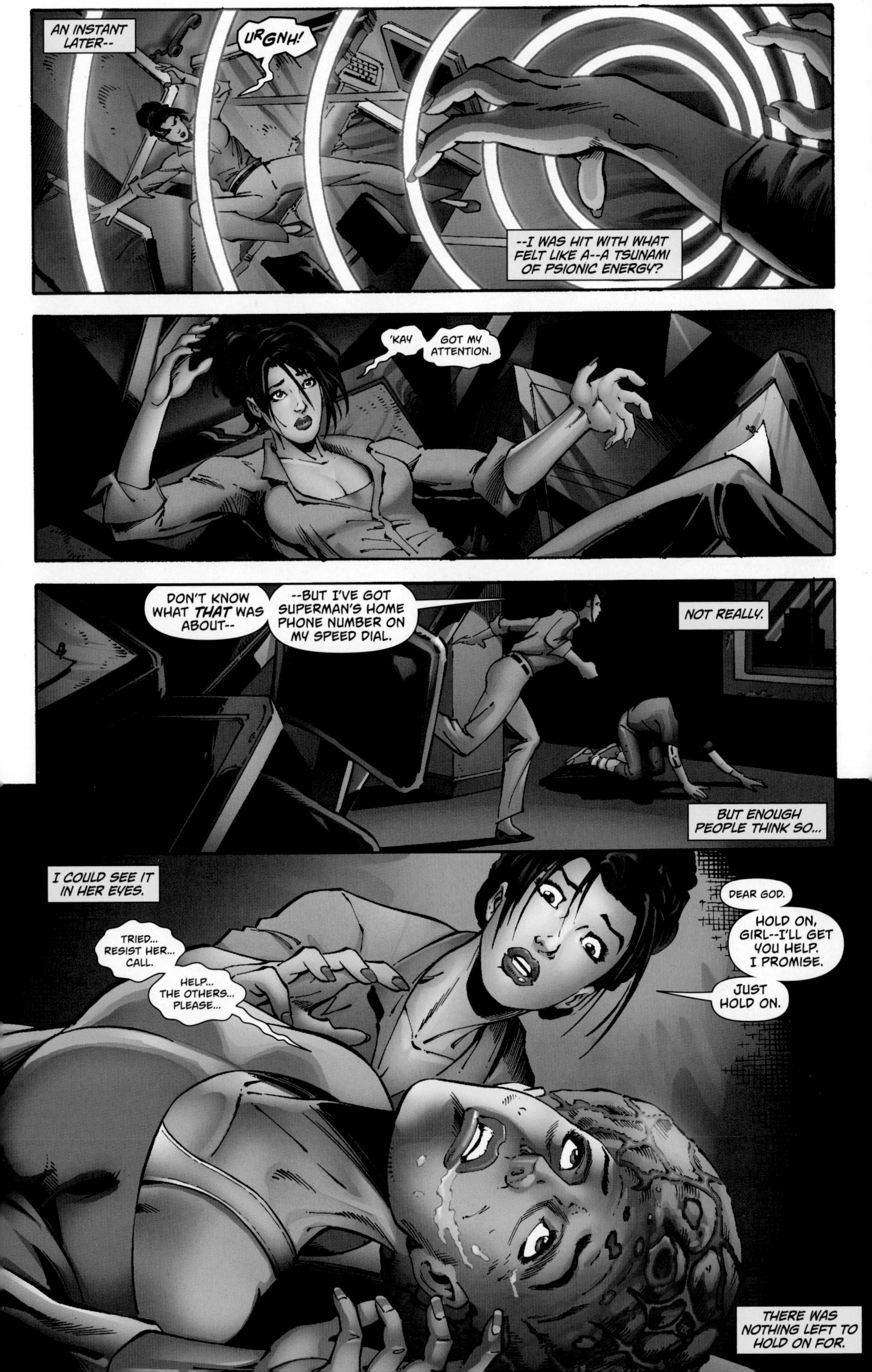
AN INSTANT LATER--
URGNH!
--I WAS HIT WITH WHAT FELT LIKE A--A TSUNAMI OF PSIONIC ENERGY?
'KAY GOT MY ATTENTION.
DON'T KNOW WHAT THAT WAS ABOUT--
--BUT I'VE GOT SUPERMAN'S HOME PHONE NUMBER ON MY SPEED DIAL.
NOT REALLY.
BUT ENOUGH PEOPLE THINK SO...
I COULD SEE IT IN HER EYES.
TRIED... RESIST HER... CALL.
HELP... THE OTHERS... PLEASE...
DEAR GOD.
HOLD ON, GIRL--I'LL GET YOU HELP. I PROMISE.
JUST HOLD ON.
THERE WAS NOTHING LEFT TO HOLD ON FOR.

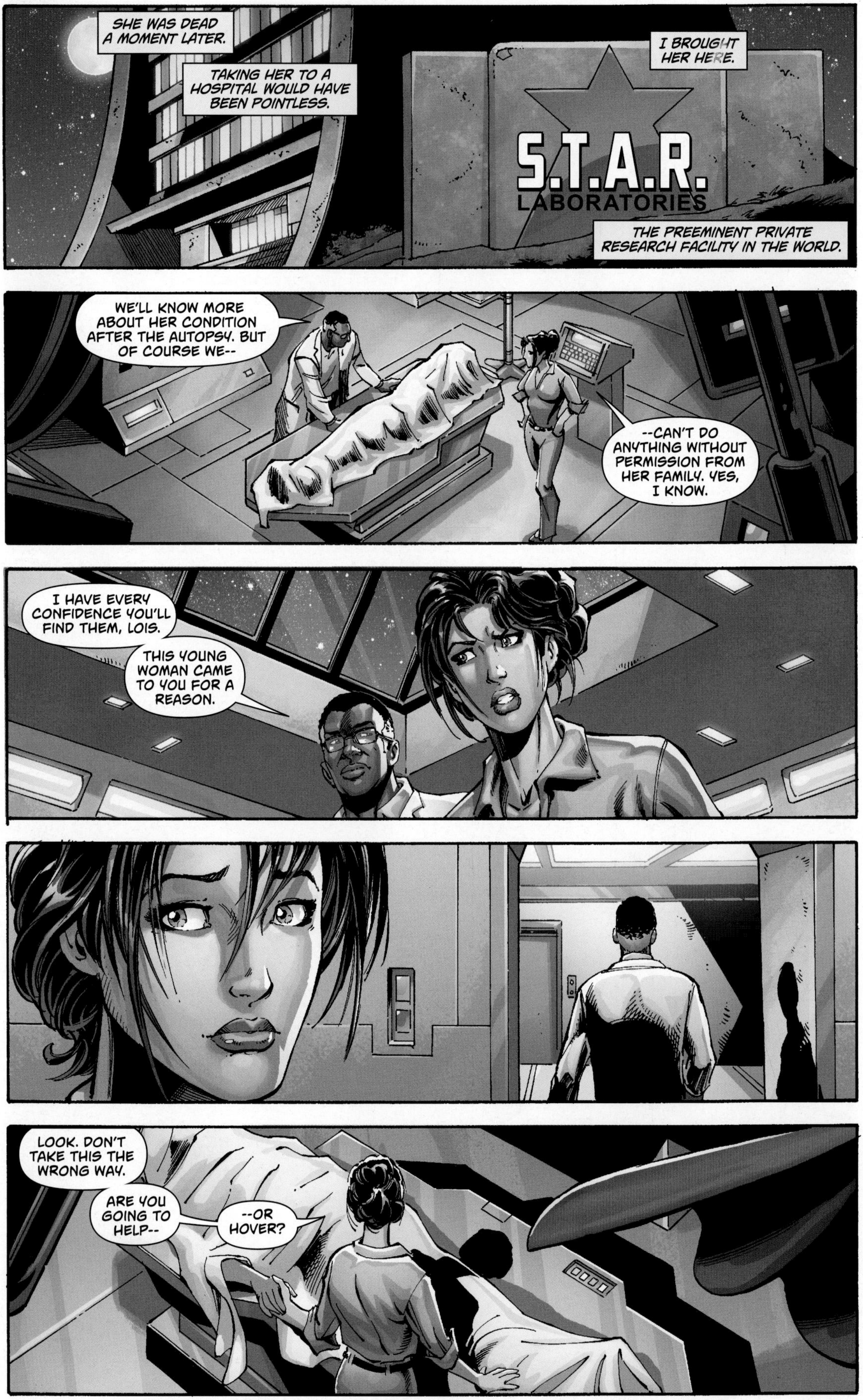
SHE WAS DEAD A MOMENT LATER.
TAKING HER TO A HOSPITAL WOULD HAVE BEEN POINTLESS.
I BROUGHT HER HERE.
S.T.A.R. LABORATORIES
THE PREEMINENT PRIVATE RESEARCH FACILITY IN THE WORLD.
WE'LL KNOW MORE ABOUT HER CONDITION AFTER THE AUTOPSY. BUT OF COURSE WE--
--CAN'T DO ANYTHING WITHOUT PERMISSION FROM HER FAMILY. YES, I KNOW.
I HAVE EVERY CONFIDENCE YOU'LL FIND THEM, LOIS.
THIS YOUNG WOMAN CAME TO YOU FOR A REASON.
LOOK. DON'T TAKE THIS THE WRONG WAY.
ARE YOU GOING TO HELP--
--OR HOVER?

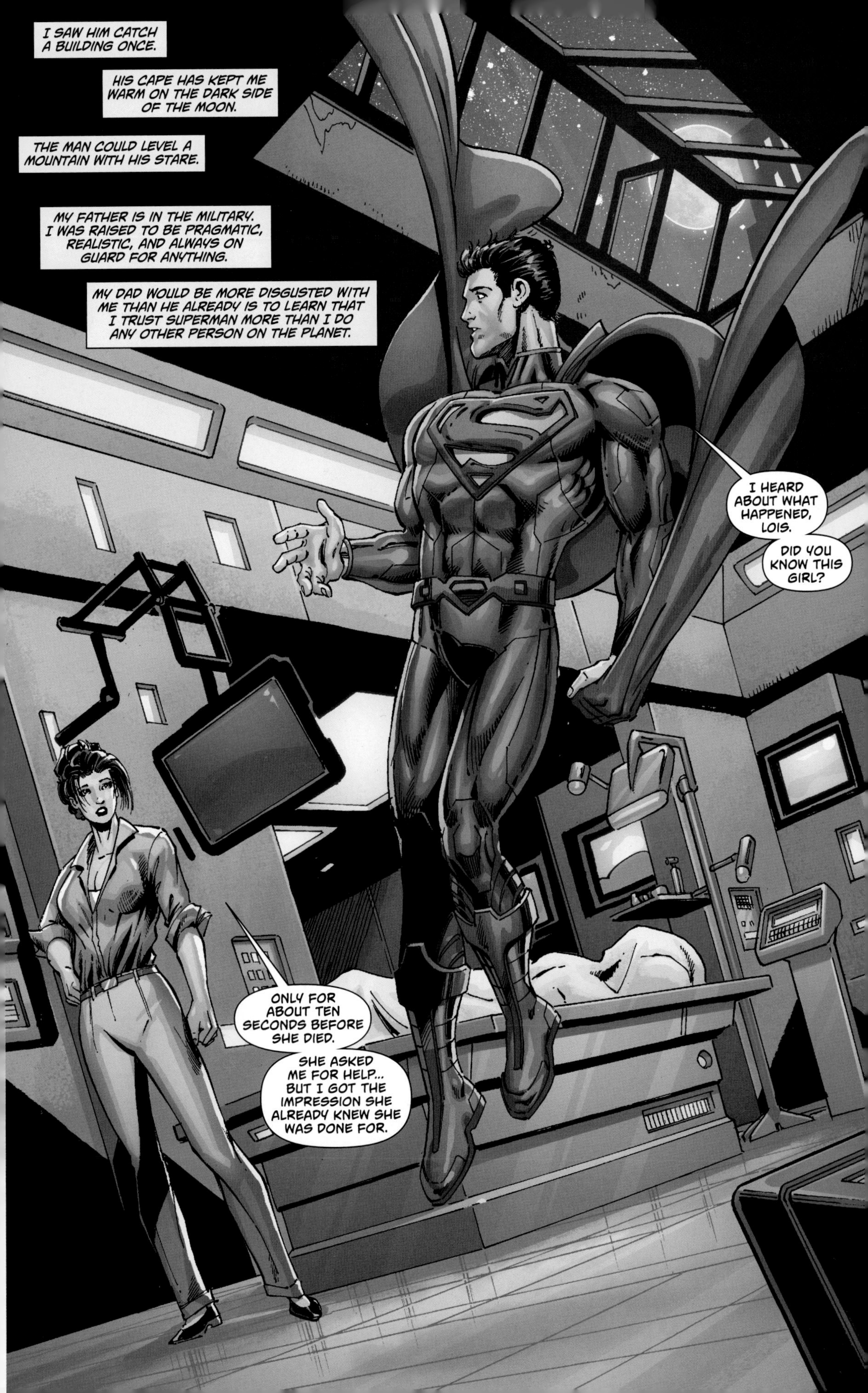
I SAW HIM CATCH A BUILDING ONCE.
HIS CAPE HAS KEPT ME WARM ON THE DARK SIDE OF THE MOON.
THE MAN COULD LEVEL A MOUNTAIN WITH HIS STARE.
MY FATHER IS IN THE MILITARY. I WAS RAISED TO BE PRAGMATIC, REALISTIC, AND ALWAYS ON GUARD FOR ANYTHING.
MY DAD WOULD BE MORE DISGUSTED WITH ME THAN HE ALREADY IS TO LEARN THAT I TRUST SUPERMAN MORE THAN I DO ANY OTHER PERSON ON THE PLANET.
I HEARD ABOUT WHAT HAPPENED, LOIS.
DID YOU KNOW THIS GIRL?
ONLY FOR ABOUT TEN SECONDS BEFORE SHE DIED.
SHE ASKED ME FOR HELP... BUT I GOT THE IMPRESSION SHE ALREADY KNEW SHE WAS DONE FOR.

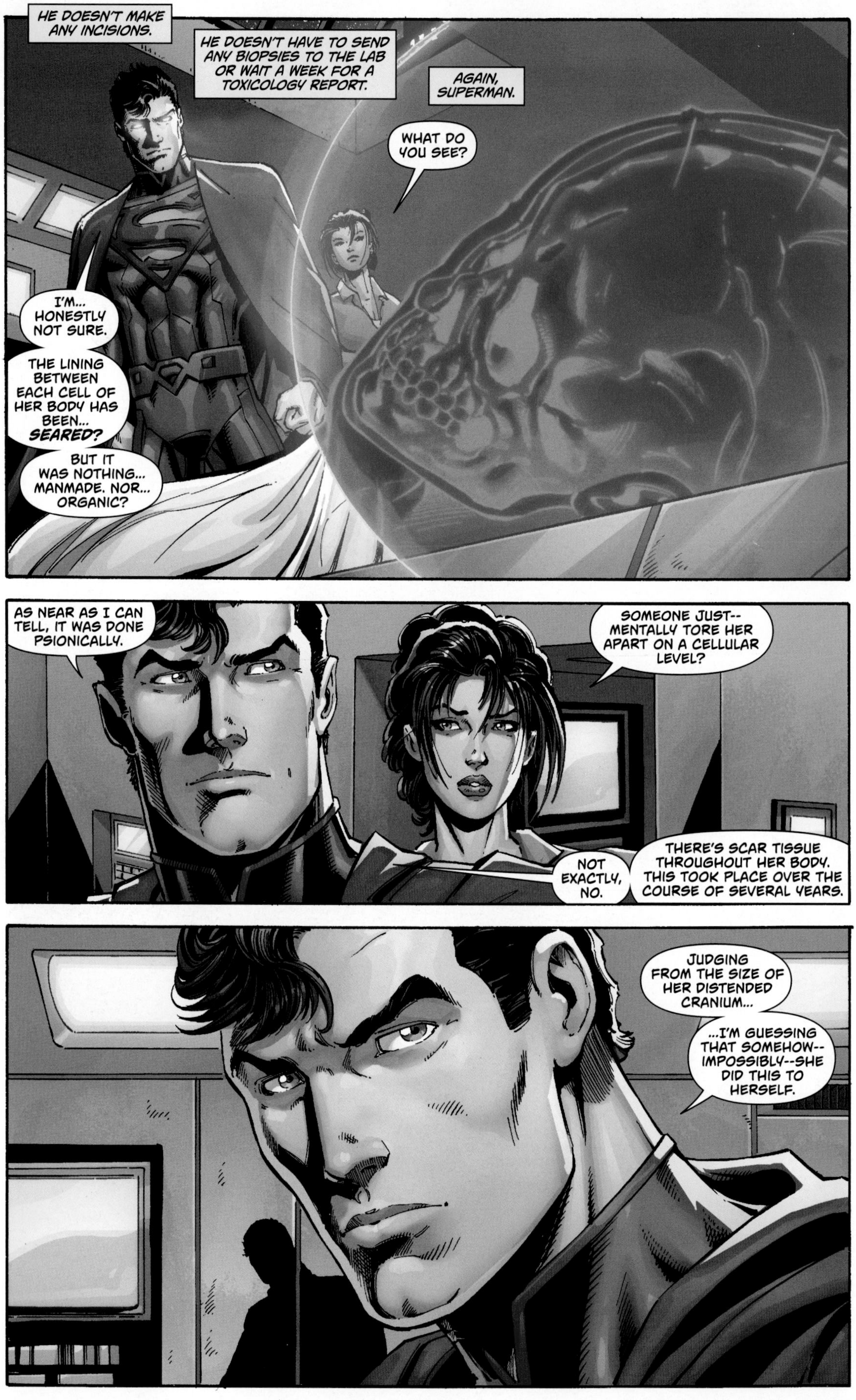
HE DOESN'T MAKE ANY INCISIONS.
HE DOESN'T HAVE TO SEND ANY BIOPSIES TO THE LAB OR WAIT A WEEK FOR A TOXICOLOGY REPORT.
AGAIN, SUPERMAN.
WHAT DO YOU SEE?
I'M... HONESTLY NOT SURE.
THE LINING BETWEEN EACH CELL OF HER BODY HAS BEEN... SEARED?
BUT IT WAS NOTHING... MANMADE. NOR... ORGANIC?
AS NEAR AS I CAN TELL, IT WAS DONE PSIONICALLY.
SOMEONE JUST--MENTALLY TORE HER APART ON A CELLULAR LEVEL?
NOT EXACTLY, NO.
THERE'S SCAR TISSUE THROUGHOUT HER BODY. THIS TOOK PLACE OVER THE COURSE OF SEVERAL YEARS.
JUDGING FROM THE SIZE OF HER DISTENDED CRANIUM...
...I'M GUESSING THAT SOMEHOW--IMPOSSIBLY--SHE DID THIS TO HERSELF.

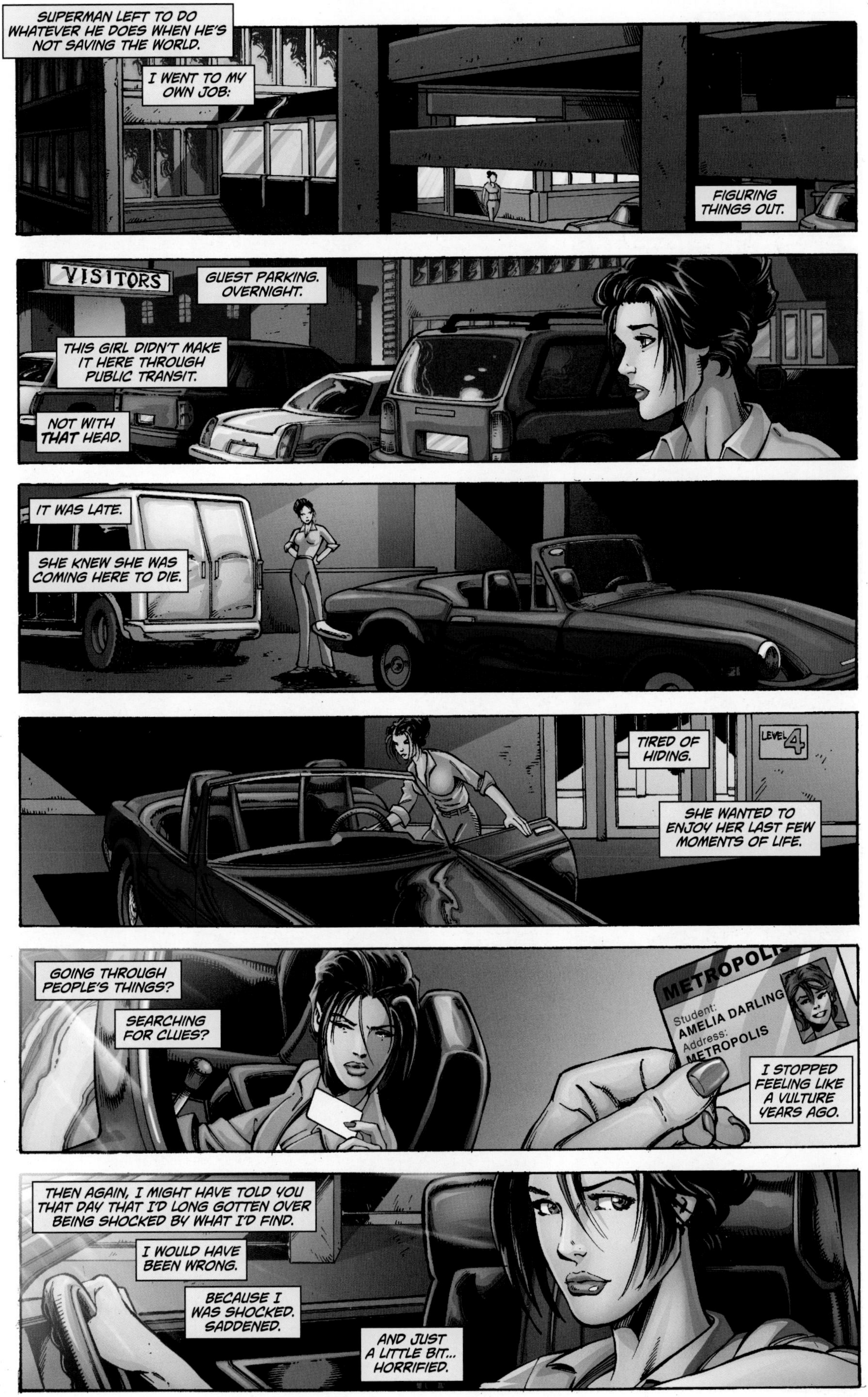
SUPERMAN LEFT TO DO WHATEVER HE DOES WHEN HE'S NOT SAVING THE WORLD.
I WENT TO MY OWN JOB:
FIGURING THINGS OUT.
VISITORS
GUEST PARKING. OVERNIGHT.
THIS GIRL DIDN'T MAKE IT HERE THROUGH PUBLIC TRANSIT.
NOT WITH THAT HEAD.
IT WAS LATE.
SHE KNEW SHE WAS COMING HERE TO DIE.
LEVEL 4
TIRED OF HIDING.
SHE WANTED TO ENJOY HER LAST FEW MOMENTS OF LIFE.
GOING THROUGH PEOPLE'S THINGS?
SEARCHING FOR CLUES?
METROPOLIS
Student: AMELIA DARLING
Address: METROPOLIS
I STOPPED FEELING LIKE A VULTURE YEARS AGO.
THEN AGAIN, I MIGHT HAVE TOLD YOU THAT DAY THAT I'D LONG GOTTEN OVER BEING SHOCKED BY WHAT I'D FIND.
I WOULD HAVE BEEN WRONG.
BECAUSE I WAS SHOCKED. SADDENED.
AND JUST A LITTLE BIT... HORRIFIED.

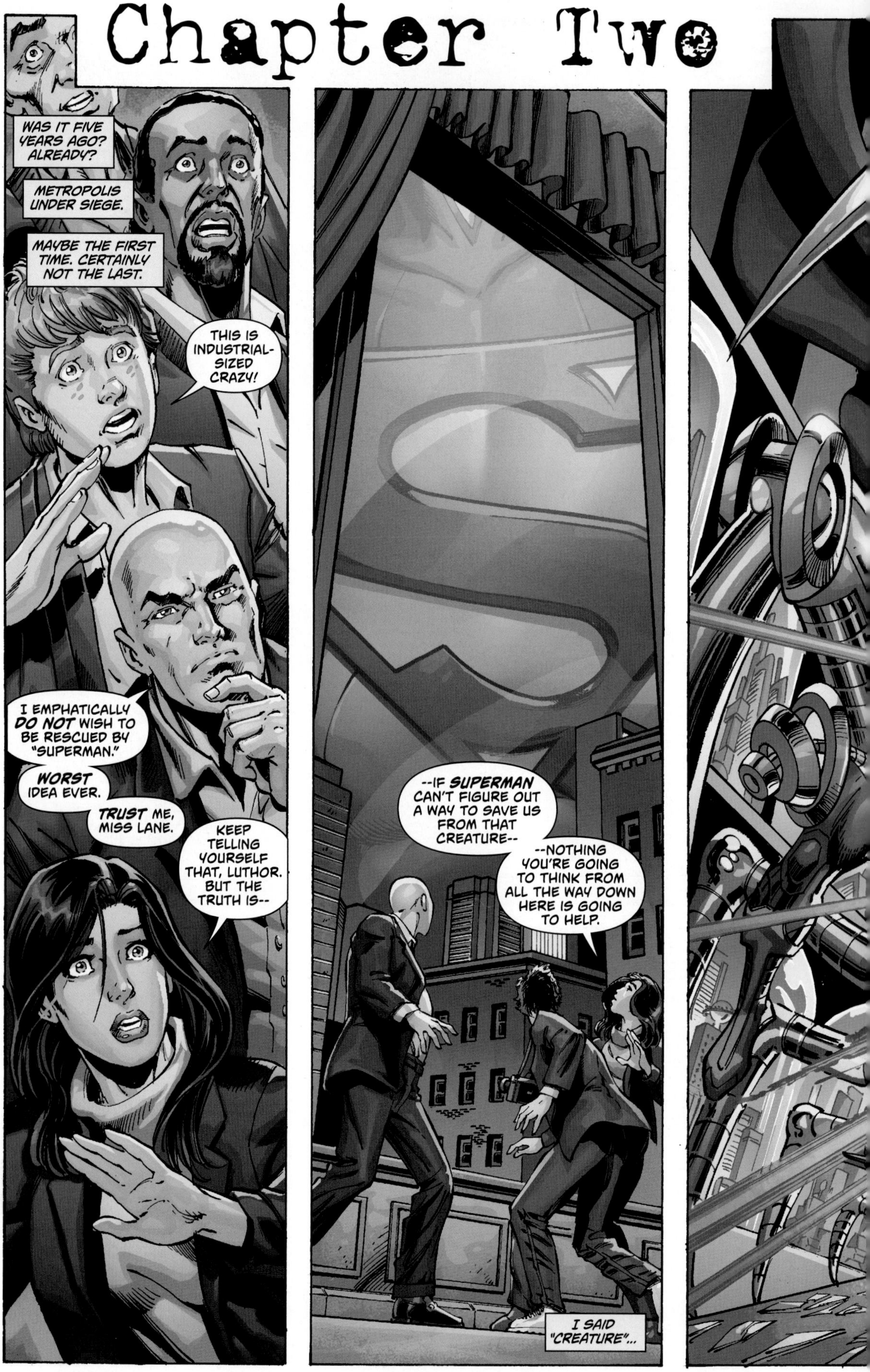
Chapter Two
WAS IT FIVE YEARS AGO? ALREADY?
METROPOLIS UNDER SIEGE.
MAYBE THE FIRST TIME. CERTAINLY NOT THE LAST.
THIS IS INDUSTRIAL-SIZED CRAZY!
I EMPHATICALLY DO NOT WISH TO BE RESCUED BY "SUPERMAN."
WORST IDEA EVER.
TRUST ME, MISS LANE.
KEEP TELLING YOURSELF THAT, LUTHOR. BUT THE TRUTH IS--
--IF SUPERMAN CAN'T FIGURE OUT A WAY TO SAVE US FROM THAT CREATURE--
--NOTHING YOU'RE GOING TO THINK FROM ALL THE WAY DOWN HERE IS GOING TO HELP.
I SAID "CREATURE"...

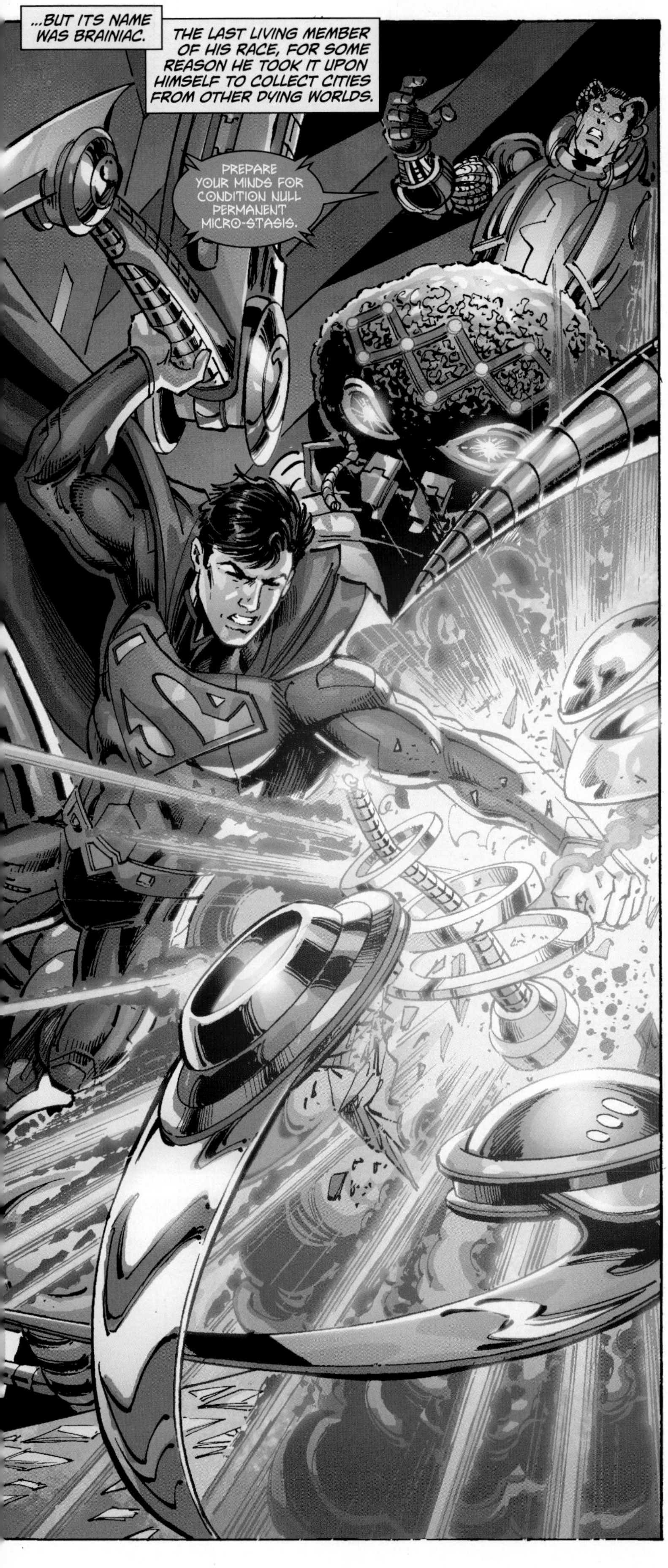
...BUT ITS NAME WAS BRAINIAC.
THE LAST LIVING MEMBER OF HIS RACE, FOR SOME REASON HE TOOK IT UPON HIMSELF TO COLLECT CITIES FROM OTHER DYING WORLDS.
PREPARE YOUR MINDS FOR CONDITION NULL PERMANENT MICRO-STASIS.

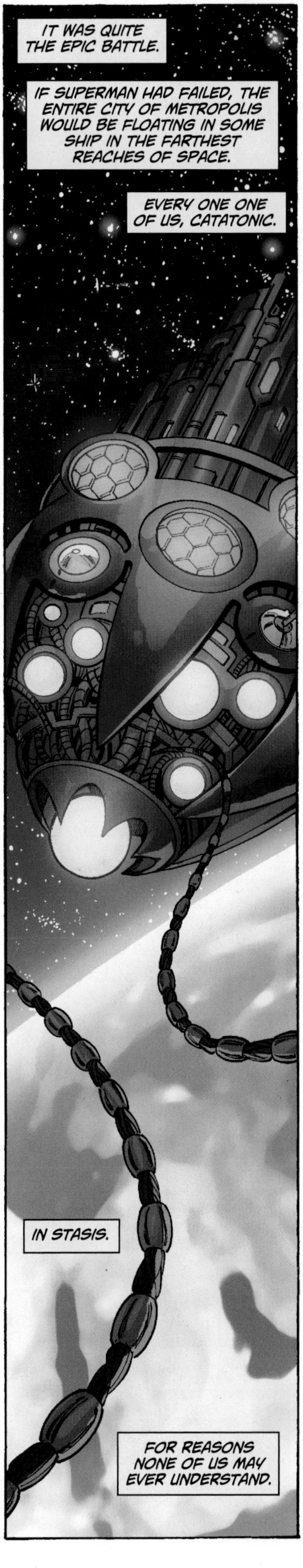
IT WAS QUITE THE EPIC BATTLE.
IF SUPERMAN HAD FAILED, THE ENTIRE CITY OF METROPOLIS WOULD BE FLOATING IN SOME SHIP IN THE FARTHEST REACHES OF SPACE.
EVERY ONE ONE OF US, CATATONIC.
IN STASIS.
FOR REASONS NONE OF US MAY EVER UNDERSTAND.

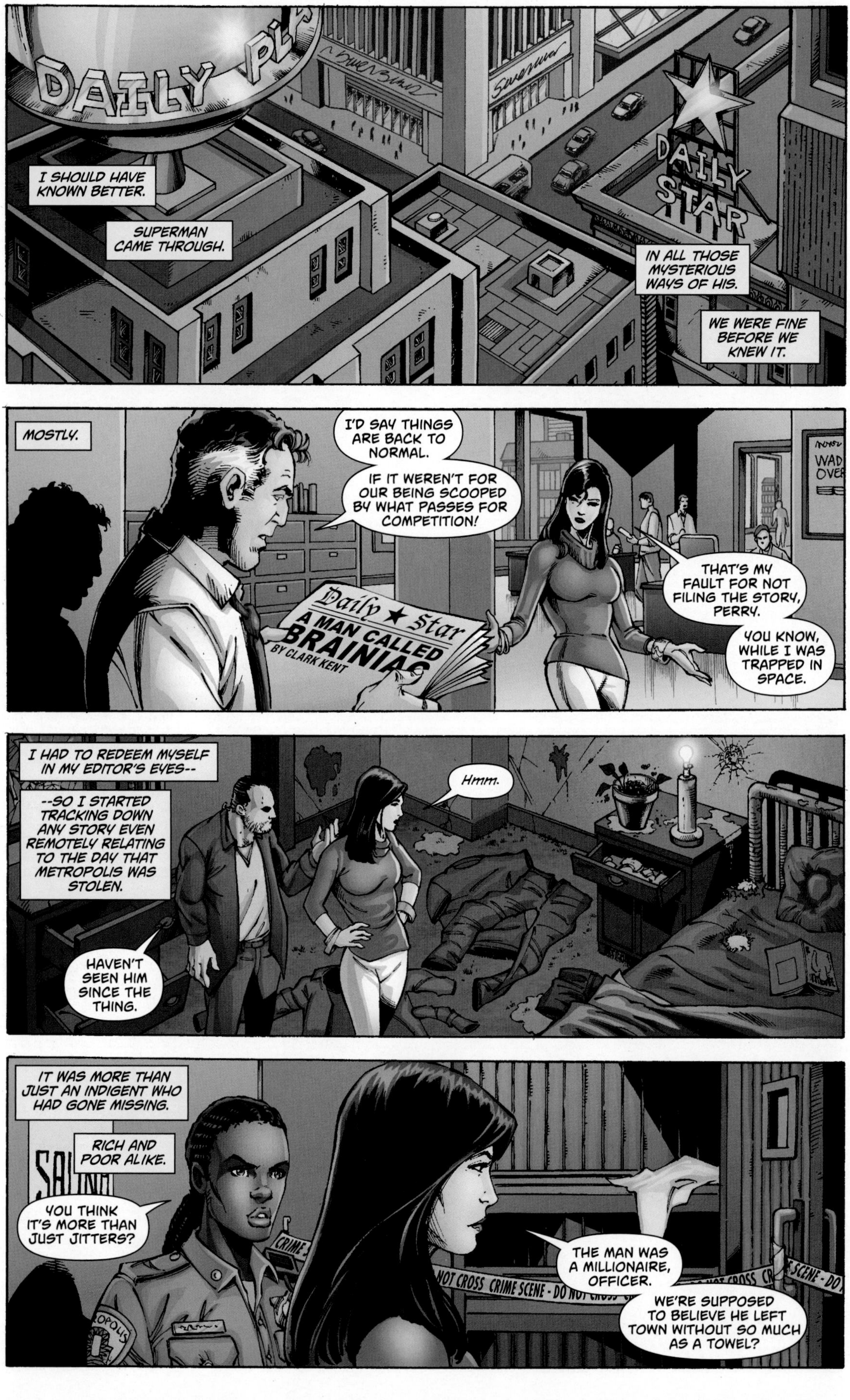
DAILY PL
DAILY STAR
I SHOULD HAVE KNOWN BETTER.
SUPERMAN CAME THROUGH.
IN ALL THOSE MYSTERIOUS WAYS OF HIS.
WE WERE FINE BEFORE WE KNEW IT.
MOSTLY.
I'D SAY THINGS ARE BACK TO NORMAL.
IF IT WEREN'T FOR OUR BEING SCOOPED BY WHAT PASSES FOR COMPETITION!
Daily ★ Star
A MAN CALLED BRAINIAC
BY CLARK KENT
THAT'S MY FAULT FOR NOT FILING THE STORY, PERRY.
YOU KNOW, WHILE I WAS TRAPPED IN SPACE.
I HAD TO REDEEM MYSELF IN MY EDITOR'S EYES--
--SO I STARTED TRACKING DOWN ANY STORY EVEN REMOTELY RELATING TO THE DAY THAT METROPOLIS WAS STOLEN.
Hmm.
HAVEN'T SEEN HIM SINCE THE THING.
IT WAS MORE THAN JUST AN INDIGENT WHO HAD GONE MISSING.
RICH AND POOR ALIKE.
YOU THINK IT'S MORE THAN JUST JITTERS?
THE MAN WAS A MILLIONAIRE, OFFICER.
WE'RE SUPPOSED TO BELIEVE HE LEFT TOWN WITHOUT SO MUCH AS A TOWEL?
NOT CROSS CRIME SCENE - DO NOT CROSS

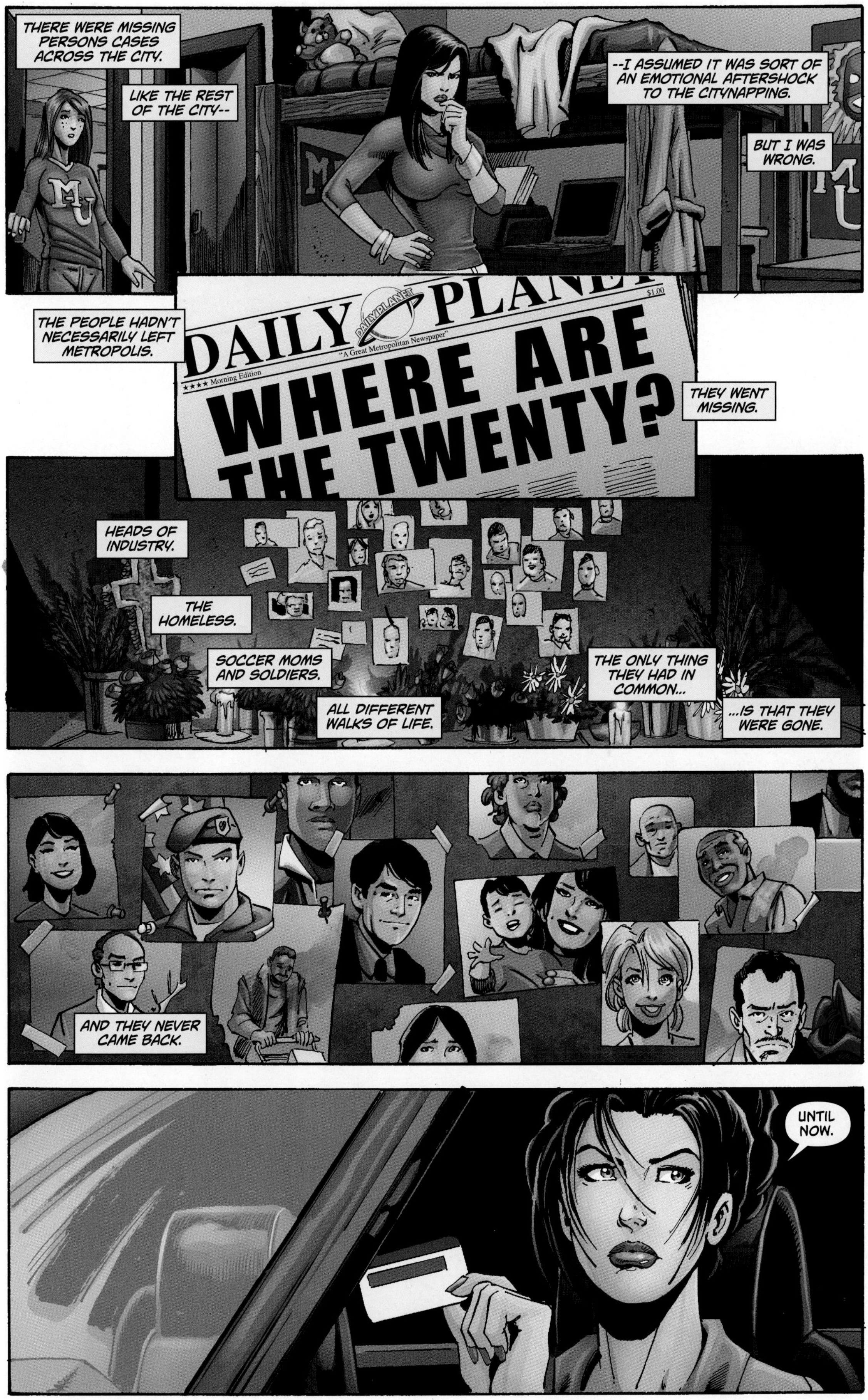
THERE WERE MISSING PERSONS CASES ACROSS THE CITY.
LIKE THE REST OF THE CITY--
--I ASSUMED IT WAS SORT OF AN EMOTIONAL AFTERSHOCK TO THE CITYNAPPING.
BUT I WAS WRONG.
THE PEOPLE HADN'T NECESSARILY LEFT METROPOLIS.
DAILY PLANET
"A Great Metropolitan Newspaper"
$1.00
Morning Edition
WHERE ARE THE TWENTY?
THEY WENT MISSING.
HEADS OF INDUSTRY.
THE HOMELESS.
SOCCER MOMS AND SOLDIERS.
ALL DIFFERENT WALKS OF LIFE.
THE ONLY THING THEY HAD IN COMMON...
...IS THAT THEY WERE GONE.
AND THEY NEVER CAME BACK.
UNTIL NOW.

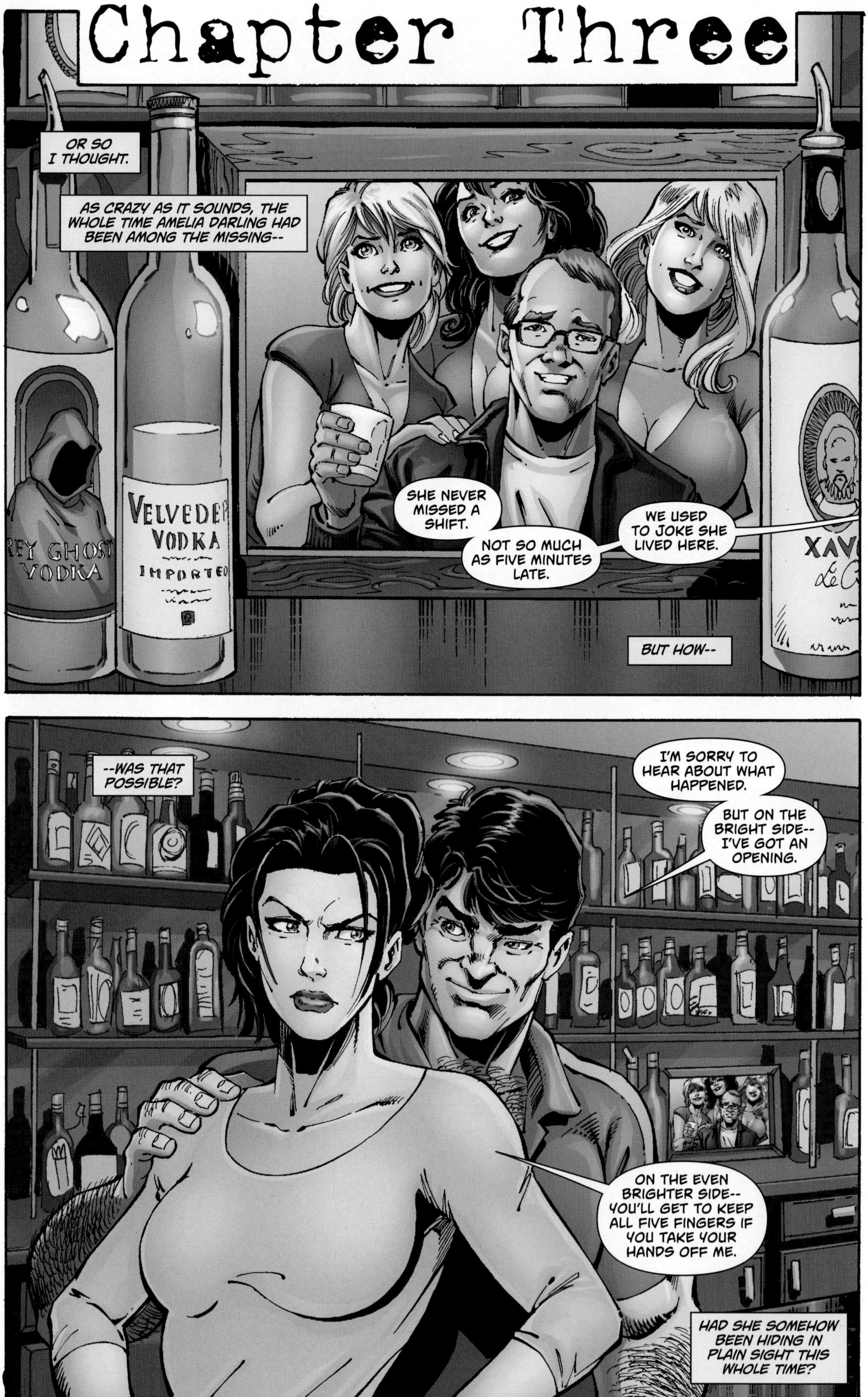
Chapter Three
OR SO I THOUGHT.
AS CRAZY AS IT SOUNDS, THE WHOLE TIME AMELIA DARLING HAD BEEN AMONG THE MISSING--
SHE NEVER MISSED A SHIFT.
NOT SO MUCH AS FIVE MINUTES LATE.
WE USED TO JOKE SHE LIVED HERE.
VELVEDER VODKA IMPORTED
REY GHOST VODKA
BUT HOW--
--WAS THAT POSSIBLE?
I'M SORRY TO HEAR ABOUT WHAT HAPPENED.
BUT ON THE BRIGHT SIDE-- I'VE GOT AN OPENING.
ON THE EVEN BRIGHTER SIDE-- YOU'LL GET TO KEEP ALL FIVE FINGERS IF YOU TAKE YOUR HANDS OFF ME.
HAD SHE SOMEHOW BEEN HIDING IN PLAIN SIGHT THIS WHOLE TIME?

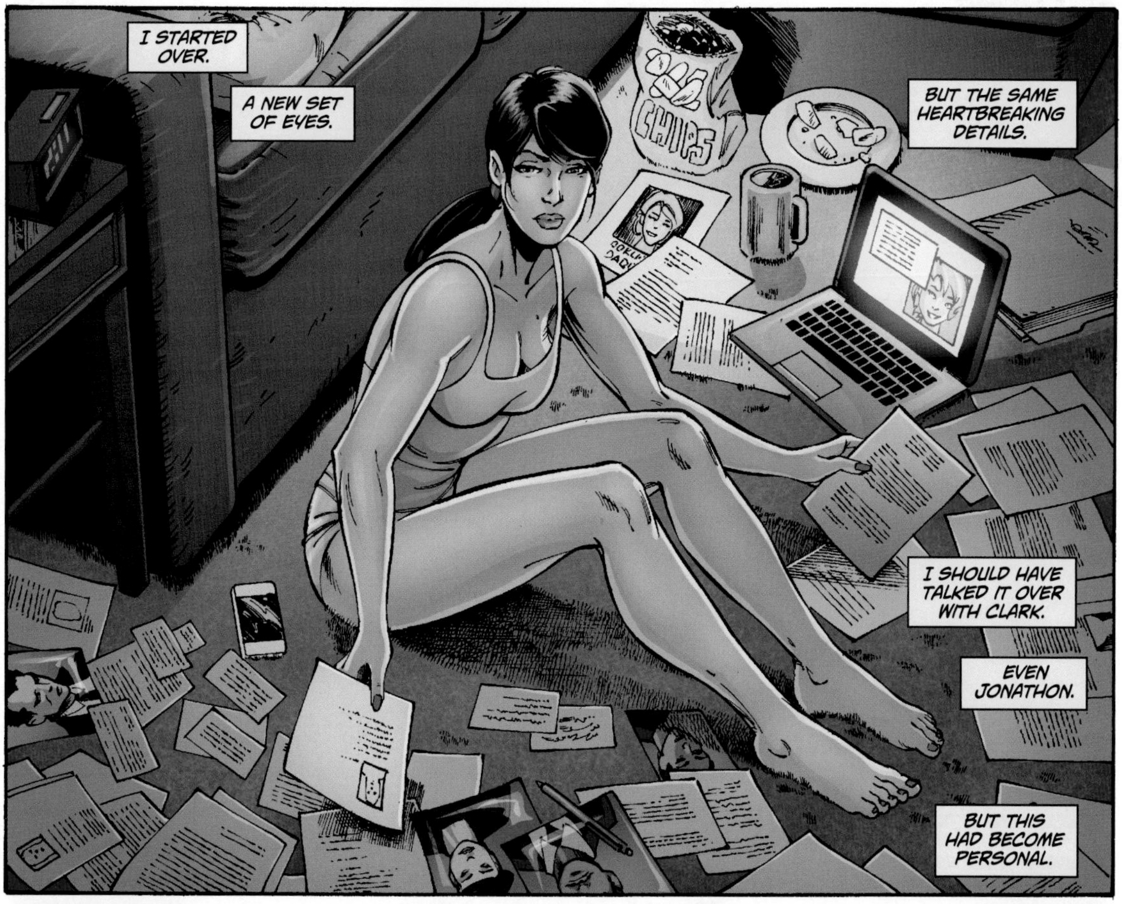
I STARTED OVER.
A NEW SET OF EYES.
BUT THE SAME HEARTBREAKING DETAILS.
I SHOULD HAVE TALKED IT OVER WITH CLARK.
EVEN JONATHON.
BUT THIS HAD BECOME PERSONAL.

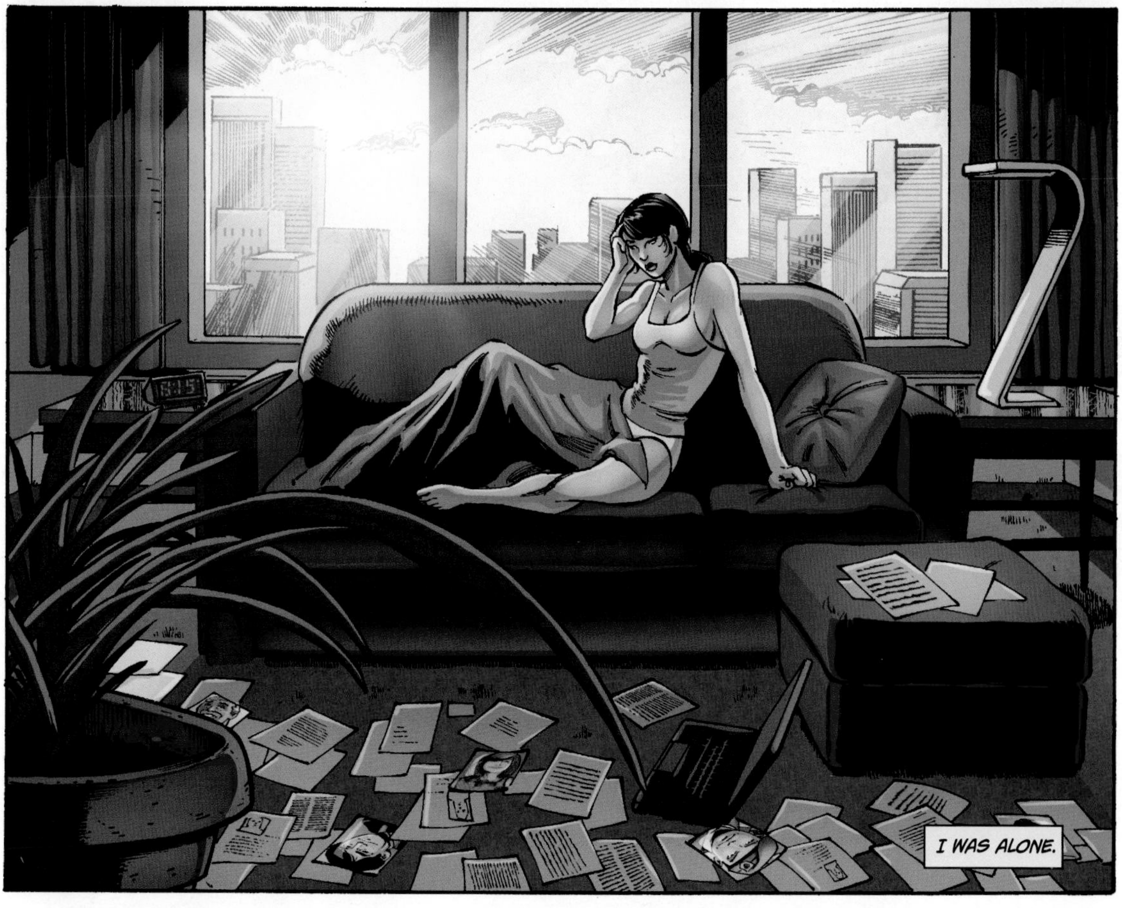
I WAS ALONE.

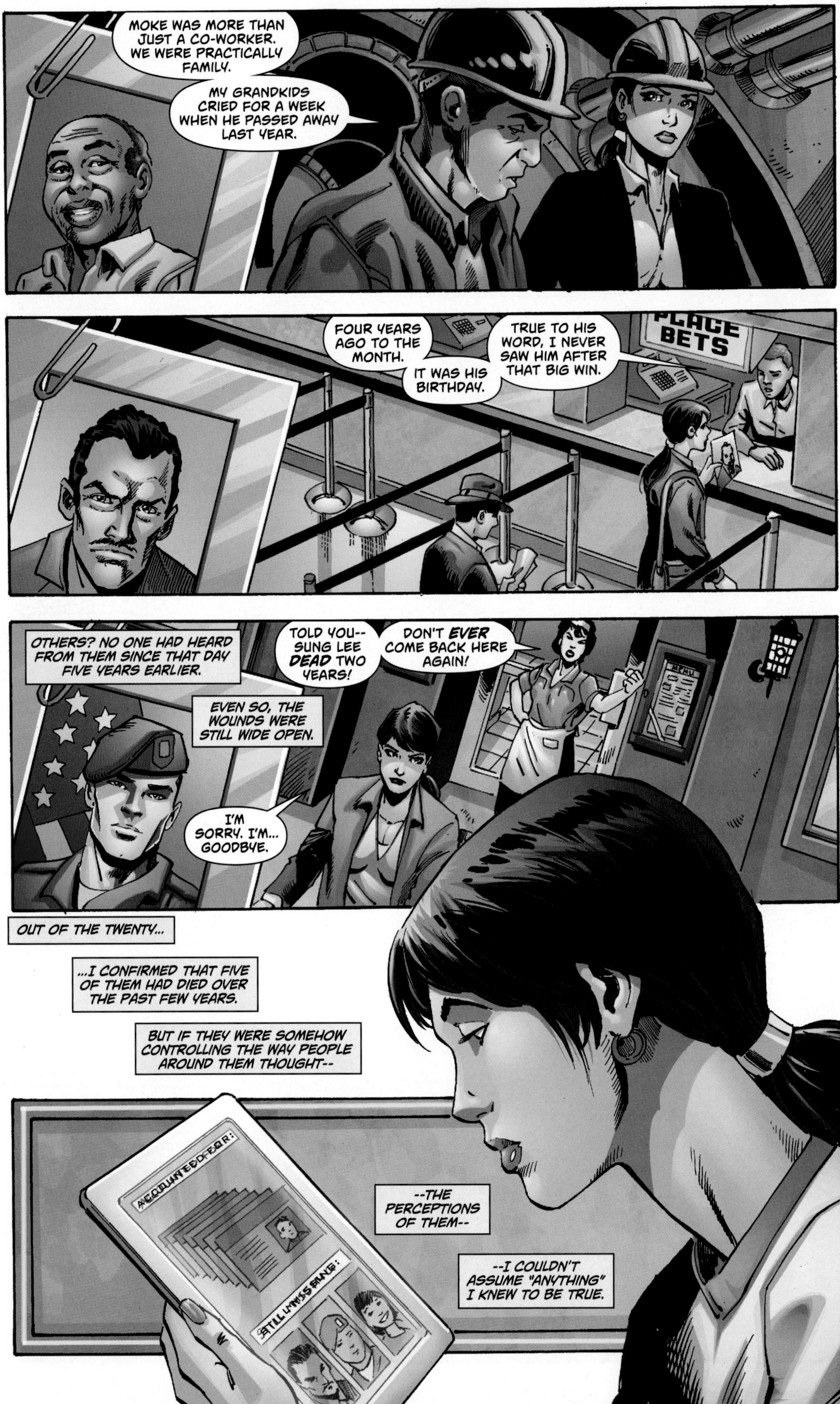
MOKE WAS MORE THAN JUST A CO-WORKER. WE WERE PRACTICALLY FAMILY.
MY GRANDKIDS CRIED FOR A WEEK WHEN HE PASSED AWAY LAST YEAR.
FOUR YEARS AGO TO THE MONTH.
IT WAS HIS BIRTHDAY.
TRUE TO HIS WORD, I NEVER SAW HIM AFTER THAT BIG WIN.
PLACE BETS
OTHERS? NO ONE HAD HEARD FROM THEM SINCE THAT DAY FIVE YEARS EARLIER.
EVEN SO, THE WOUNDS WERE STILL WIDE OPEN.
TOLD YOU-- SUNG LEE **DEAD** TWO YEARS!
DON'T **EVER** COME BACK HERE AGAIN!
I'M SORRY. I'M... GOODBYE.
OUT OF THE TWENTY...
...I CONFIRMED THAT FIVE OF THEM HAD DIED OVER THE PAST FEW YEARS.
BUT IF THEY WERE SOMEHOW CONTROLLING THE WAY PEOPLE AROUND THEM THOUGHT--
--THE PERCEPTIONS OF THEM--
--I COULDN'T ASSUME "ANYTHING" I KNEW TO BE TRUE.

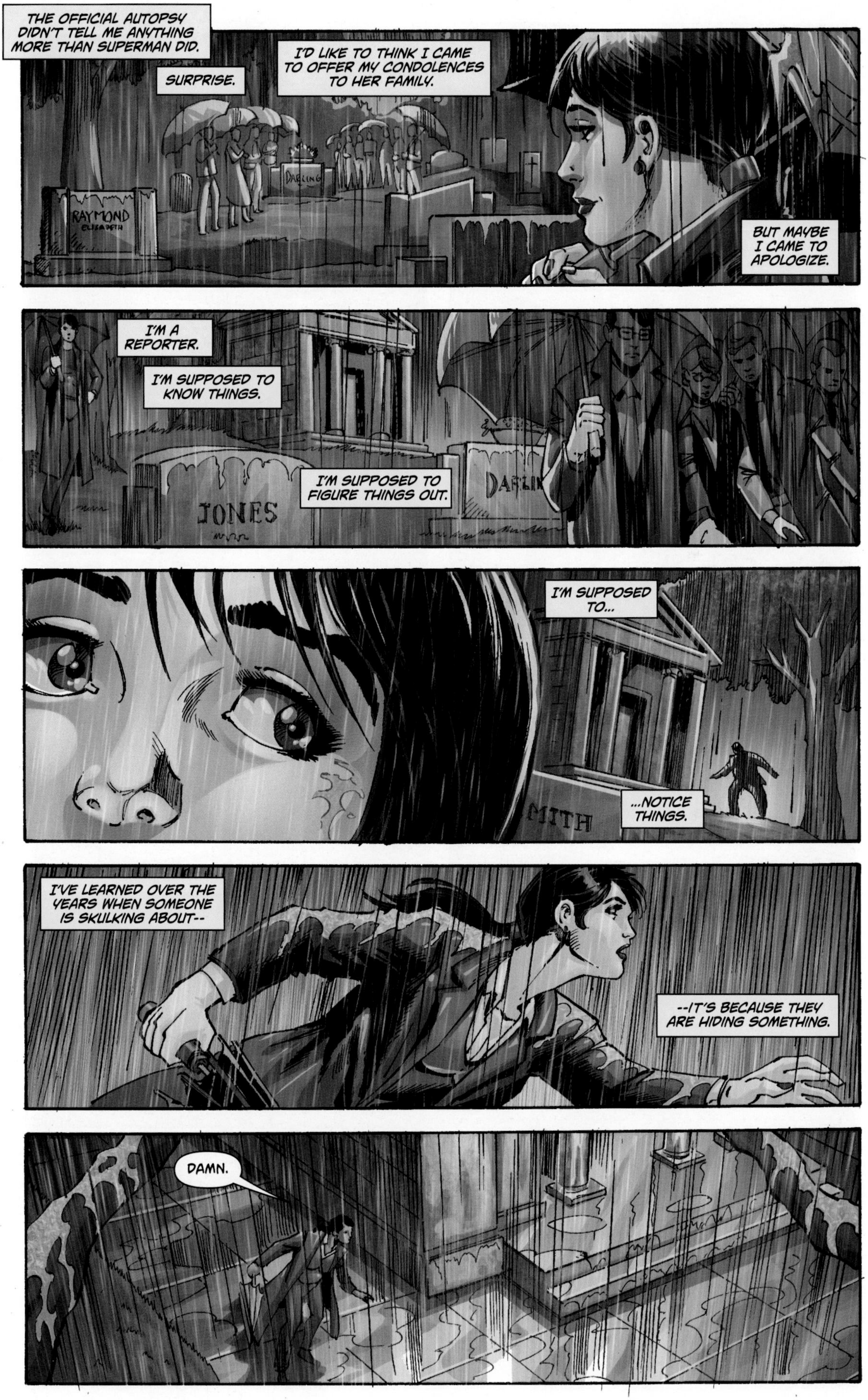
THE OFFICIAL AUTOPSY DIDN'T TELL ME ANYTHING MORE THAN SUPERMAN DID.
SURPRISE.
I'D LIKE TO THINK I CAME TO OFFER MY CONDOLENCES TO HER FAMILY.
RAYMOND
ELIZABETH
DARLING
BUT MAYBE I CAME TO APOLOGIZE.
I'M A REPORTER.
I'M SUPPOSED TO KNOW THINGS.
I'M SUPPOSED TO FIGURE THINGS OUT.
JONES
I'M SUPPOSED TO...
...NOTICE THINGS.
MITH
I'VE LEARNED OVER THE YEARS WHEN SOMEONE IS SKULKING ABOUT--
--IT'S BECAUSE THEY ARE HIDING SOMETHING.
DAMN.

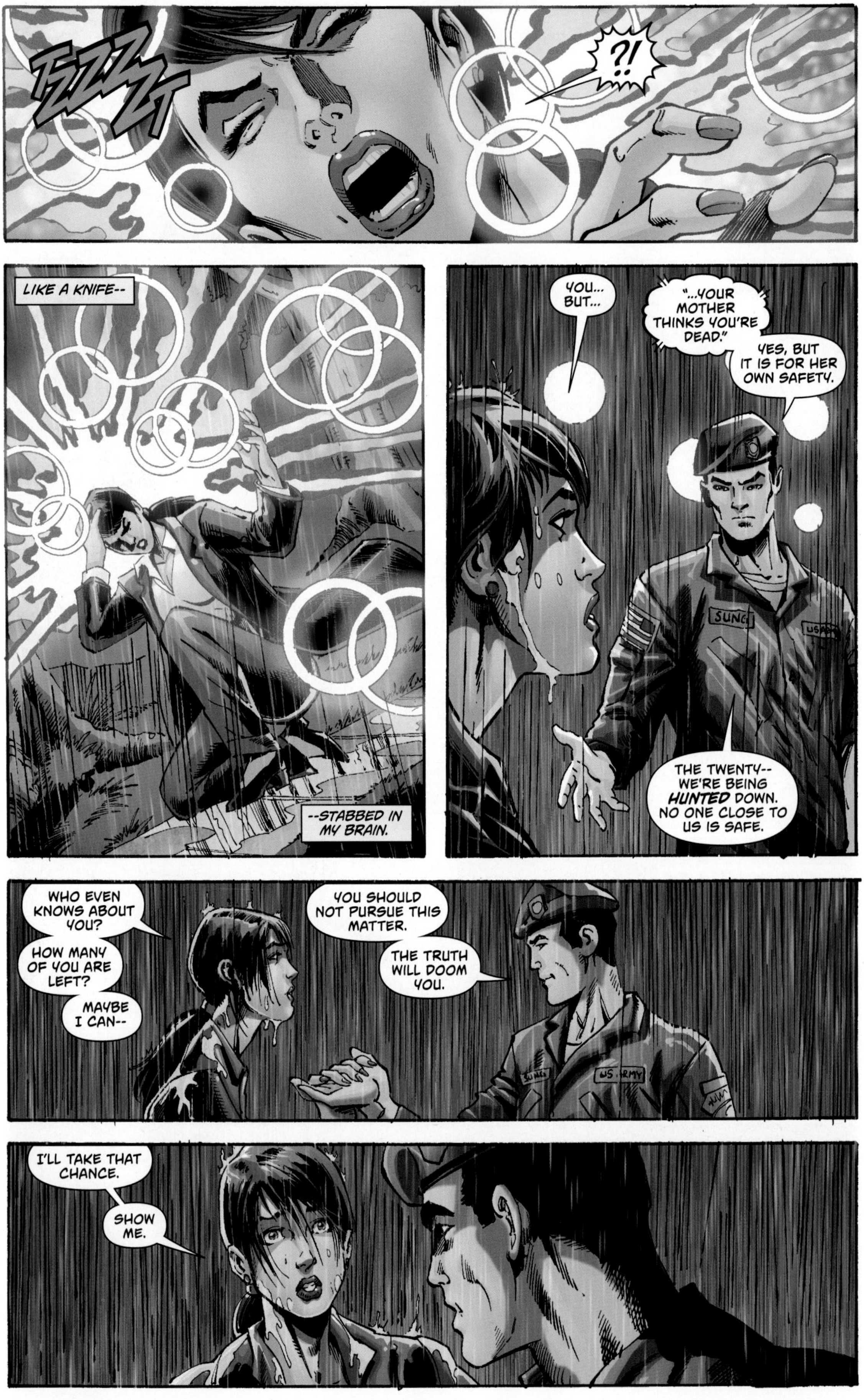
TZZZZT
?!
LIKE A KNIFE--
--STABBED IN MY BRAIN.
YOU... BUT...
"...YOUR MOTHER THINKS YOU'RE DEAD."
YES, BUT IT IS FOR HER OWN SAFETY.
THE TWENTY-- WE'RE BEING HUNTED DOWN. NO ONE CLOSE TO US IS SAFE.
WHO EVEN KNOWS ABOUT YOU?
HOW MANY OF YOU ARE LEFT?
MAYBE I CAN--
YOU SHOULD NOT PURSUE THIS MATTER.
THE TRUTH WILL DOOM YOU.
I'LL TAKE THAT CHANCE.
SHOW ME.

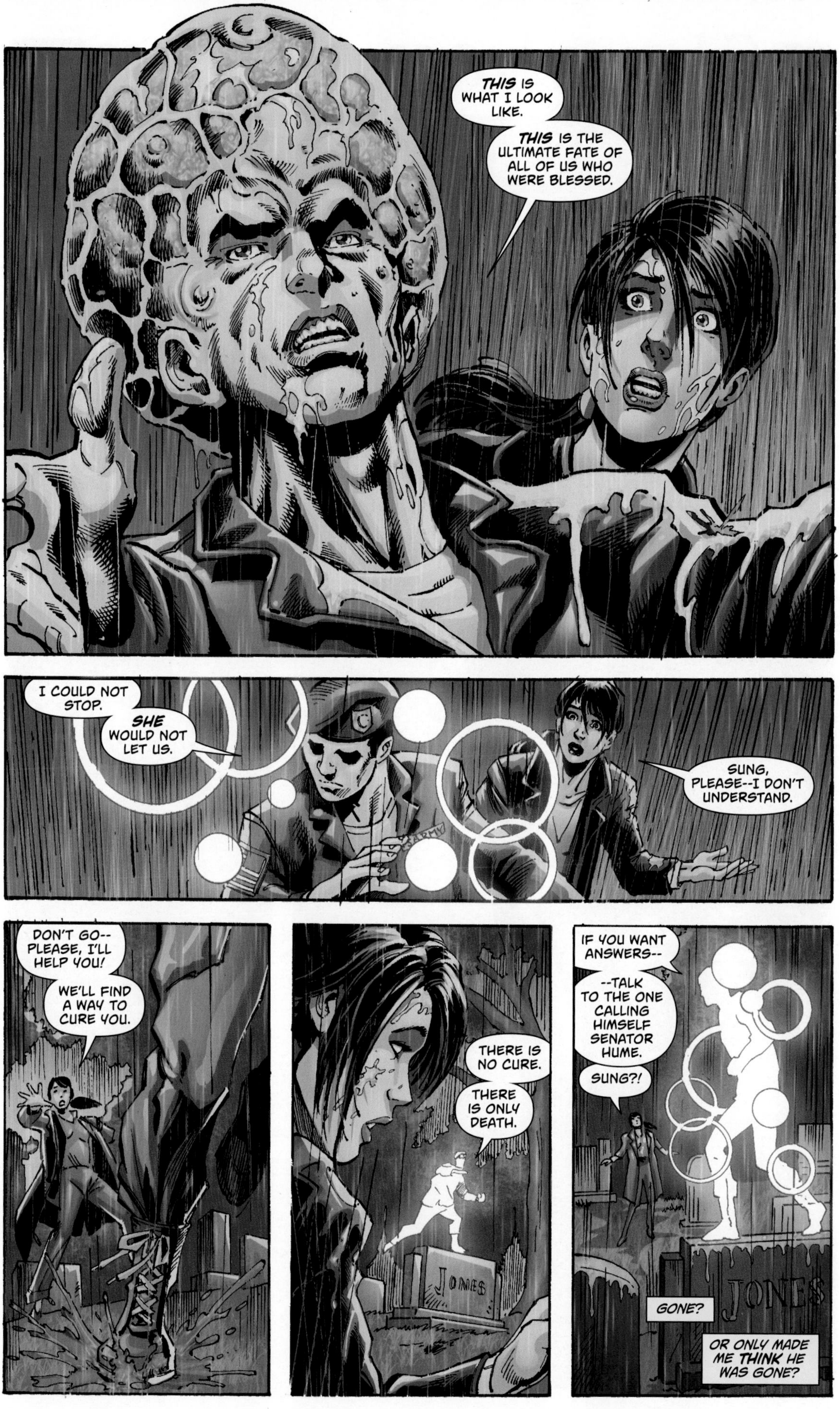
THIS IS WHAT I LOOK LIKE.
THIS IS THE ULTIMATE FATE OF ALL OF US WHO WERE BLESSED.
I COULD NOT STOP.
SHE WOULD NOT LET US.
SUNG, PLEASE--I DON'T UNDERSTAND.
DON'T GO-- PLEASE, I'LL HELP YOU!
WE'LL FIND A WAY TO CURE YOU.
THERE IS NO CURE.
THERE IS ONLY DEATH.
JONES
IF YOU WANT ANSWERS--
--TALK TO THE ONE CALLING HIMSELF SENATOR HUME.
SUNG?!
JONES
GONE?
OR ONLY MADE ME THINK HE WAS GONE?

Chapter Four

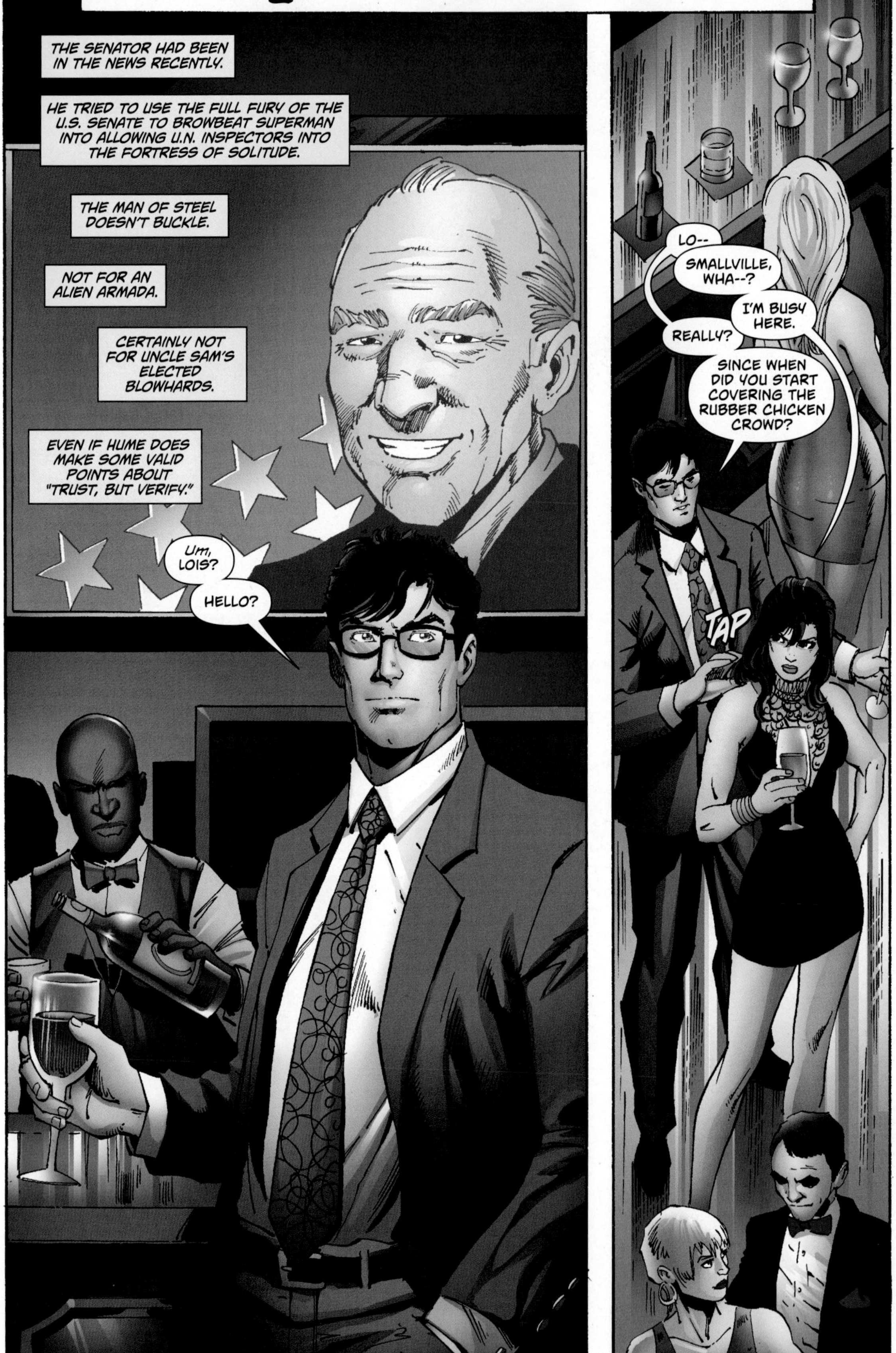
THE SENATOR HAD BEEN IN THE NEWS RECENTLY.
HE TRIED TO USE THE FULL FURY OF THE U.S. SENATE TO BROWBEAT SUPERMAN INTO ALLOWING U.N. INSPECTORS INTO THE FORTRESS OF SOLITUDE.
THE MAN OF STEEL DOESN'T BUCKLE.
NOT FOR AN ALIEN ARMADA.
CERTAINLY NOT FOR UNCLE SAM'S ELECTED BLOWHARDS.
EVEN IF HUME DOES MAKE SOME VALID POINTS ABOUT "TRUST, BUT VERIFY."
Um, LOIS?
HELLO?
LO--
SMALLVILLE, WHA--?
I'M BUSY HERE.
REALLY?
SINCE WHEN DID YOU START COVERING THE RUBBER CHICKEN CROWD?
TAP

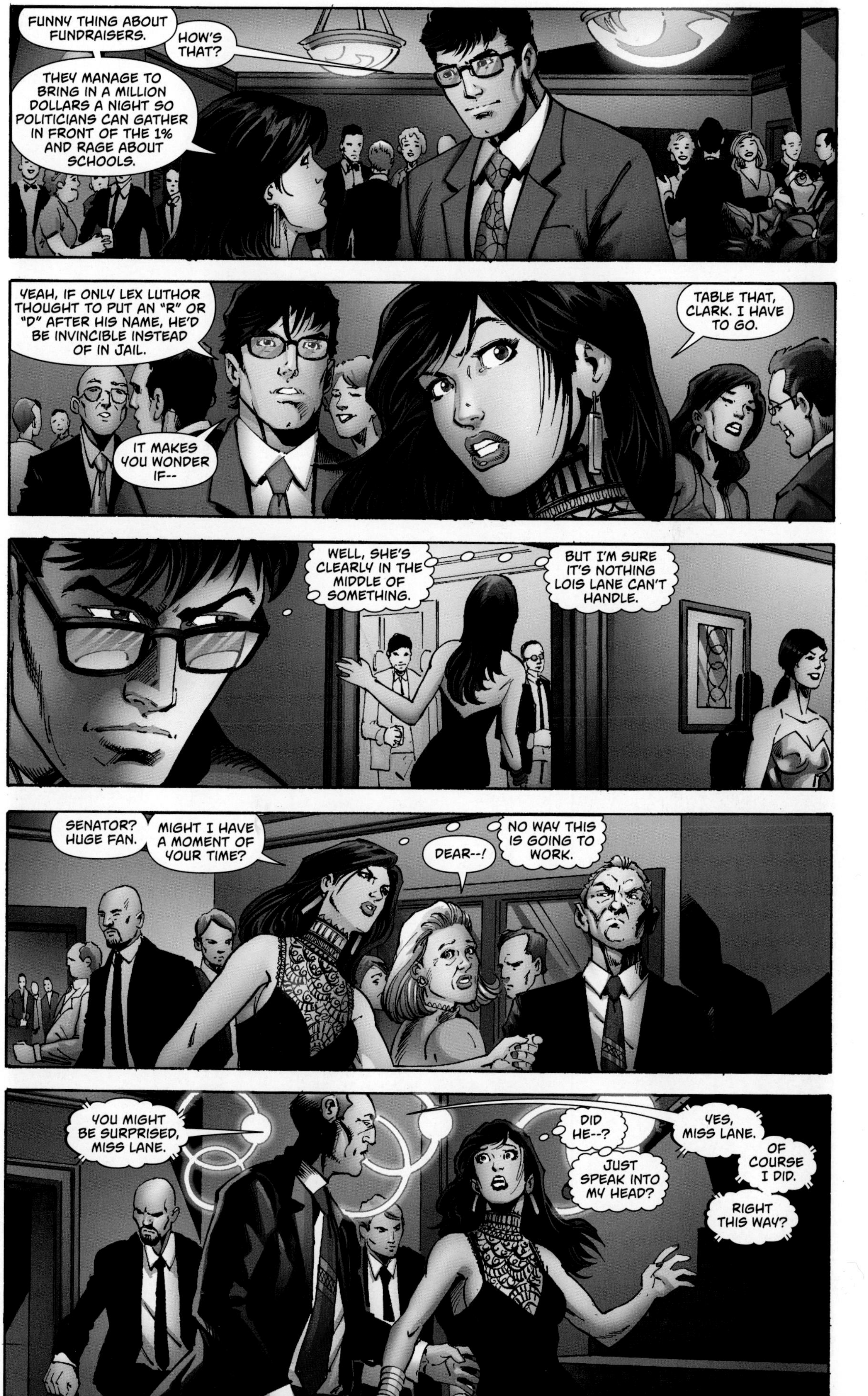
FUNNY THING ABOUT FUNDRAISERS.
HOW'S THAT?
THEY MANAGE TO BRING IN A MILLION DOLLARS A NIGHT SO POLITICIANS CAN GATHER IN FRONT OF THE 1% AND RAGE ABOUT SCHOOLS.
YEAH, IF ONLY LEX LUTHOR THOUGHT TO PUT AN "R" OR "D" AFTER HIS NAME, HE'D BE INVINCIBLE INSTEAD OF IN JAIL.
IT MAKES YOU WONDER IF--
TABLE THAT, CLARK. I HAVE TO GO.
WELL, SHE'S CLEARLY IN THE MIDDLE OF SOMETHING.
BUT I'M SURE IT'S NOTHING LOIS LANE CAN'T HANDLE.
SENATOR? HUGE FAN.
MIGHT I HAVE A MOMENT OF YOUR TIME?
DEAR--!
NO WAY THIS IS GOING TO WORK.
YOU MIGHT BE SURPRISED, MISS LANE.
DID HE--?
JUST SPEAK INTO MY HEAD?
YES, MISS LANE.
OF COURSE I DID.
RIGHT THIS WAY?

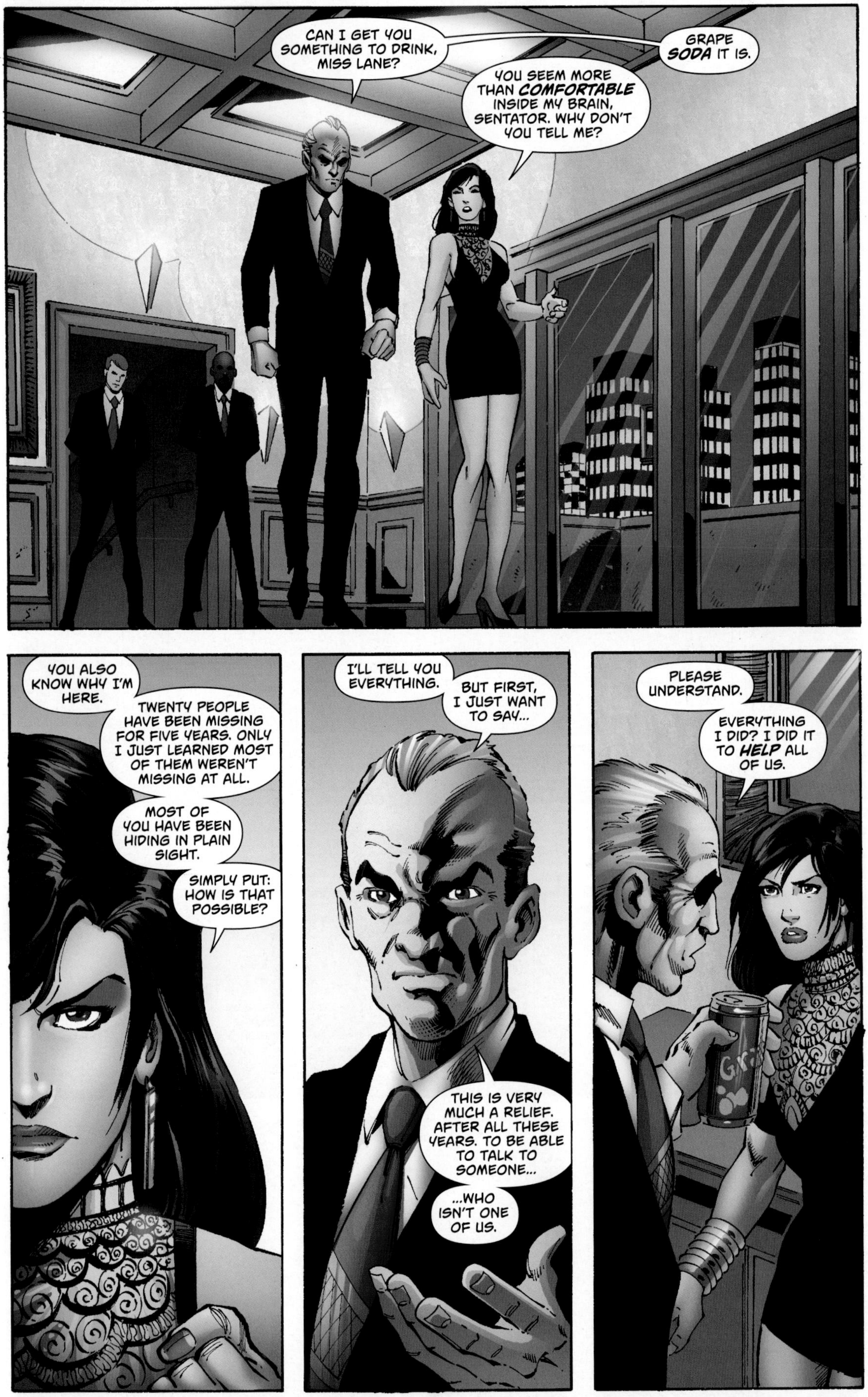
CAN I GET YOU SOMETHING TO DRINK, MISS LANE?
YOU SEEM MORE THAN COMFORTABLE INSIDE MY BRAIN, SENTATOR. WHY DON'T YOU TELL ME?
GRAPE SODA IT IS.
YOU ALSO KNOW WHY I'M HERE.
TWENTY PEOPLE HAVE BEEN MISSING FOR FIVE YEARS. ONLY I JUST LEARNED MOST OF THEM WEREN'T MISSING AT ALL.
MOST OF YOU HAVE BEEN HIDING IN PLAIN SIGHT.
SIMPLY PUT: HOW IS THAT POSSIBLE?
I'LL TELL YOU EVERYTHING.
BUT FIRST, I JUST WANT TO SAY...
THIS IS VERY MUCH A RELIEF. AFTER ALL THESE YEARS. TO BE ABLE TO TALK TO SOMEONE...
...WHO ISN'T ONE OF US.
PLEASE UNDERSTAND.
EVERYTHING I DID? I DID IT TO HELP ALL OF US.

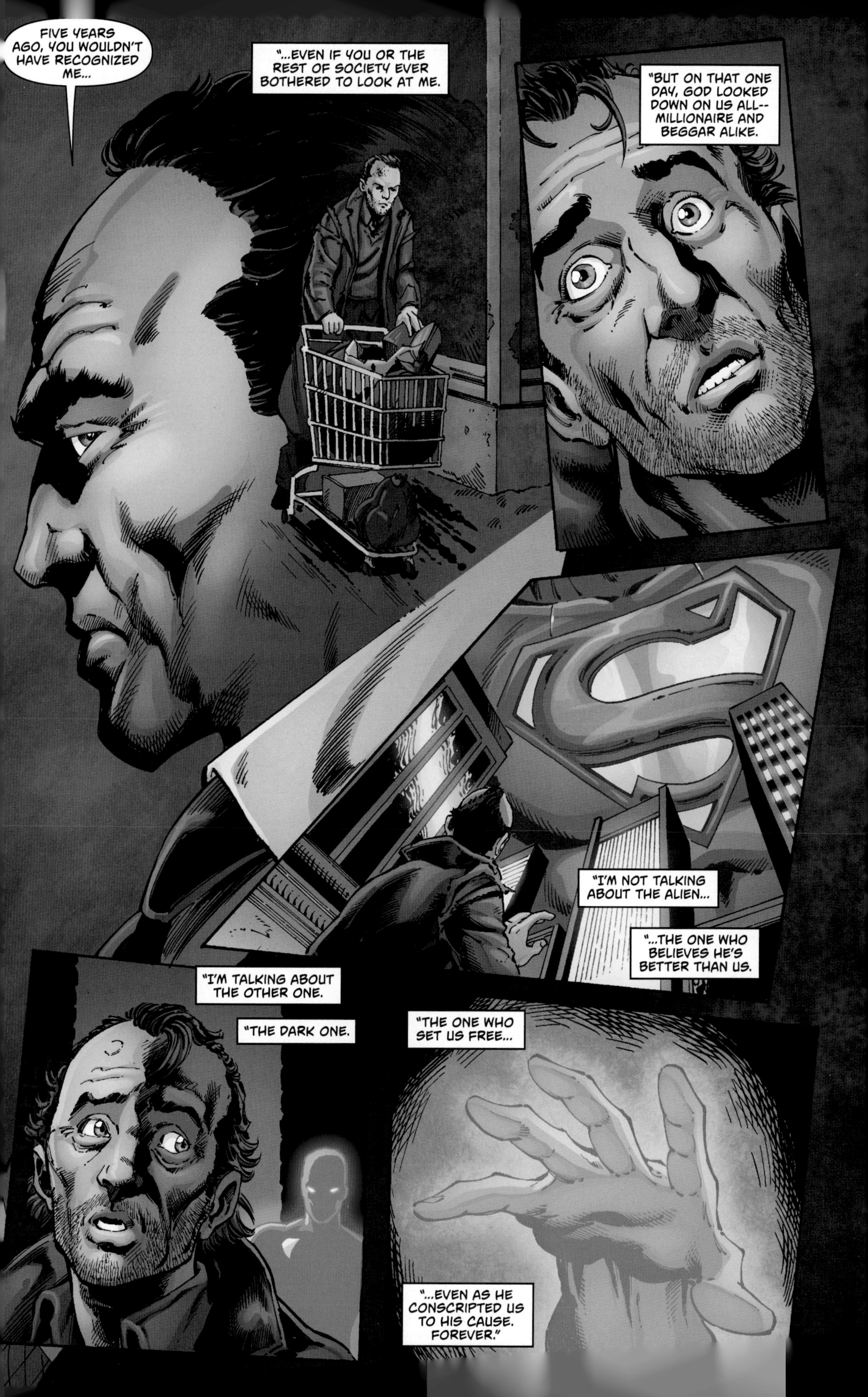
FIVE YEARS AGO, YOU WOULDN'T HAVE RECOGNIZED ME...
"...EVEN IF YOU OR THE REST OF SOCIETY EVER BOTHERED TO LOOK AT ME.
"BUT ON THAT ONE DAY, GOD LOOKED DOWN ON US ALL-- MILLIONAIRE AND BEGGAR ALIKE.
"I'M NOT TALKING ABOUT THE ALIEN...
"...THE ONE WHO BELIEVES HE'S BETTER THAN US.
"I'M TALKING ABOUT THE OTHER ONE.
"THE DARK ONE.
"THE ONE WHO SET US FREE...
"...EVEN AS HE CONSCRIPTED US TO HIS CAUSE. FOREVER."

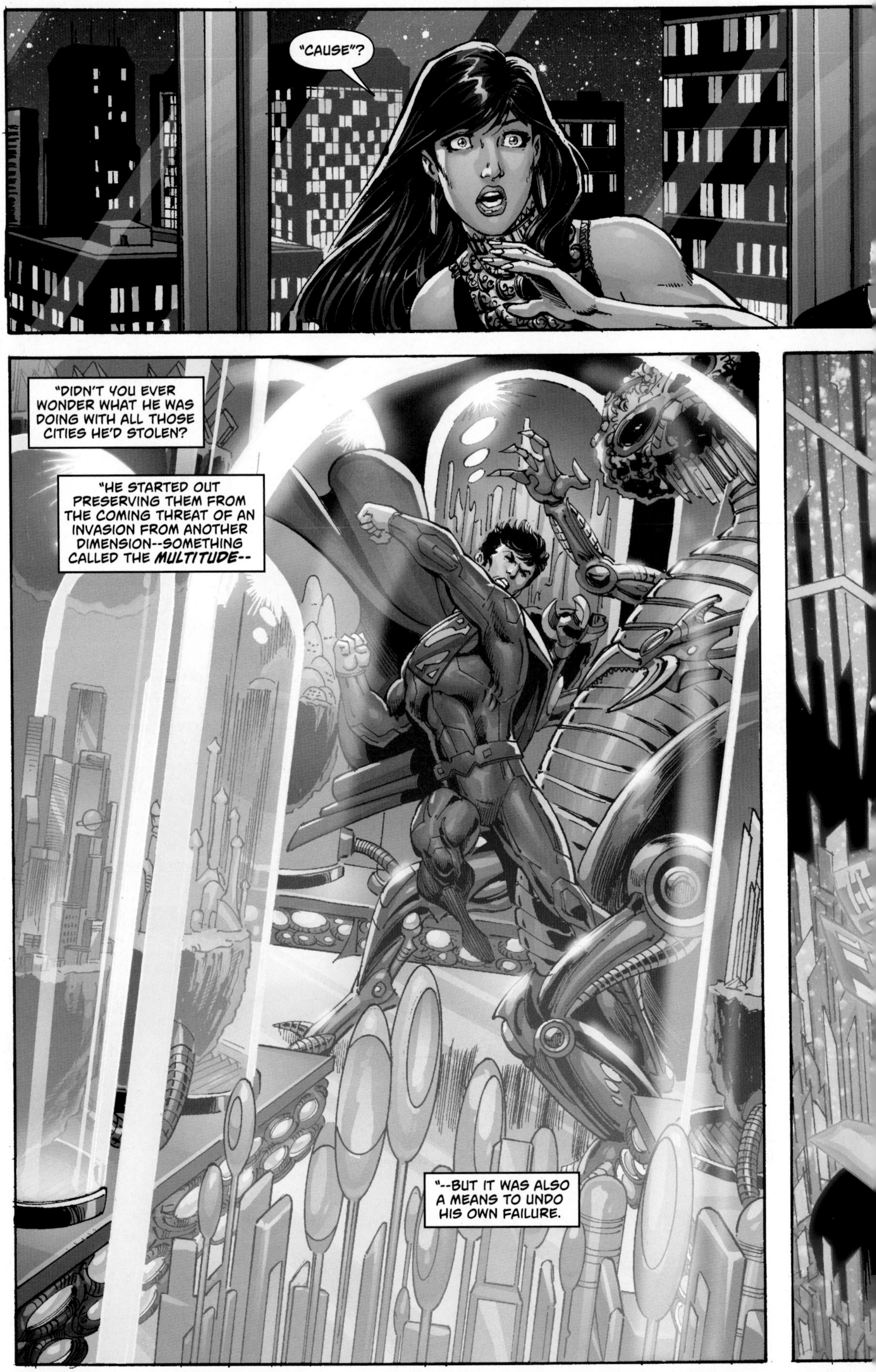
"CAUSE"?
"DIDN'T YOU EVER WONDER WHAT HE WAS DOING WITH ALL THOSE CITIES HE'D STOLEN?
"HE STARTED OUT PRESERVING THEM FROM THE COMING THREAT OF AN INVASION FROM ANOTHER DIMENSION--SOMETHING CALLED THE *MULTITUDE*--
"--BUT IT WAS ALSO A MEANS TO UNDO HIS OWN FAILURE.

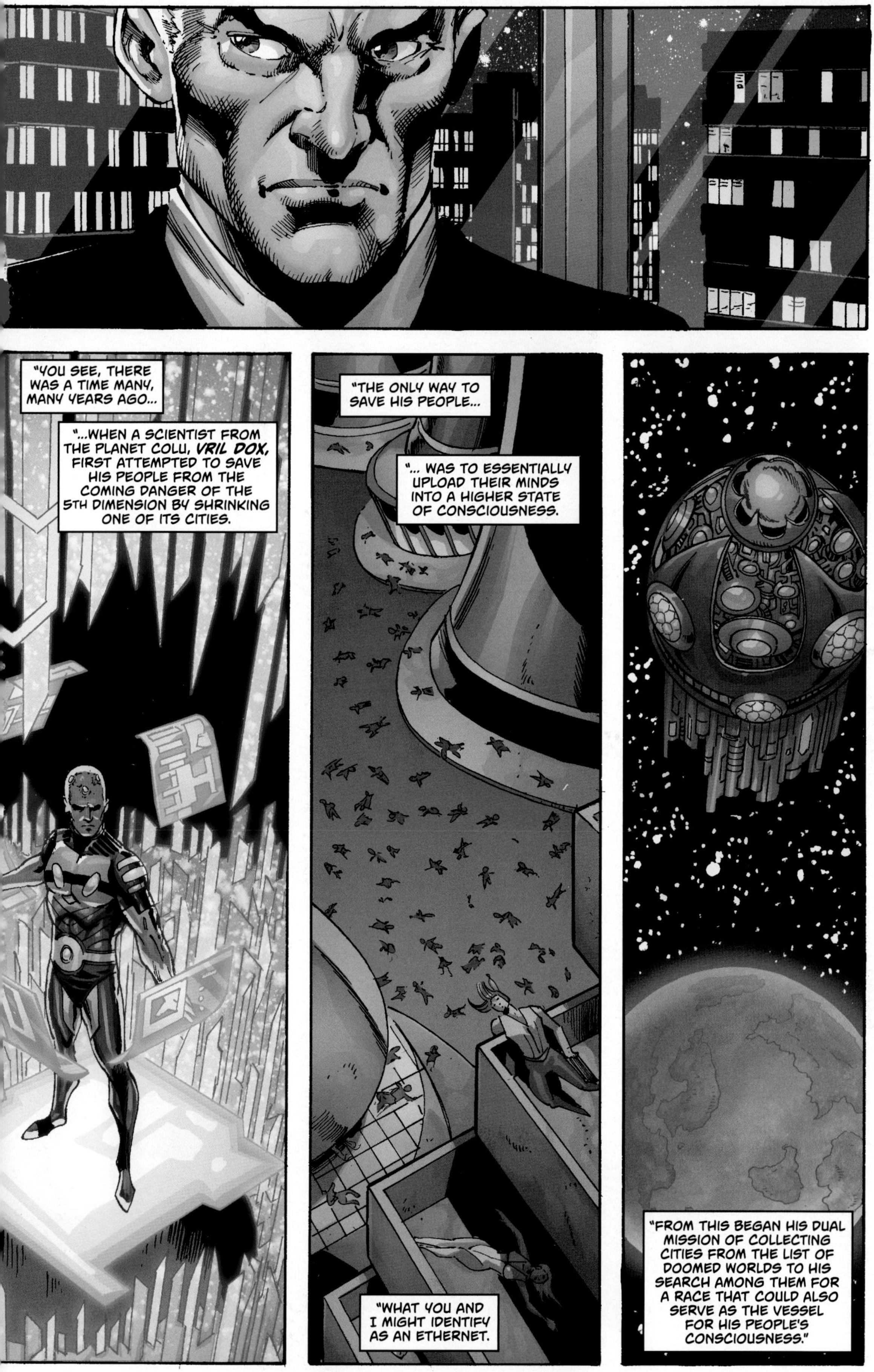
"YOU SEE, THERE WAS A TIME MANY, MANY YEARS AGO...
"...WHEN A SCIENTIST FROM THE PLANET COLU, *VRIL DOX,* FIRST ATTEMPTED TO SAVE HIS PEOPLE FROM THE COMING DANGER OF THE 5TH DIMENSION BY SHRINKING ONE OF ITS CITIES.
"THE ONLY WAY TO SAVE HIS PEOPLE...
"... WAS TO ESSENTIALLY UPLOAD THEIR MINDS INTO A HIGHER STATE OF CONSCIOUSNESS.
"WHAT YOU AND I MIGHT IDENTIFY AS AN ETHERNET.
"FROM THIS BEGAN HIS DUAL MISSION OF COLLECTING CITIES FROM THE LIST OF DOOMED WORLDS TO HIS SEARCH AMONG THEM FOR A RACE THAT COULD ALSO SERVE AS THE VESSEL FOR HIS PEOPLE'S CONSCIOUSNESS."

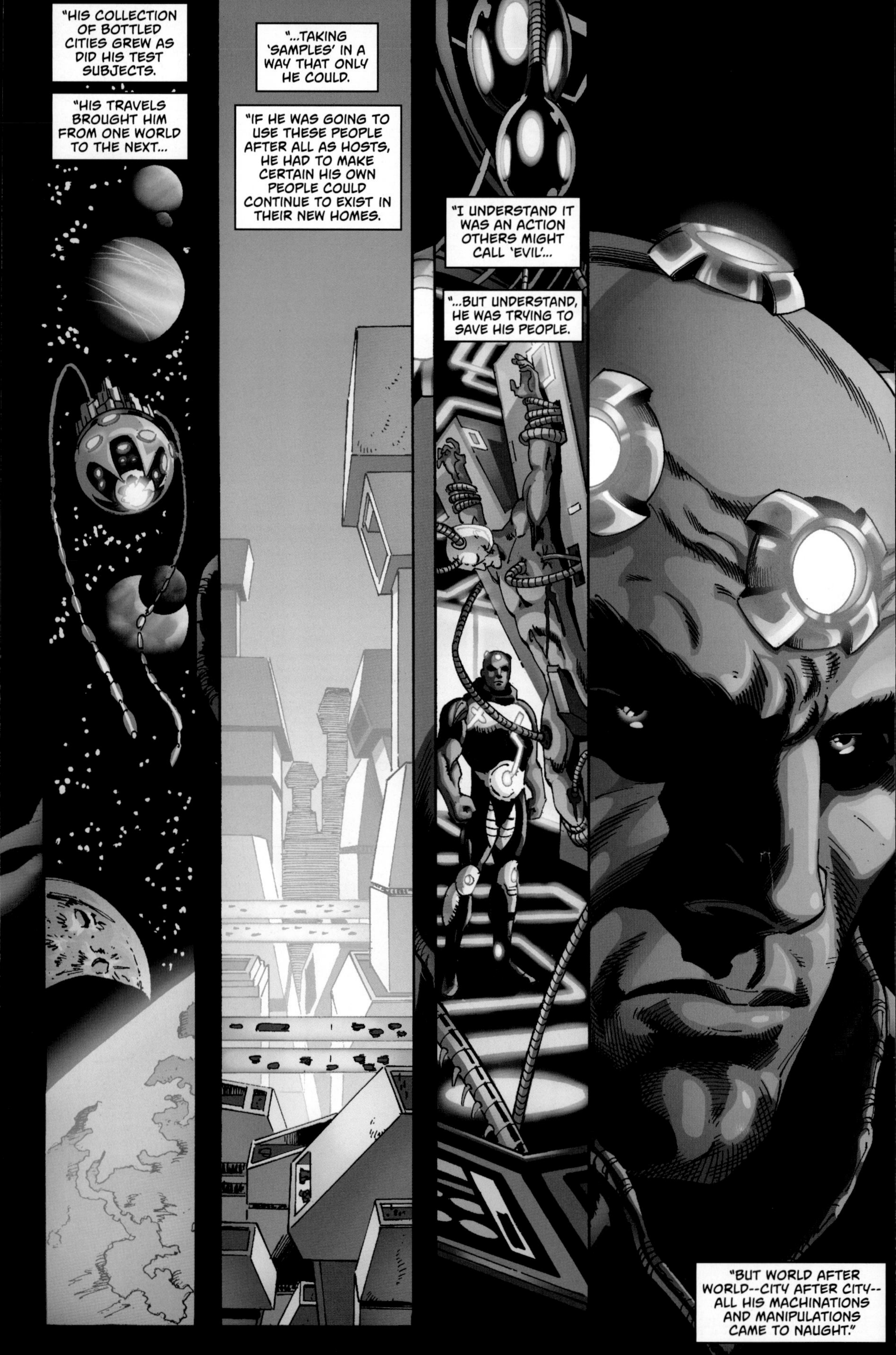
"HIS COLLECTION OF BOTTLED CITIES GREW AS DID HIS TEST SUBJECTS.
"HIS TRAVELS BROUGHT HIM FROM ONE WORLD TO THE NEXT...
"...TAKING 'SAMPLES' IN A WAY THAT ONLY HE COULD.
"IF HE WAS GOING TO USE THESE PEOPLE AFTER ALL AS HOSTS, HE HAD TO MAKE CERTAIN HIS OWN PEOPLE COULD CONTINUE TO EXIST IN THEIR NEW HOMES.
"I UNDERSTAND IT WAS AN ACTION OTHERS MIGHT CALL 'EVIL'...
"...BUT UNDERSTAND, HE WAS TRYING TO SAVE HIS PEOPLE.
"BUT WORLD AFTER WORLD--CITY AFTER CITY--ALL HIS MACHINATIONS AND MANIPULATIONS CAME TO NAUGHT."

"THAT WAS UNTIL FIVE YEARS AGO. IN TAKING METROPOLIS, BRAINIAC 'INFECTED' SOME OF US."

"AT A TOUCH OF HIS ALIEN TECHNOLOGY, HE ELEVATED THE BRAINS OF TWENTY RANDOM HUMANS TO THE 12TH LEVEL!"

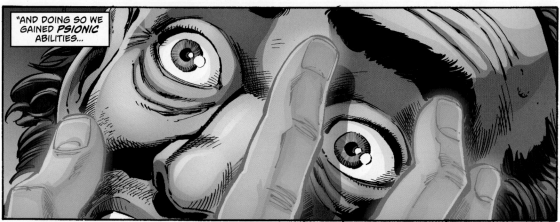

"AND DOING SO WE GAINED *PSIONIC* ABILITIES..."

"WE CAME TO RECOGNIZE EACH OTHER AT A GLANCE.

"AS YOU'VE NO DOUBT DISCOVERED, SOME OF US USED OUR POWERS FOR OUR OWN MEANS...

"FOR FUN. FOR PROFIT.

"OTHERS LIKE ME WERE MORE... PRECISE.

"I TURNED MY LIFE AROUND BECAUSE I WANTED TO HELP."

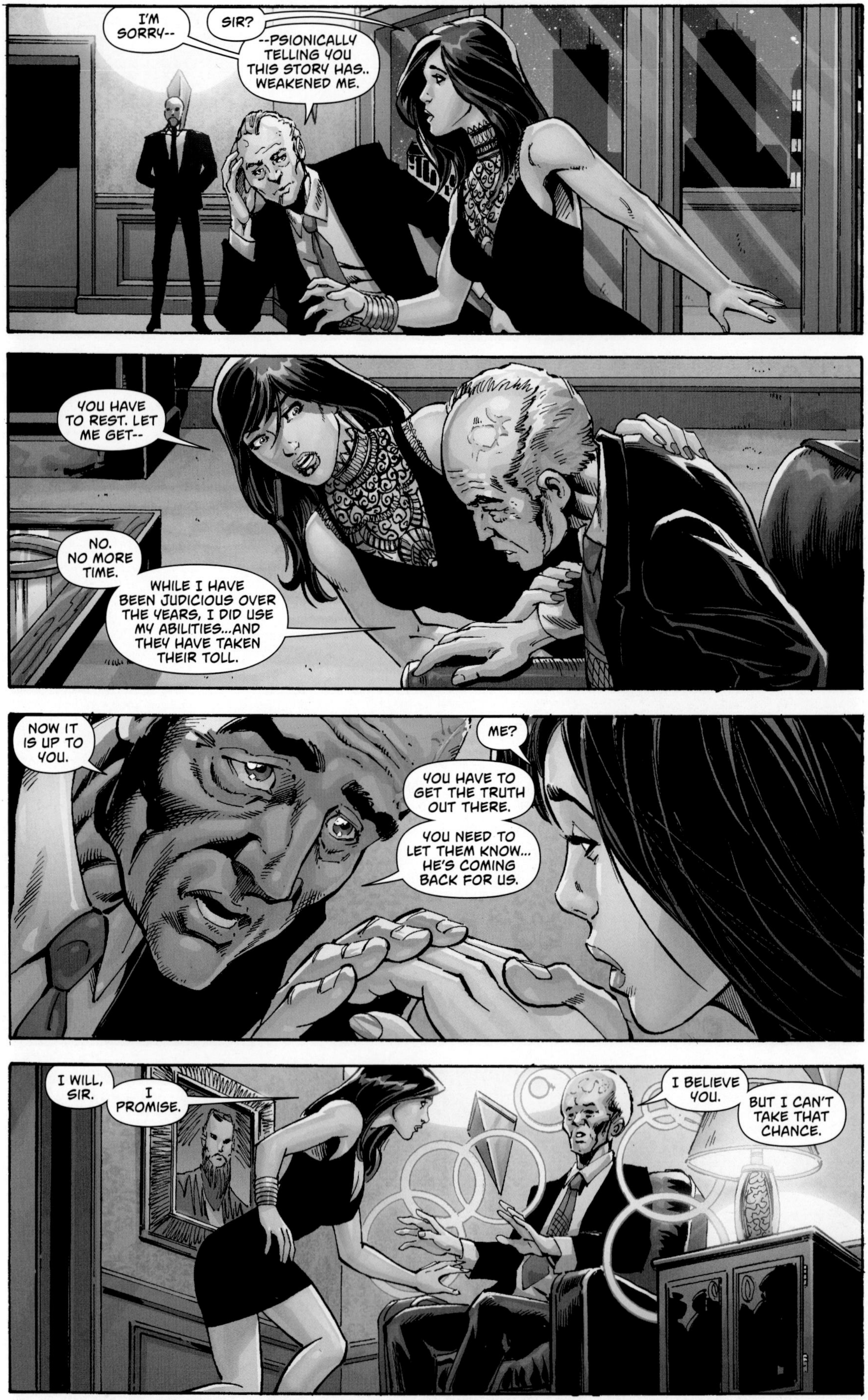
I'M SORRY--
SIR?
--PSIONICALLY TELLING YOU THIS STORY HAS.. WEAKENED ME.
YOU HAVE TO REST. LET ME GET--
NO. NO MORE TIME.
WHILE I HAVE BEEN JUDICIOUS OVER THE YEARS, I DID USE MY ABILITIES...AND THEY HAVE TAKEN THEIR TOLL.
NOW IT IS UP TO YOU.
ME?
YOU HAVE TO GET THE TRUTH OUT THERE.
YOU NEED TO LET THEM KNOW... HE'S COMING BACK FOR US.
I WILL, SIR.
I PROMISE.
I BELIEVE YOU.
BUT I CAN'T TAKE THAT CHANCE.

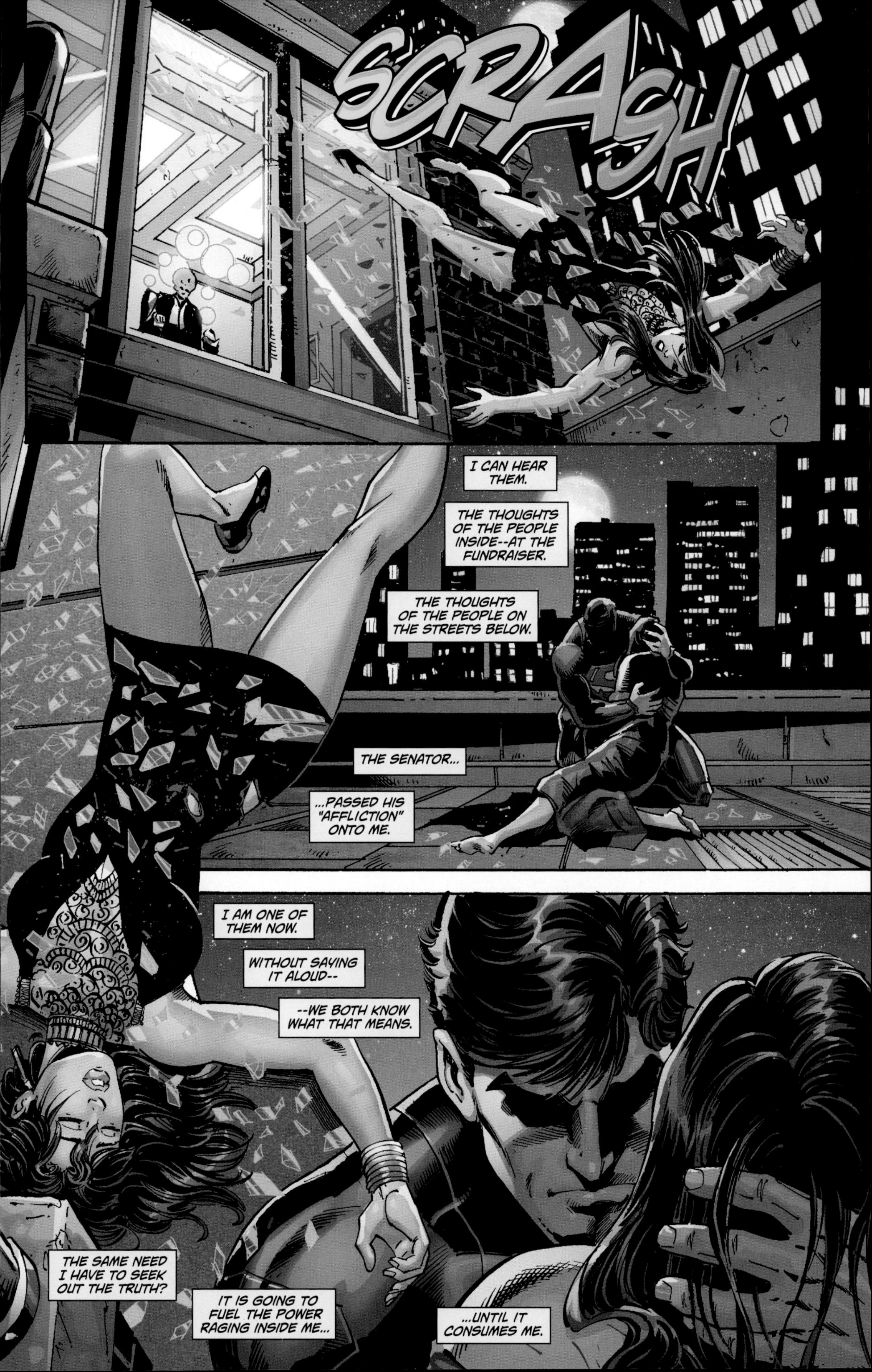
SCRASH
I CAN HEAR THEM.
THE THOUGHTS OF THE PEOPLE INSIDE--AT THE FUNDRAISER.
THE THOUGHTS OF THE PEOPLE ON THE STREETS BELOW.
THE SENATOR...
...PASSED HIS "AFFLICTION" ONTO ME.
I AM ONE OF THEM NOW.
WITHOUT SAYING IT ALOUD--
--WE BOTH KNOW WHAT THAT MEANS.
THE SAME NEED I HAVE TO SEEK OUT THE TRUTH?
IT IS GOING TO FUEL THE POWER RAGING INSIDE ME...
...UNTIL IT CONSUMES ME.

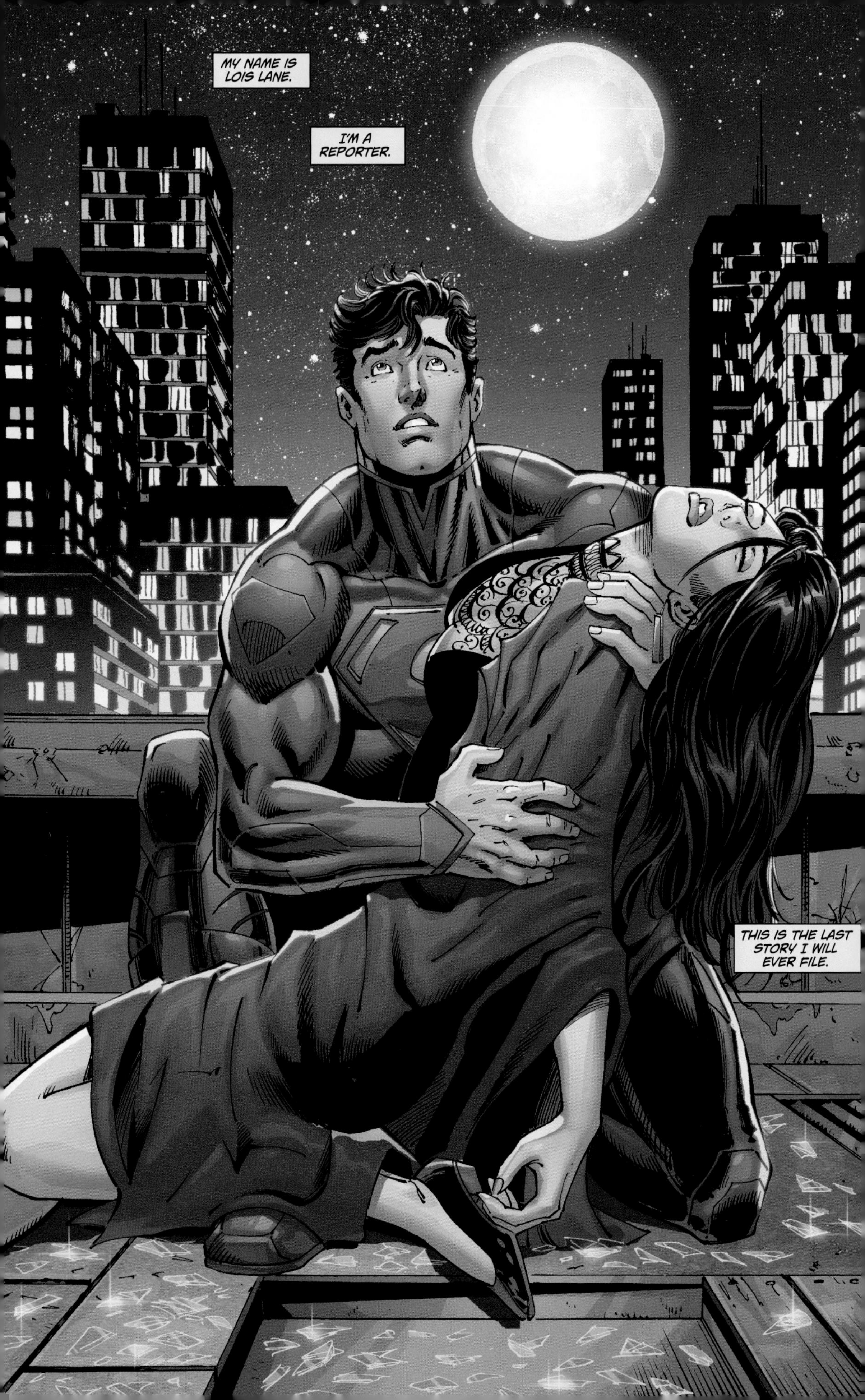
MY NAME IS LOIS LANE.
I'M A REPORTER.
THIS IS THE LAST STORY I WILL EVER FILE.

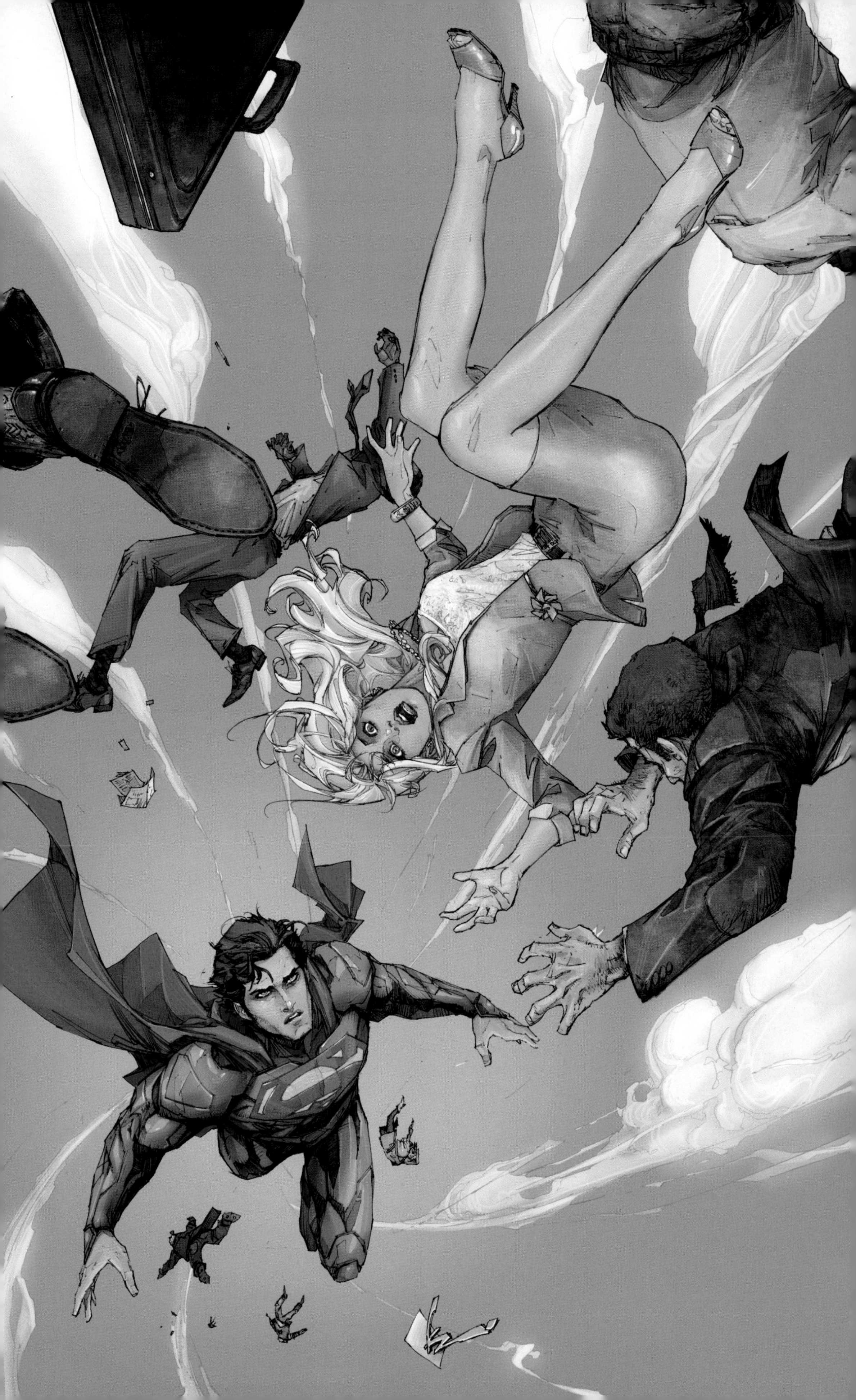

METROPOLITAN NIGHTMARE

SCOTT LOBDELL writer **AARON KUDER** – PGS 1-4 & 17-20 **TYLER KIRKHAM** – PGS 5-9 **ROBSON ROCHA** – PGS 10-16 pencillers
AARON KUDER – PGS 1-4 & 17-20 **JAIME MENDOZA** – PGS 10-16 inkers cover art by **KENNETH ROCAFORT**

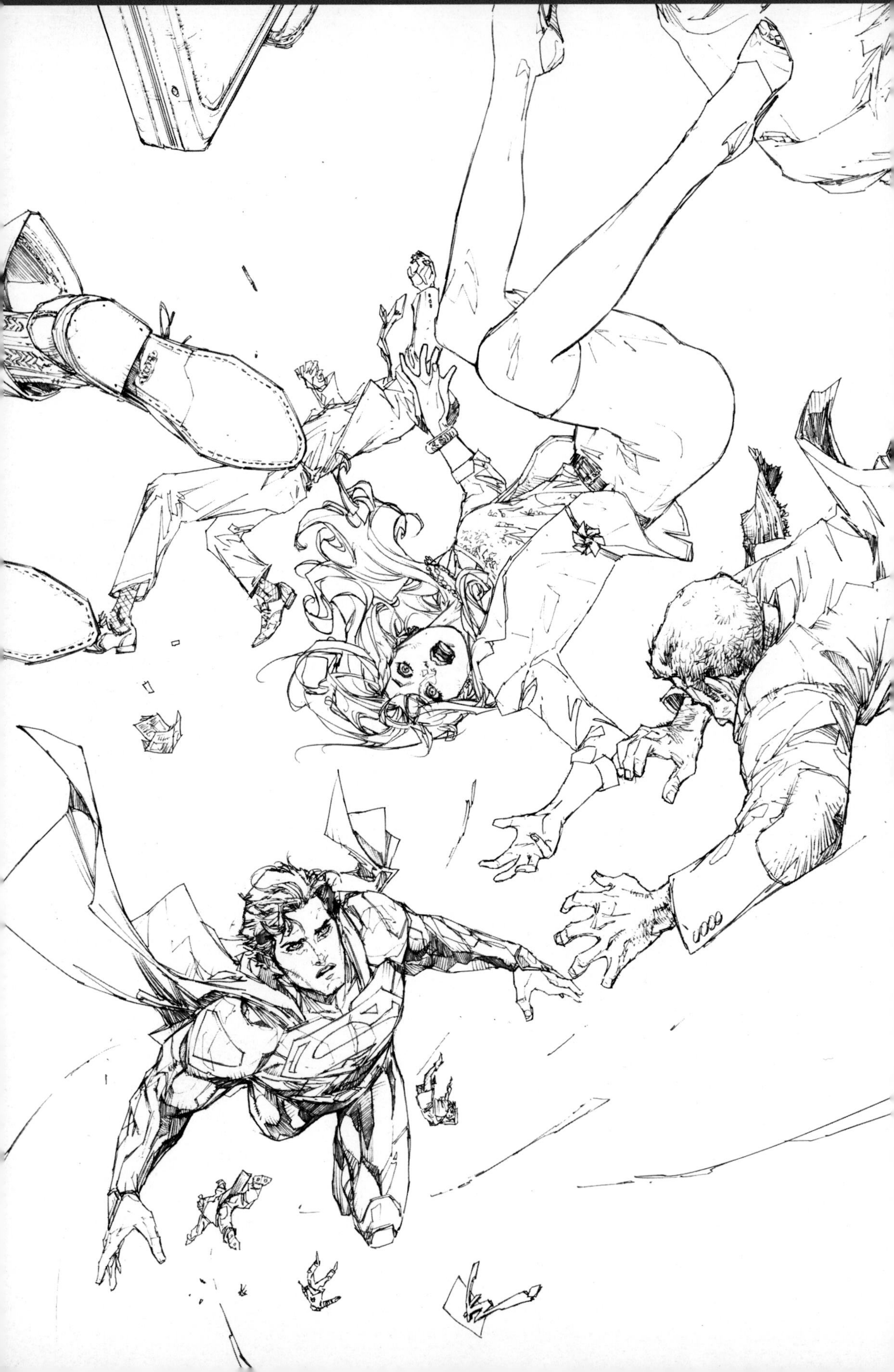

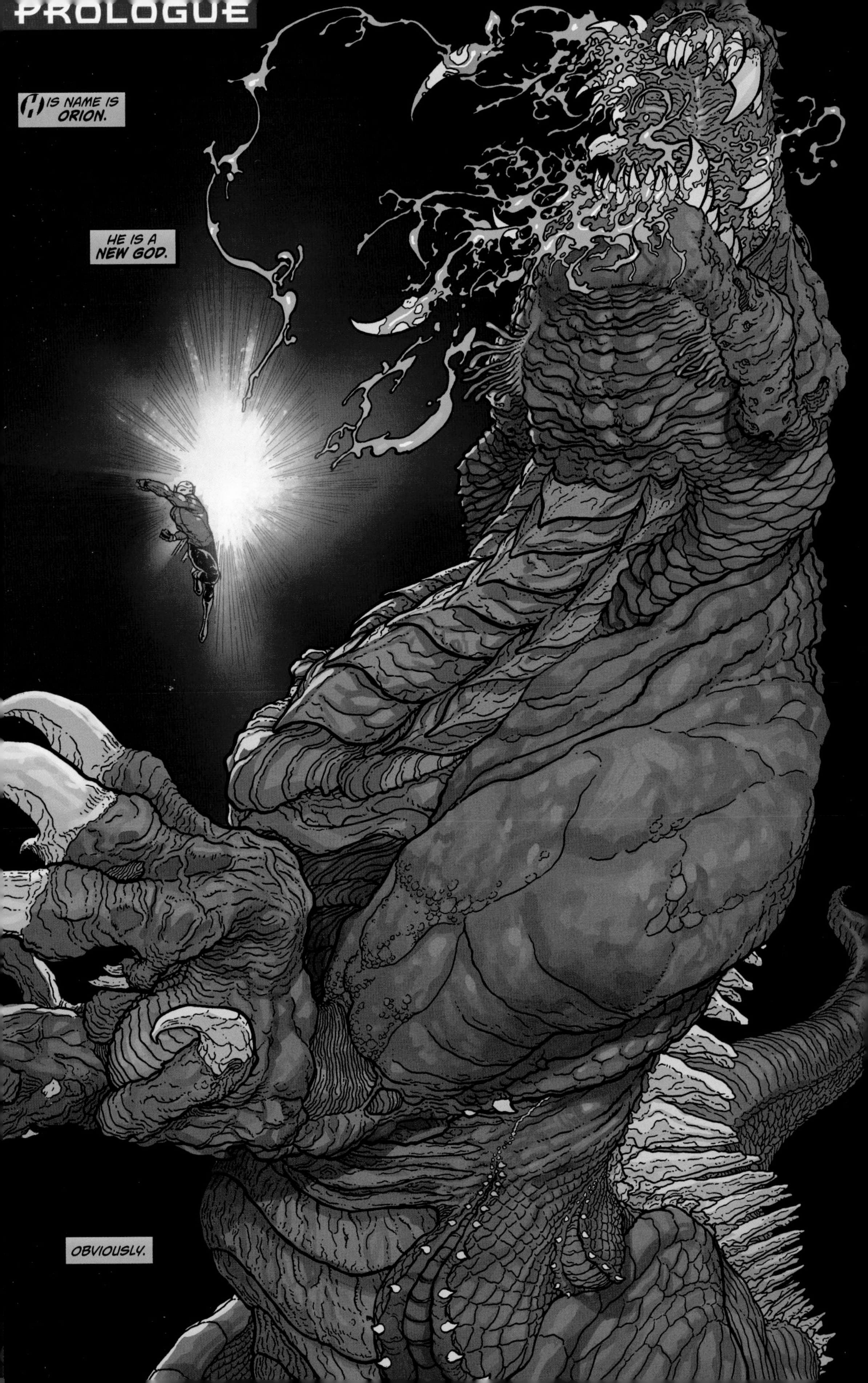
PROLOGUE
HIS NAME IS ORION.
HE IS A NEW GOD.
OBVIOUSLY.

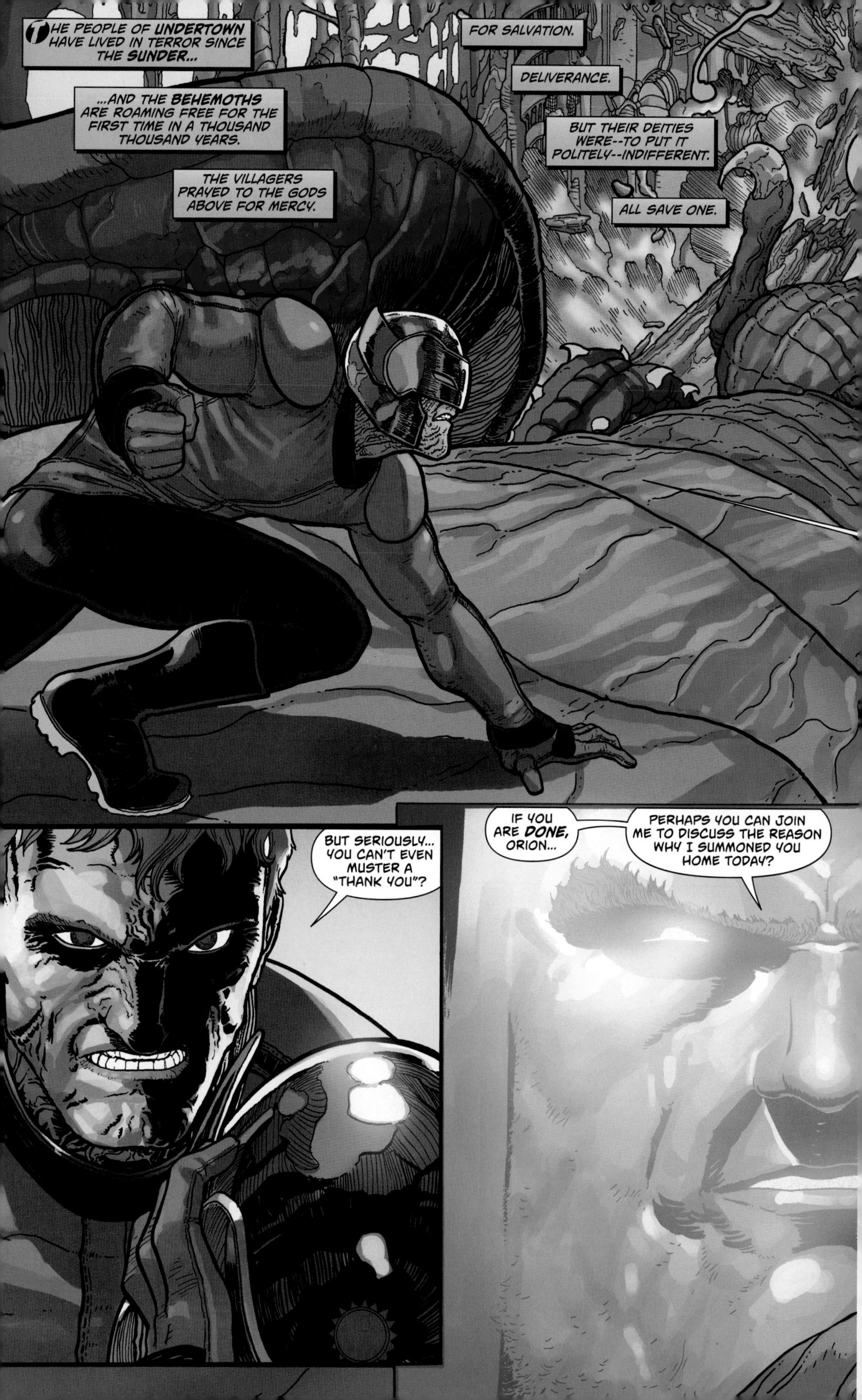
THE PEOPLE OF UNDERTOWN HAVE LIVED IN TERROR SINCE THE SUNDER...
...AND THE BEHEMOTHS ARE ROAMING FREE FOR THE FIRST TIME IN A THOUSAND THOUSAND YEARS.
THE VILLAGERS PRAYED TO THE GODS ABOVE FOR MERCY.
FOR SALVATION.
DELIVERANCE.
BUT THEIR DEITIES WERE--TO PUT IT POLITELY--INDIFFERENT.
ALL SAVE ONE.
BUT SERIOUSLY... YOU CAN'T EVEN MUSTER A "THANK YOU"?
IF YOU ARE DONE, ORION...
PERHAPS YOU CAN JOIN ME TO DISCUSS THE REASON WHY I SUMMONED YOU HOME TODAY?

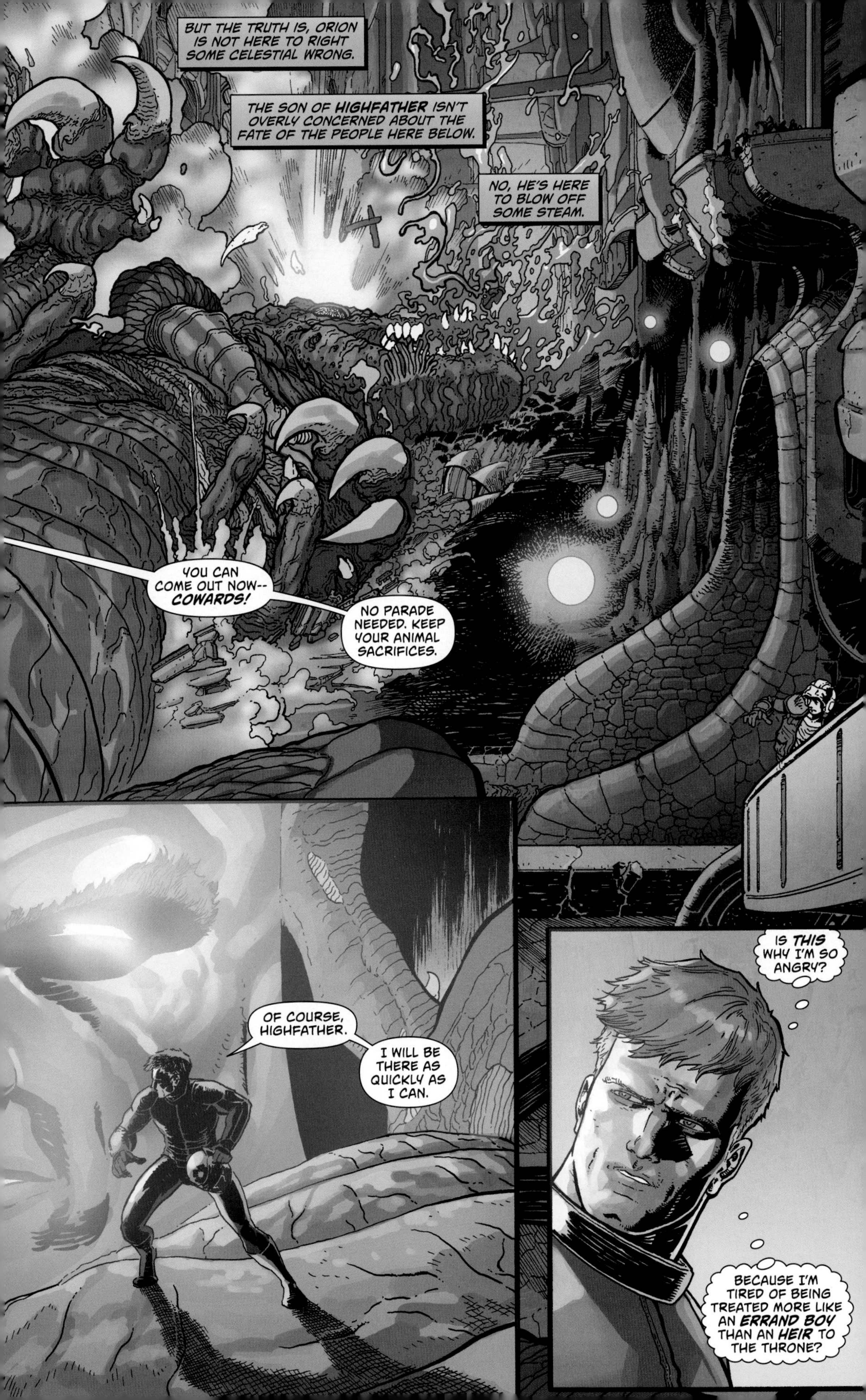
BUT THE TRUTH IS, ORION IS NOT HERE TO RIGHT SOME CELESTIAL WRONG.
THE SON OF HIGHFATHER ISN'T OVERLY CONCERNED ABOUT THE FATE OF THE PEOPLE HERE BELOW.
NO, HE'S HERE TO BLOW OFF SOME STEAM.
YOU CAN COME OUT NOW-- COWARDS!
NO PARADE NEEDED. KEEP YOUR ANIMAL SACRIFICES.
OF COURSE, HIGHFATHER.
I WILL BE THERE AS QUICKLY AS I CAN.
IS THIS WHY I'M SO ANGRY?
BECAUSE I'M TIRED OF BEING TREATED MORE LIKE AN ERRAND BOY THAN AN HEIR TO THE THRONE?

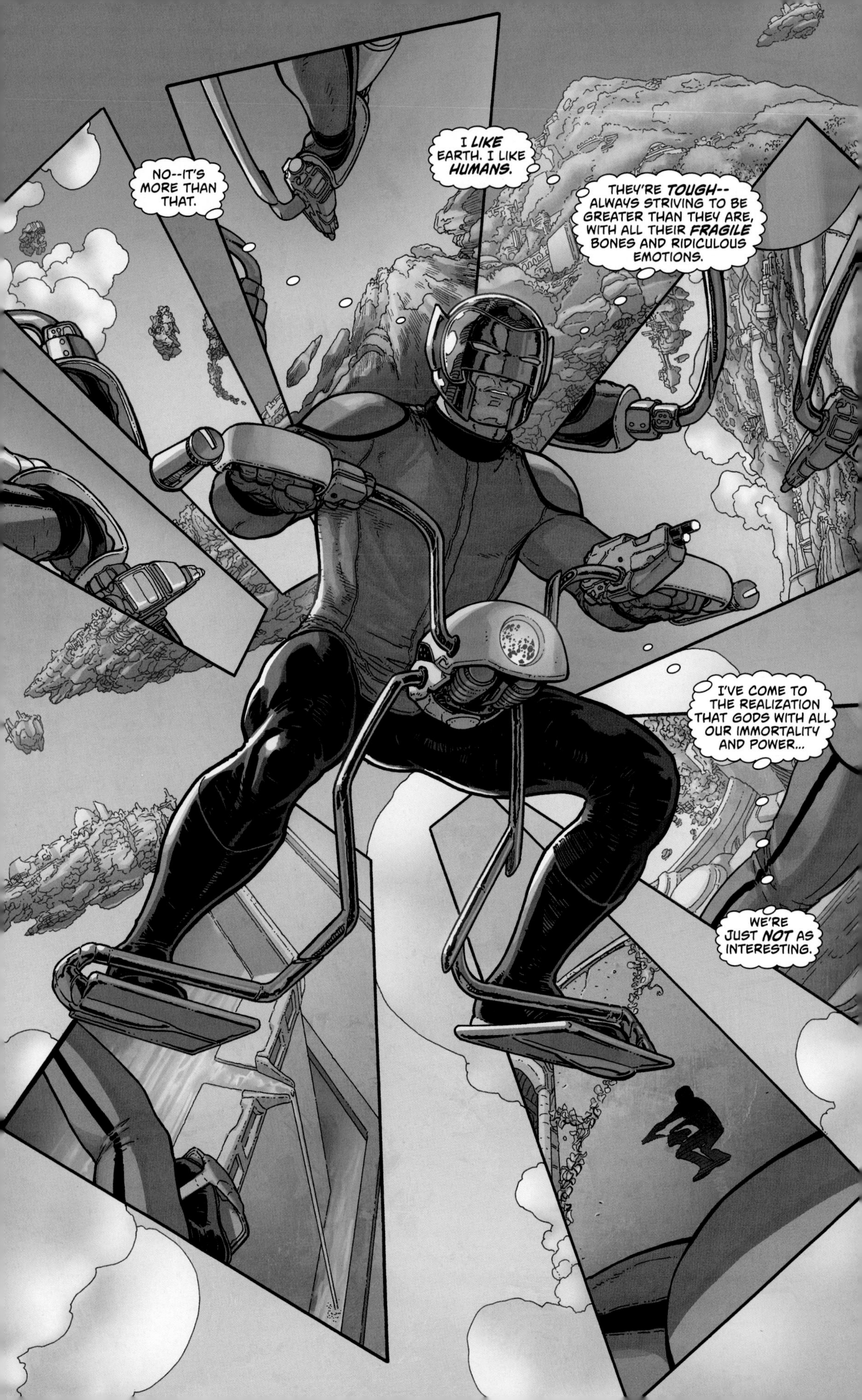
NO--IT'S MORE THAN THAT.
I LIKE EARTH. I LIKE HUMANS.
THEY'RE TOUGH-- ALWAYS STRIVING TO BE GREATER THAN THEY ARE, WITH ALL THEIR FRAGILE BONES AND RIDICULOUS EMOTIONS.
I'VE COME TO THE REALIZATION THAT GODS WITH ALL OUR IMMORTALITY AND POWER...
WE'RE JUST NOT AS INTERESTING.

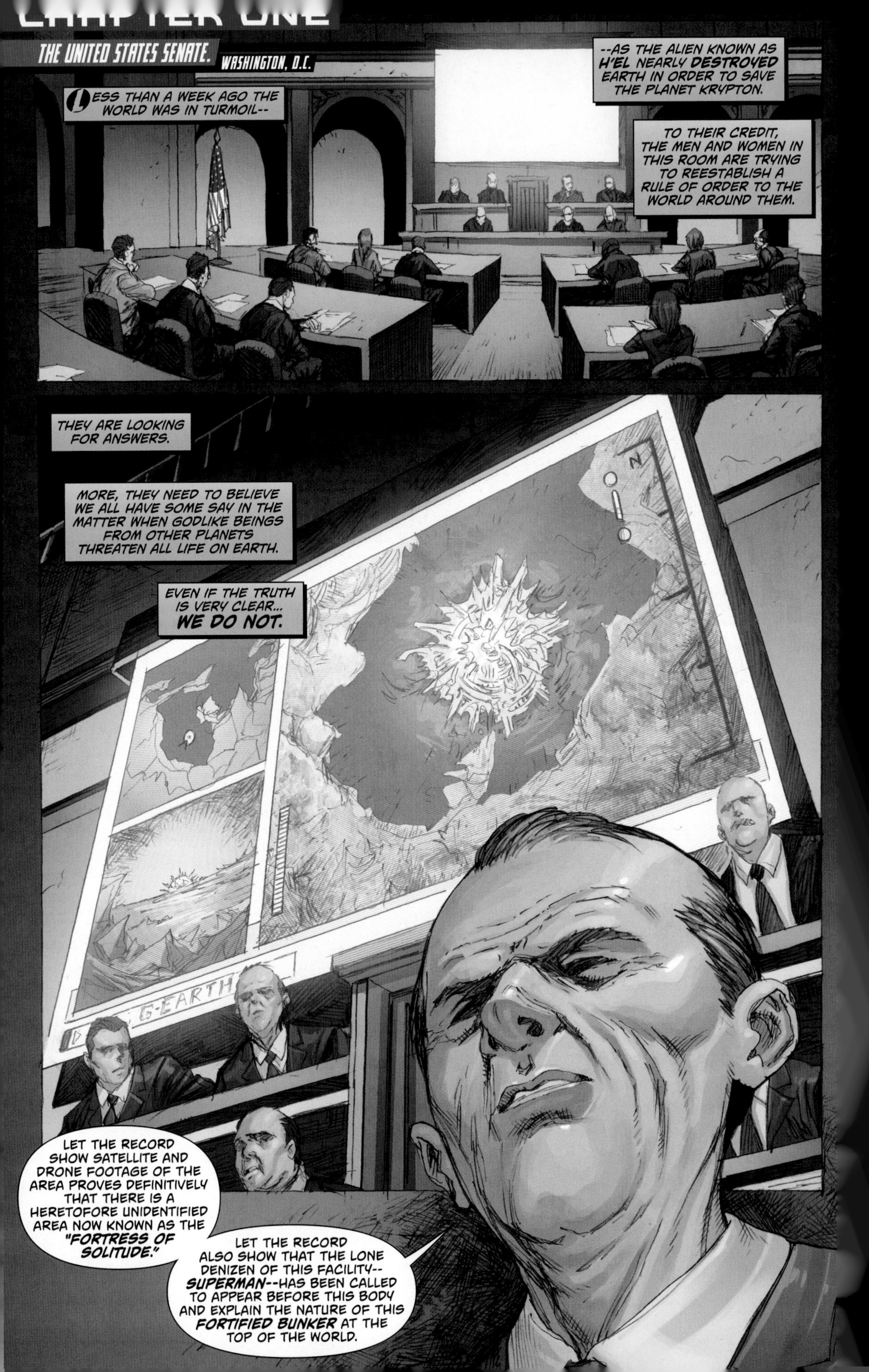
THE UNITED STATES SENATE.
WASHINGTON, D.C.
LESS THAN A WEEK AGO THE WORLD WAS IN TURMOIL--
--AS THE ALIEN KNOWN AS H'EL NEARLY DESTROYED EARTH IN ORDER TO SAVE THE PLANET KRYPTON.
TO THEIR CREDIT, THE MEN AND WOMEN IN THIS ROOM ARE TRYING TO REESTABLISH A RULE OF ORDER TO THE WORLD AROUND THEM.
THEY ARE LOOKING FOR ANSWERS.
MORE, THEY NEED TO BELIEVE WE ALL HAVE SOME SAY IN THE MATTER WHEN GODLIKE BEINGS FROM OTHER PLANETS THREATEN ALL LIFE ON EARTH.
EVEN IF THE TRUTH IS VERY CLEAR... WE DO NOT.
G-EARTH
LET THE RECORD SHOW SATELLITE AND DRONE FOOTAGE OF THE AREA PROVES DEFINITIVELY THAT THERE IS A HERETOFORE UNIDENTIFIED AREA NOW KNOWN AS THE "FORTRESS OF SOLITUDE."
LET THE RECORD ALSO SHOW THAT THE LONE DENIZEN OF THIS FACILITY--SUPERMAN--HAS BEEN CALLED TO APPEAR BEFORE THIS BODY AND EXPLAIN THE NATURE OF THIS FORTIFIED BUNKER AT THE TOP OF THE WORLD.

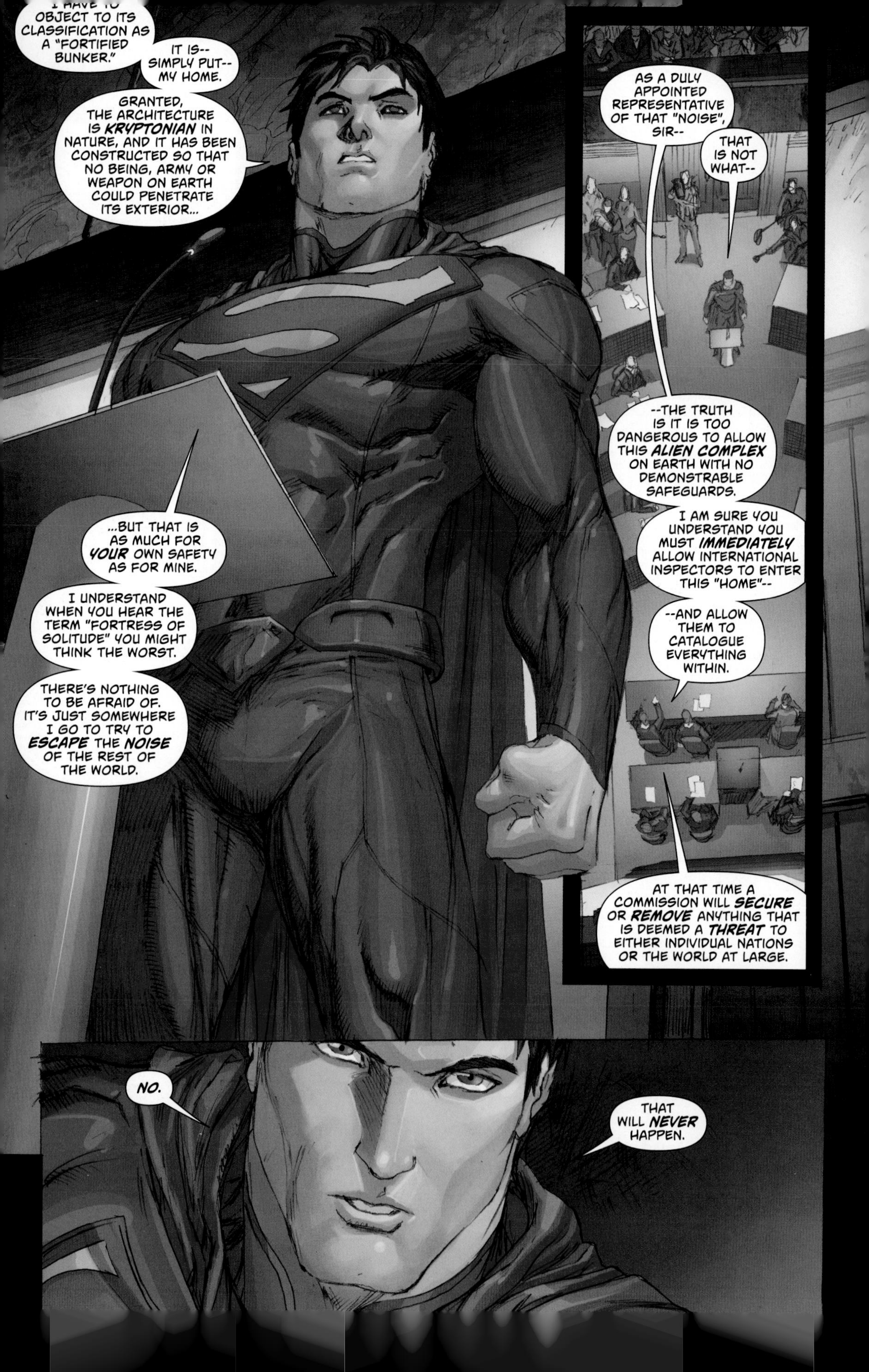
I HAVE TO OBJECT TO ITS CLASSIFICATION AS A "FORTIFIED BUNKER."
IT IS-- SIMPLY PUT-- MY HOME.
GRANTED, THE ARCHITECTURE IS KRYPTONIAN IN NATURE, AND IT HAS BEEN CONSTRUCTED SO THAT NO BEING, ARMY OR WEAPON ON EARTH COULD PENETRATE ITS EXTERIOR...
...BUT THAT IS AS MUCH FOR YOUR OWN SAFETY AS FOR MINE.
I UNDERSTAND WHEN YOU HEAR THE TERM "FORTRESS OF SOLITUDE" YOU MIGHT THINK THE WORST.
THERE'S NOTHING TO BE AFRAID OF. IT'S JUST SOMEWHERE I GO TO TRY TO ESCAPE THE NOISE OF THE REST OF THE WORLD.
AS A DULY APPOINTED REPRESENTATIVE OF THAT "NOISE", SIR--
THAT IS NOT WHAT--
--THE TRUTH IS IT IS TOO DANGEROUS TO ALLOW THIS ALIEN COMPLEX ON EARTH WITH NO DEMONSTRABLE SAFEGUARDS.
I AM SURE YOU UNDERSTAND YOU MUST IMMEDIATELY ALLOW INTERNATIONAL INSPECTORS TO ENTER THIS "HOME"--
--AND ALLOW THEM TO CATALOGUE EVERYTHING WITHIN.
AT THAT TIME A COMMISSION WILL SECURE OR REMOVE ANYTHING THAT IS DEEMED A THREAT TO EITHER INDIVIDUAL NATIONS OR THE WORLD AT LARGE.
NO.
THAT WILL NEVER HAPPEN.

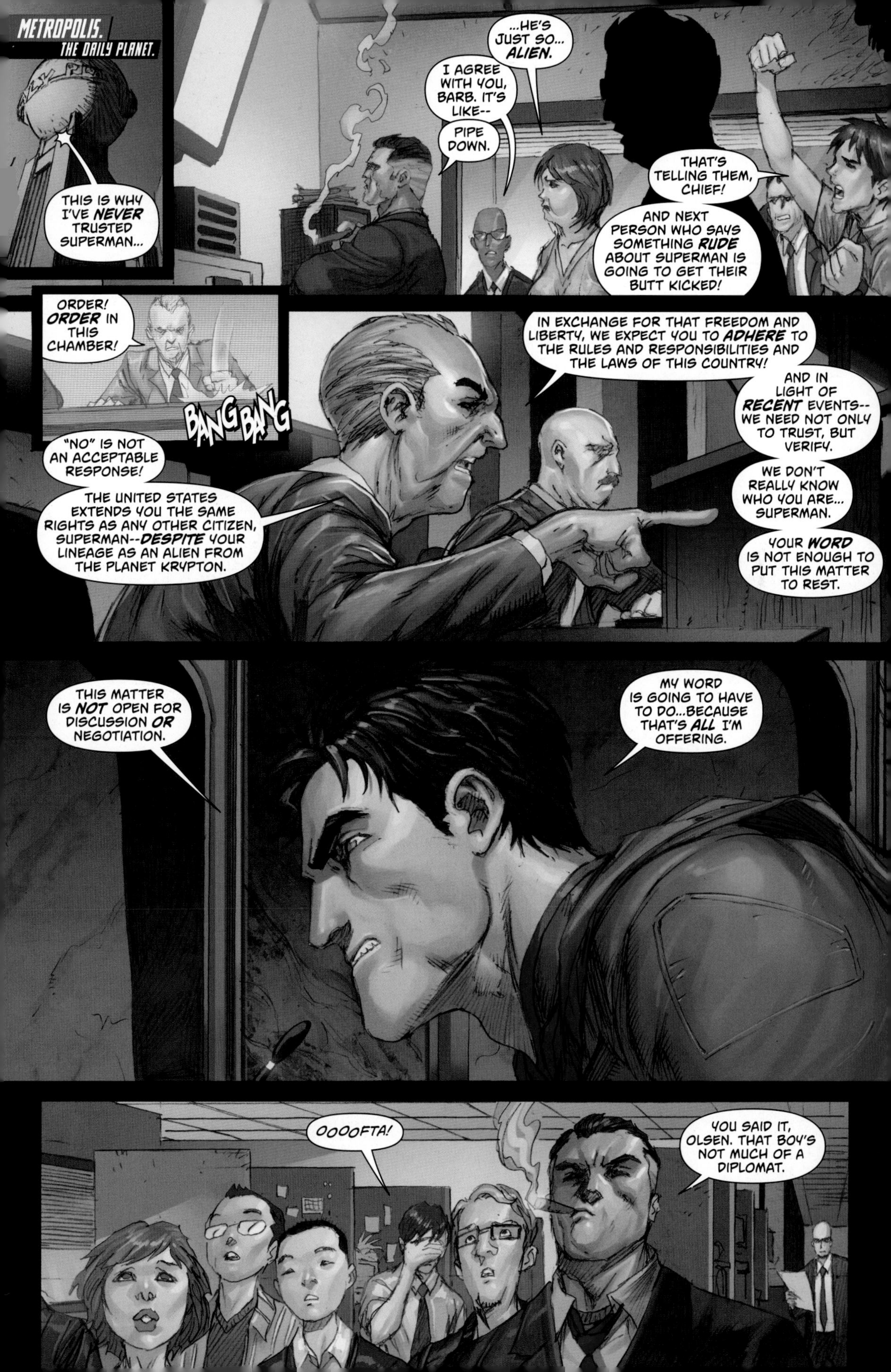
METROPOLIS.
THE DAILY PLANET.
THIS IS WHY I'VE NEVER TRUSTED SUPERMAN...
I AGREE WITH YOU, BARB. IT'S LIKE--
...HE'S JUST SO... ALIEN.
PIPE DOWN.
THAT'S TELLING THEM, CHIEF!
AND NEXT PERSON WHO SAYS SOMETHING RUDE ABOUT SUPERMAN IS GOING TO GET THEIR BUTT KICKED!
ORDER! ORDER IN THIS CHAMBER!
BANG BANG
"NO" IS NOT AN ACCEPTABLE RESPONSE!
THE UNITED STATES EXTENDS YOU THE SAME RIGHTS AS ANY OTHER CITIZEN, SUPERMAN--DESPITE YOUR LINEAGE AS AN ALIEN FROM THE PLANET KRYPTON.
IN EXCHANGE FOR THAT FREEDOM AND LIBERTY, WE EXPECT YOU TO ADHERE TO THE RULES AND RESPONSIBILITIES AND THE LAWS OF THIS COUNTRY!
AND IN LIGHT OF RECENT EVENTS--WE NEED NOT ONLY TO TRUST, BUT VERIFY.
WE DON'T REALLY KNOW WHO YOU ARE... SUPERMAN.
YOUR WORD IS NOT ENOUGH TO PUT THIS MATTER TO REST.
THIS MATTER IS NOT OPEN FOR DISCUSSION OR NEGOTIATION.
MY WORD IS GOING TO HAVE TO DO...BECAUSE THAT'S ALL I'M OFFERING.
OOOOFTA!
YOU SAID IT, OLSEN. THAT BOY'S NOT MUCH OF A DIPLOMAT.

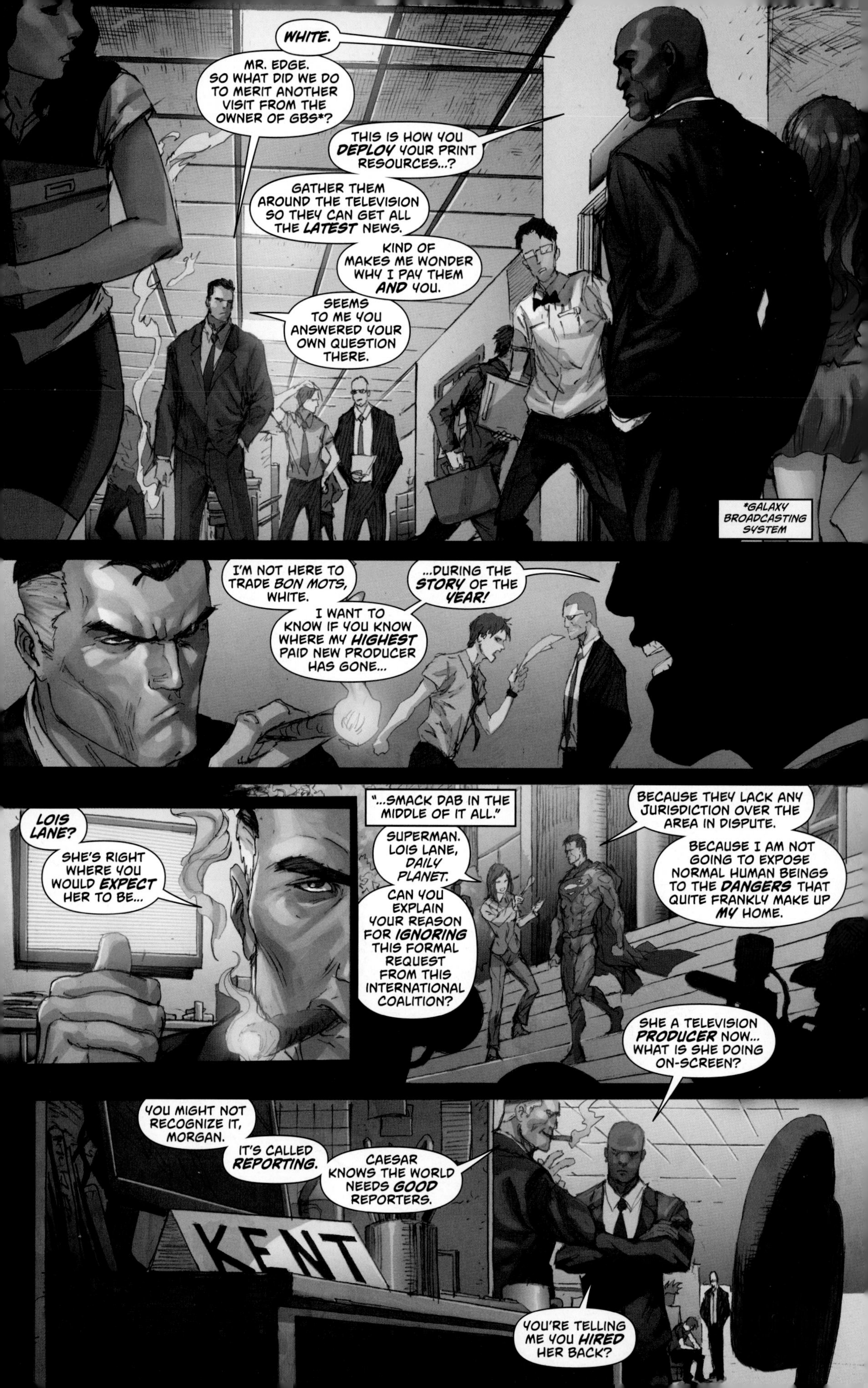
WHITE.
MR. EDGE. SO WHAT DID WE DO TO MERIT ANOTHER VISIT FROM THE OWNER OF GBS*?
THIS IS HOW YOU DEPLOY YOUR PRINT RESOURCES...?
GATHER THEM AROUND THE TELEVISION SO THEY CAN GET ALL THE LATEST NEWS.
KIND OF MAKES ME WONDER WHY I PAY THEM AND YOU.
SEEMS TO ME YOU ANSWERED YOUR OWN QUESTION THERE.
*GALAXY BROADCASTING SYSTEM
I'M NOT HERE TO TRADE BON MOTS, WHITE.
I WANT TO KNOW IF YOU KNOW WHERE MY HIGHEST PAID NEW PRODUCER HAS GONE...
...DURING THE STORY OF THE YEAR!
LOIS LANE?
SHE'S RIGHT WHERE YOU WOULD EXPECT HER TO BE...
"...SMACK DAB IN THE MIDDLE OF IT ALL."
SUPERMAN. LOIS LANE, DAILY PLANET.
CAN YOU EXPLAIN YOUR REASON FOR IGNORING THIS FORMAL REQUEST FROM THIS INTERNATIONAL COALITION?
BECAUSE THEY LACK ANY JURISDICTION OVER THE AREA IN DISPUTE.
BECAUSE I AM NOT GOING TO EXPOSE NORMAL HUMAN BEINGS TO THE DANGERS THAT QUITE FRANKLY MAKE UP MY HOME.
SHE A TELEVISION PRODUCER NOW... WHAT IS SHE DOING ON-SCREEN?
YOU MIGHT NOT RECOGNIZE IT, MORGAN.
IT'S CALLED REPORTING.
CAESAR KNOWS THE WORLD NEEDS GOOD REPORTERS.
KENT
YOU'RE TELLING ME YOU HIRED HER BACK?

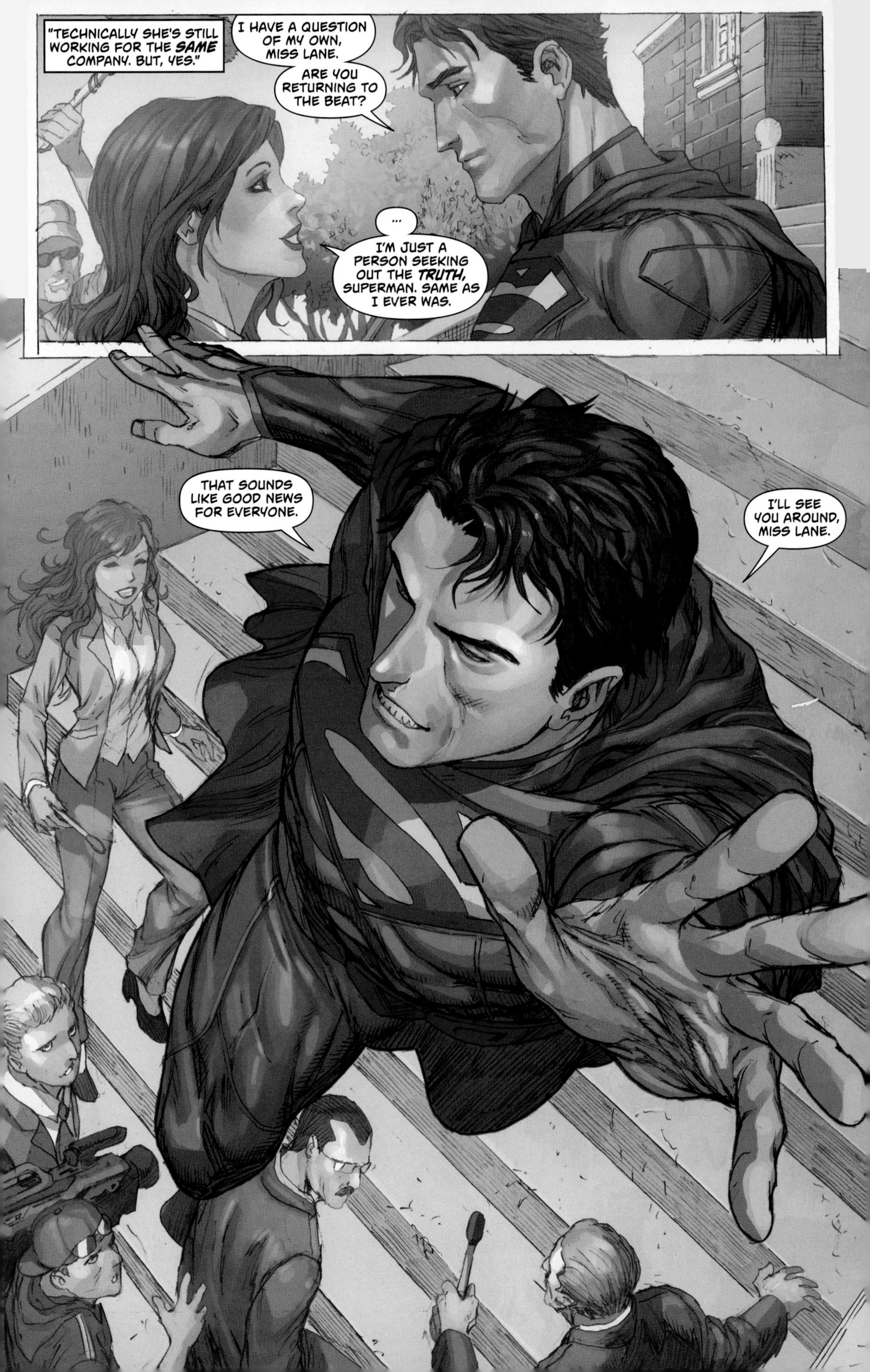
"TECHNICALLY SHE'S STILL WORKING FOR THE *SAME* COMPANY. BUT, YES."
I HAVE A QUESTION OF MY OWN, MISS LANE.
ARE YOU RETURNING TO THE BEAT?
...
I'M JUST A PERSON SEEKING OUT THE *TRUTH,* SUPERMAN. SAME AS I EVER WAS.
THAT SOUNDS LIKE GOOD NEWS FOR EVERYONE.
I'LL SEE YOU AROUND, MISS LANE.

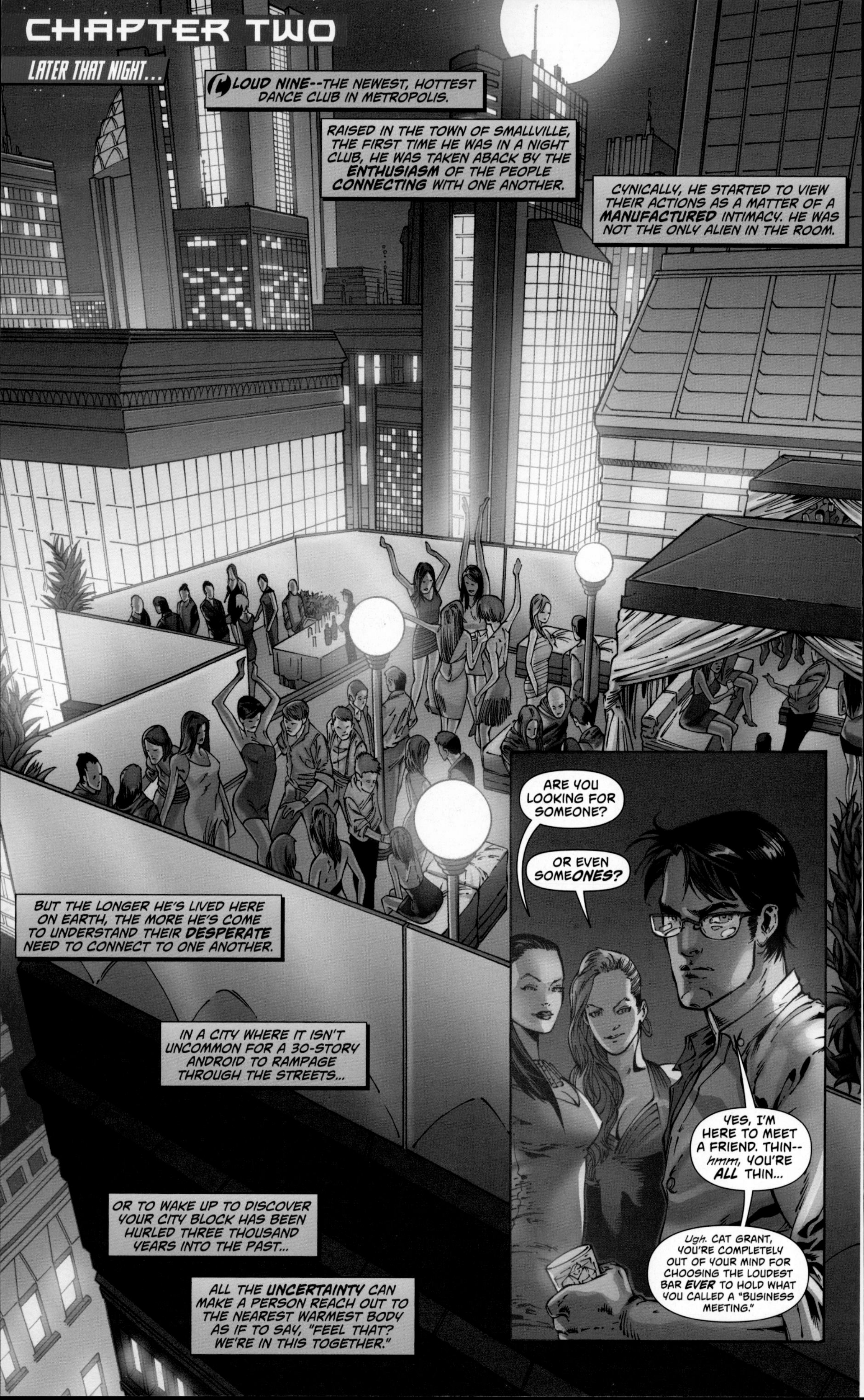
CHAPTER TWO
LATER THAT NIGHT...
CLOUD NINE--THE NEWEST, HOTTEST DANCE CLUB IN METROPOLIS.
RAISED IN THE TOWN OF SMALLVILLE, THE FIRST TIME HE WAS IN A NIGHT CLUB, HE WAS TAKEN ABACK BY THE ENTHUSIASM OF THE PEOPLE CONNECTING WITH ONE ANOTHER.
CYNICALLY, HE STARTED TO VIEW THEIR ACTIONS AS A MATTER OF A MANUFACTURED INTIMACY. HE WAS NOT THE ONLY ALIEN IN THE ROOM.
BUT THE LONGER HE'S LIVED HERE ON EARTH, THE MORE HE'S COME TO UNDERSTAND THEIR DESPERATE NEED TO CONNECT TO ONE ANOTHER.
IN A CITY WHERE IT ISN'T UNCOMMON FOR A 30-STORY ANDROID TO RAMPAGE THROUGH THE STREETS...
OR TO WAKE UP TO DISCOVER YOUR CITY BLOCK HAS BEEN HURLED THREE THOUSAND YEARS INTO THE PAST...
ALL THE UNCERTAINTY CAN MAKE A PERSON REACH OUT TO THE NEAREST WARMEST BODY AS IF TO SAY, "FEEL THAT? WE'RE IN THIS TOGETHER."
ARE YOU LOOKING FOR SOMEONE?
OR EVEN SOMEONES?
YES, I'M HERE TO MEET A FRIEND. THIN-- hmm, YOU'RE ALL THIN...
Ugh. CAT GRANT, YOU'RE COMPLETELY OUT OF YOUR MIND FOR CHOOSING THE LOUDEST BAR EVER TO HOLD WHAT YOU CALLED A "BUSINESS MEETING."

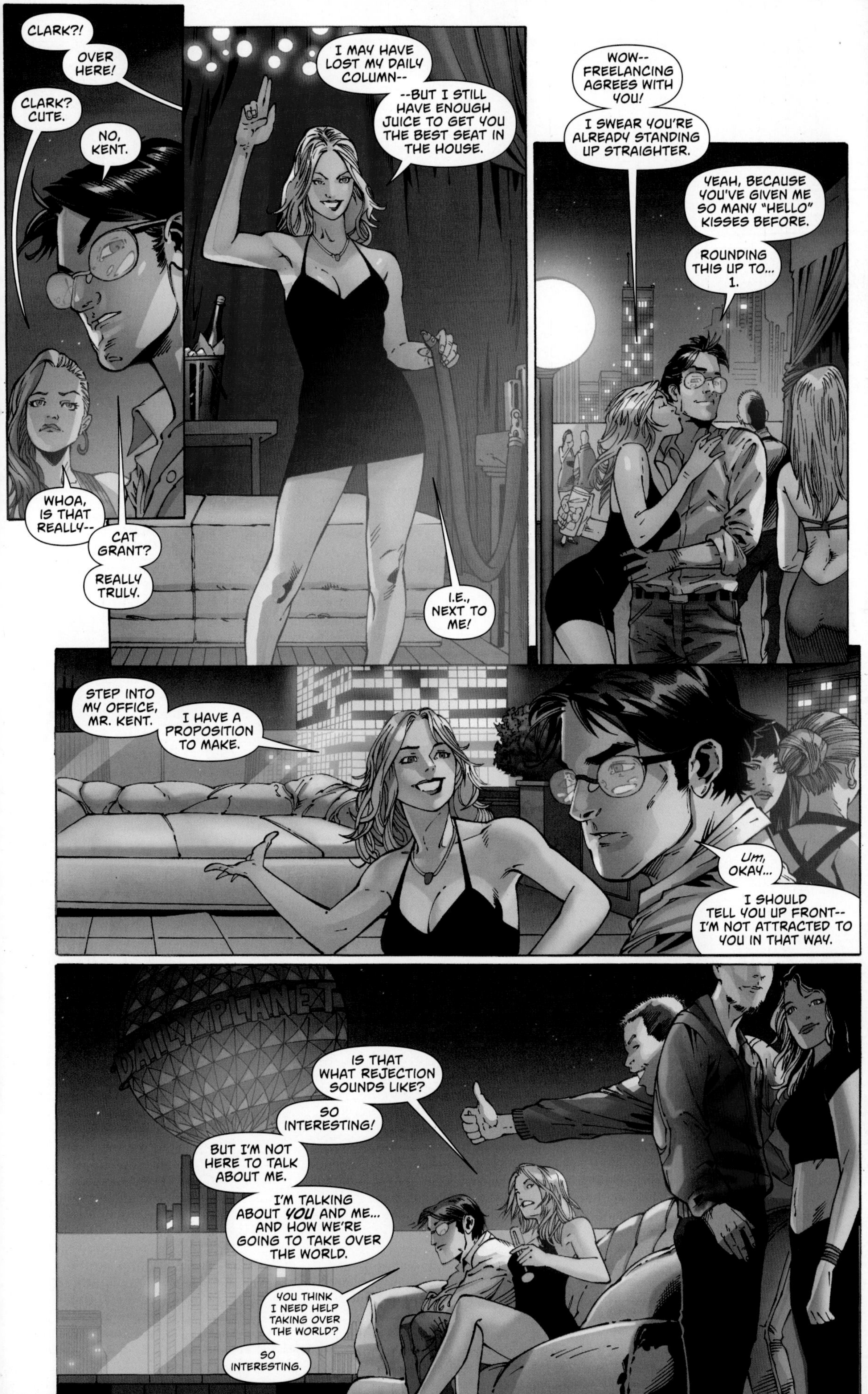
CLARK?!
OVER HERE!
CLARK? CUTE.
NO, KENT.
WHOA, IS THAT REALLY--
CAT GRANT?
REALLY TRULY.
I MAY HAVE LOST MY DAILY COLUMN--
--BUT I STILL HAVE ENOUGH JUICE TO GET YOU THE BEST SEAT IN THE HOUSE.
I.E., NEXT TO ME!
WOW-- FREELANCING AGREES WITH YOU!
I SWEAR YOU'RE ALREADY STANDING UP STRAIGHTER.
YEAH, BECAUSE YOU'VE GIVEN ME SO MANY "HELLO" KISSES BEFORE.
ROUNDING THIS UP TO... 1.
STEP INTO MY OFFICE, MR. KENT.
I HAVE A PROPOSITION TO MAKE.
UM, OKAY...
I SHOULD TELL YOU UP FRONT-- I'M NOT ATTRACTED TO YOU IN THAT WAY.
DAILY PLANET
IS THAT WHAT REJECTION SOUNDS LIKE?
SO INTERESTING!
BUT I'M NOT HERE TO TALK ABOUT ME.
I'M TALKING ABOUT YOU AND ME... AND HOW WE'RE GOING TO TAKE OVER THE WORLD.
YOU THINK I NEED HELP TAKING OVER THE WORLD?
SO INTERESTING.

WHAT CAN I GET YOU BOTH?

I'D LIKE A--

TWO CHAMPAGNES.

WE'RE CELEBRATING.

CELEBRATING, WHAT-- UNEMPLOYMENT?

MY YOGI SAYS I NEED TO LOOK FOR OBSTACTUNITIES IN LIFE.

OBSTACWHAT?

"WHEN WE'RE PRESENTED WITH AN OBSTACLE--

--WE HAVE TO TURN IT INTO AN OPPORTUNITY!"

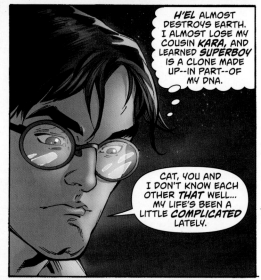

H'EL ALMOST DESTROYS EARTH. I ALMOST LOSE MY COUSIN KARA, AND LEARNED SUPERBOY IS A CLONE MADE UP--IN PART--OF MY DNA.

CAT, YOU AND I DON'T KNOW EACH OTHER THAT WELL... MY LIFE'S BEEN A LITTLE COMPLICATED LATELY.

TRY PAYING YOUR RENT WITH A SMILE. FOR ME IT WORKS, BUT...

RELAX--WHILE YOU'VE BEEN BUSY RESEARCHING SOME BIG NEWS THING...

...I TOOK IT UPON MYSELF TO SOLVE ALL OUR PROBLEMS AT ONCE.

CAT!

WHAT AM I LOOKING AT?

THE FUTURE, CLARK.

OUR FUTURE.

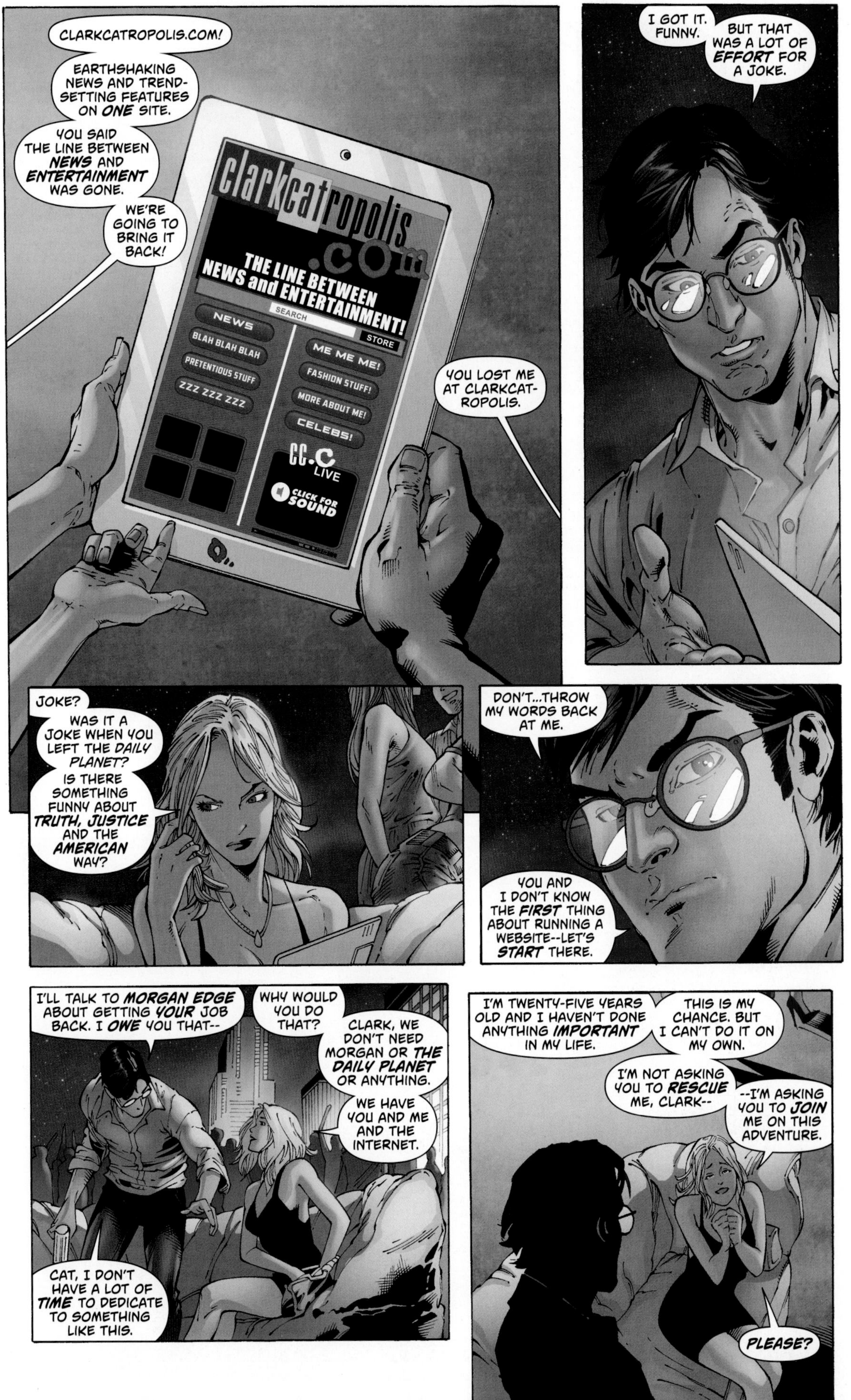
CLARKCATROPOLIS.COM!
EARTHSHAKING NEWS AND TREND-SETTING FEATURES ON ONE SITE.
YOU SAID THE LINE BETWEEN NEWS AND ENTERTAINMENT WAS GONE.
WE'RE GOING TO BRING IT BACK!
clarkcatropolis.com
THE LINE BETWEEN NEWS and ENTERTAINMENT!
SEARCH
STORE
NEWS
BLAH BLAH BLAH
PRETENTIOUS STUFF
ZZZ ZZZ ZZZ
ME ME ME!
FASHION STUFF!
MORE ABOUT ME!
CELEBS!
CC.C LIVE
CLICK FOR SOUND
YOU LOST ME AT CLARKCAT-ROPOLIS.
I GOT IT. FUNNY.
BUT THAT WAS A LOT OF EFFORT FOR A JOKE.
JOKE?
WAS IT A JOKE WHEN YOU LEFT THE DAILY PLANET?
IS THERE SOMETHING FUNNY ABOUT TRUTH, JUSTICE AND THE AMERICAN WAY?
DON'T...THROW MY WORDS BACK AT ME.
YOU AND I DON'T KNOW THE FIRST THING ABOUT RUNNING A WEBSITE--LET'S START THERE.
I'LL TALK TO MORGAN EDGE ABOUT GETTING YOUR JOB BACK. I OWE YOU THAT--
WHY WOULD YOU DO THAT?
CLARK, WE DON'T NEED MORGAN OR THE DAILY PLANET OR ANYTHING.
WE HAVE YOU AND ME AND THE INTERNET.
CAT, I DON'T HAVE A LOT OF TIME TO DEDICATE TO SOMETHING LIKE THIS.
I'M TWENTY-FIVE YEARS OLD AND I HAVEN'T DONE ANYTHING IMPORTANT IN MY LIFE.
THIS IS MY CHANCE. BUT I CAN'T DO IT ON MY OWN.
I'M NOT ASKING YOU TO RESCUE ME, CLARK--
--I'M ASKING YOU TO JOIN ME ON THIS ADVENTURE.
PLEASE?

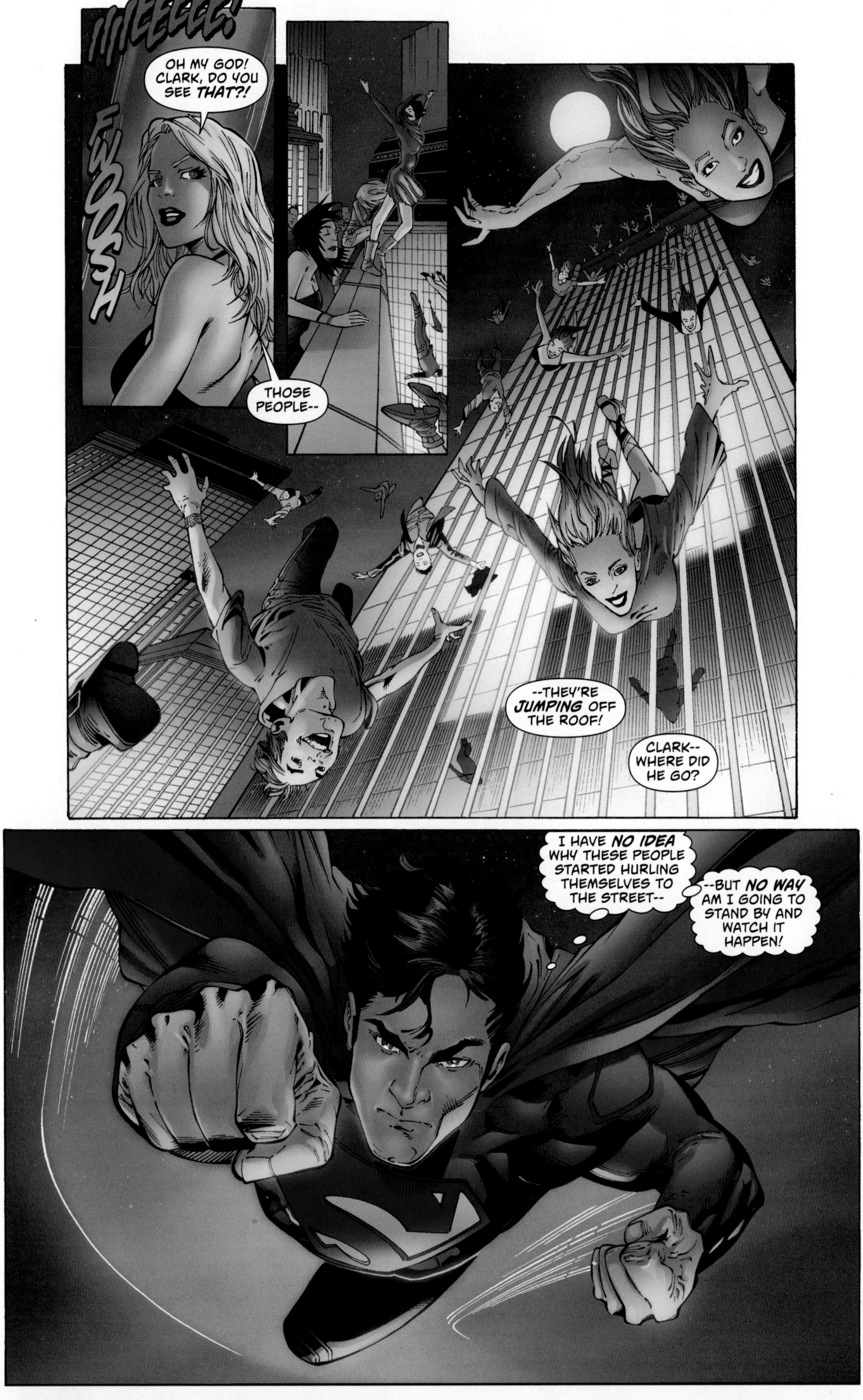
IIIIEEEEEE!
OH MY GOD! CLARK, DO YOU SEE THAT?!
FWOOOSH
THOSE PEOPLE--
--THEY'RE JUMPING OFF THE ROOF!
CLARK-- WHERE DID HE GO?
I HAVE NO IDEA WHY THESE PEOPLE STARTED HURLING THEMSELVES TO THE STREET--
--BUT NO WAY AM I GOING TO STAND BY AND WATCH IT HAPPEN!

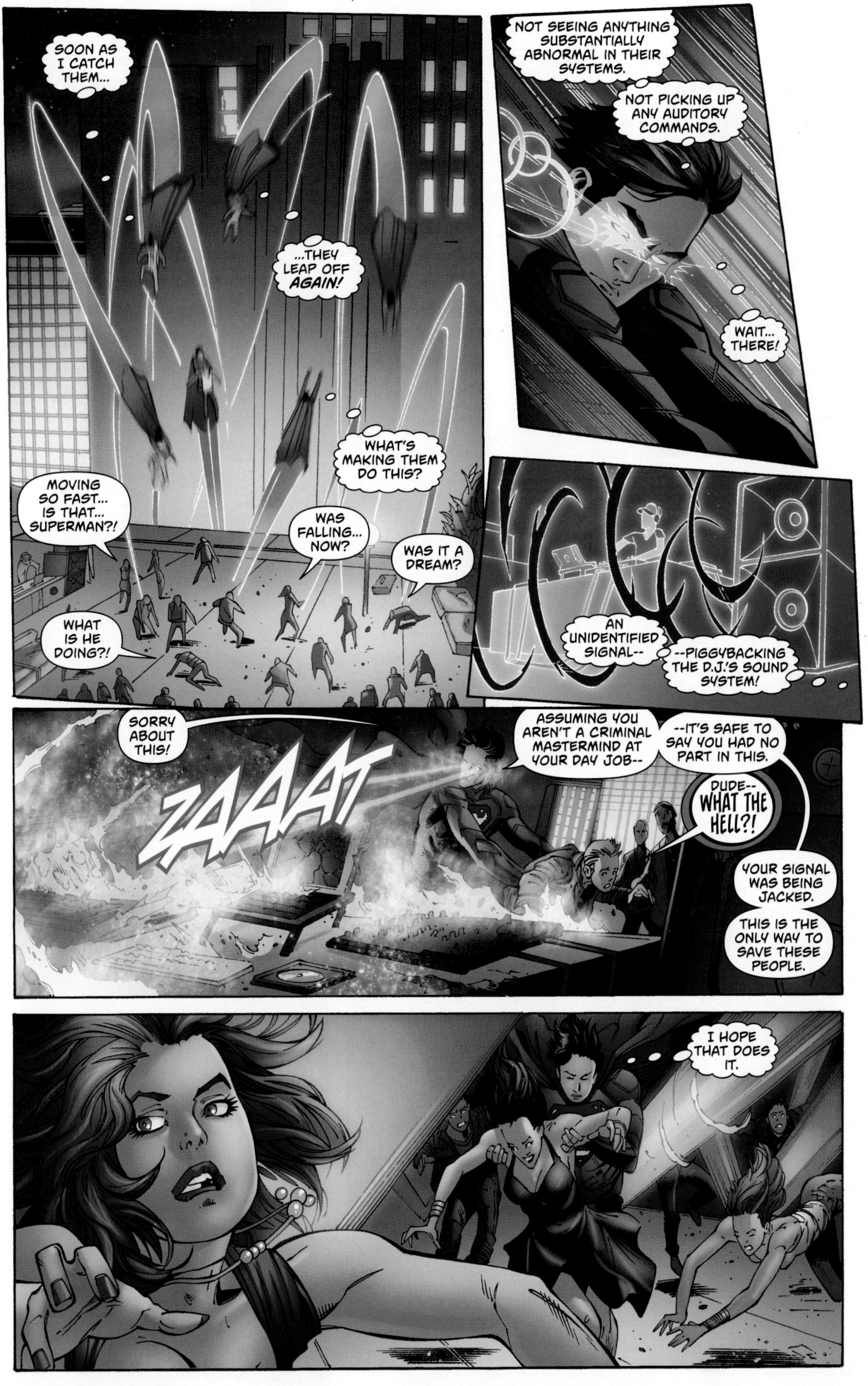
SOON AS I CATCH THEM...
...THEY LEAP OFF AGAIN!
WHAT'S MAKING THEM DO THIS?
MOVING SO FAST... IS THAT... SUPERMAN?!
WAS FALLING... NOW?
WAS IT A DREAM?
WHAT IS HE DOING?!
NOT SEEING ANYTHING SUBSTANTIALLY ABNORMAL IN THEIR SYSTEMS.
NOT PICKING UP ANY AUDITORY COMMANDS.
WAIT... THERE!
AN UNIDENTIFIED SIGNAL--
--PIGGYBACKING THE D.J.'S SOUND SYSTEM!
SORRY ABOUT THIS!
ZAAAT
ASSUMING YOU AREN'T A CRIMINAL MASTERMIND AT YOUR DAY JOB--
--IT'S SAFE TO SAY YOU HAD NO PART IN THIS.
DUDE-- WHAT THE HELL?!
YOUR SIGNAL WAS BEING JACKED.
THIS IS THE ONLY WAY TO SAVE THESE PEOPLE.
I HOPE THAT DOES IT.

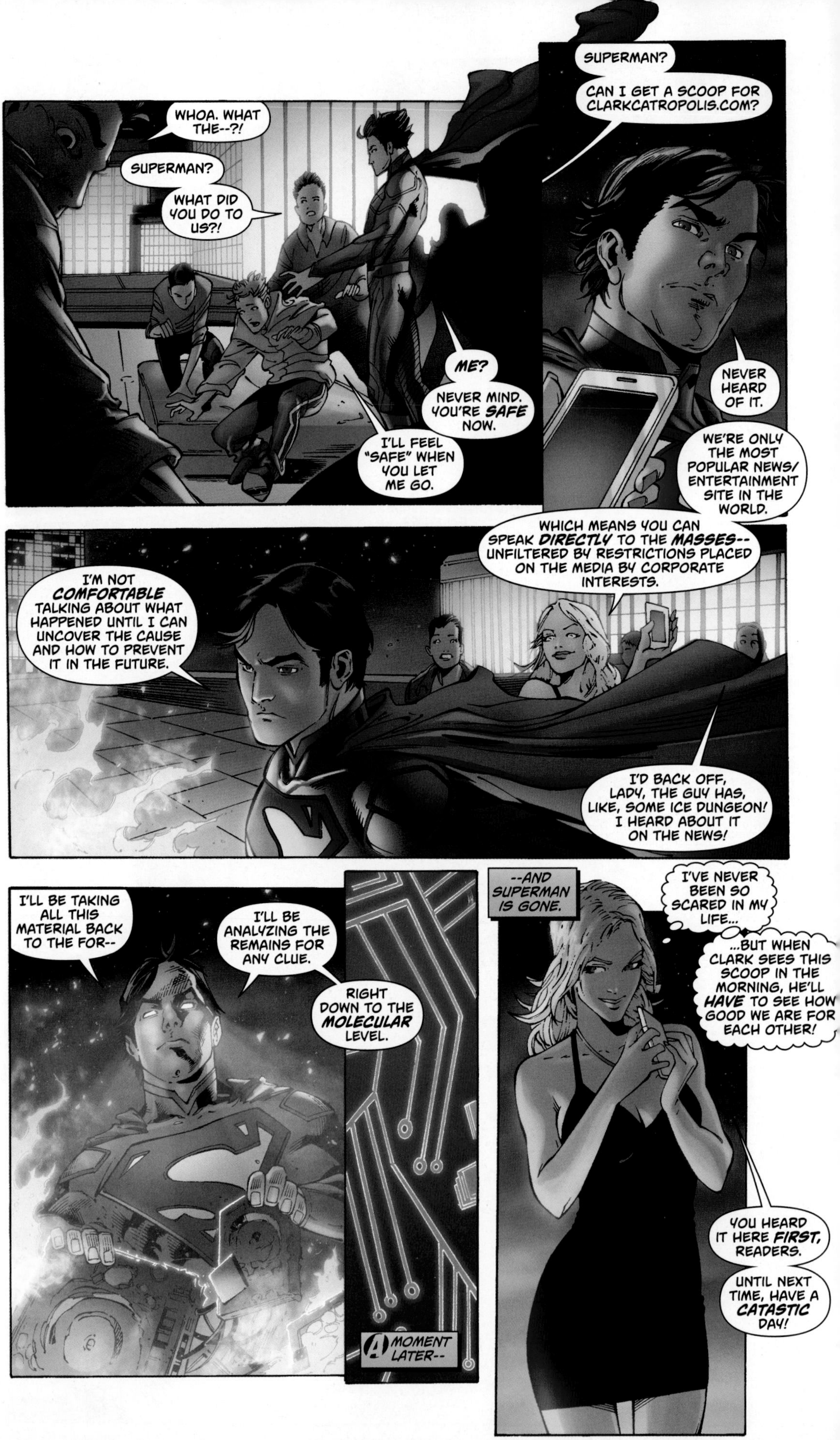
WHOA. WHAT THE--?!
SUPERMAN?
WHAT DID YOU DO TO US?!
ME?
NEVER MIND. YOU'RE SAFE NOW.
I'LL FEEL "SAFE" WHEN YOU LET ME GO.
SUPERMAN?
CAN I GET A SCOOP FOR CLARKCATROPOLIS.COM?
NEVER HEARD OF IT.
WE'RE ONLY THE MOST POPULAR NEWS/ ENTERTAINMENT SITE IN THE WORLD.
WHICH MEANS YOU CAN SPEAK DIRECTLY TO THE MASSES-- UNFILTERED BY RESTRICTIONS PLACED ON THE MEDIA BY CORPORATE INTERESTS.
I'M NOT COMFORTABLE TALKING ABOUT WHAT HAPPENED UNTIL I CAN UNCOVER THE CAUSE AND HOW TO PREVENT IT IN THE FUTURE.
I'D BACK OFF, LADY, THE GUY HAS, LIKE, SOME ICE DUNGEON! I HEARD ABOUT IT ON THE NEWS!
I'LL BE TAKING ALL THIS MATERIAL BACK TO THE FOR--
I'LL BE ANALYZING THE REMAINS FOR ANY CLUE.
RIGHT DOWN TO THE MOLECULAR LEVEL.
A MOMENT LATER--
--AND SUPERMAN IS GONE.
I'VE NEVER BEEN SO SCARED IN MY LIFE...
...BUT WHEN CLARK SEES THIS SCOOP IN THE MORNING, HE'LL HAVE TO SEE HOW GOOD WE ARE FOR EACH OTHER!
YOU HEARD IT HERE FIRST, READERS.
UNTIL NEXT TIME, HAVE A CATASTIC DAY!

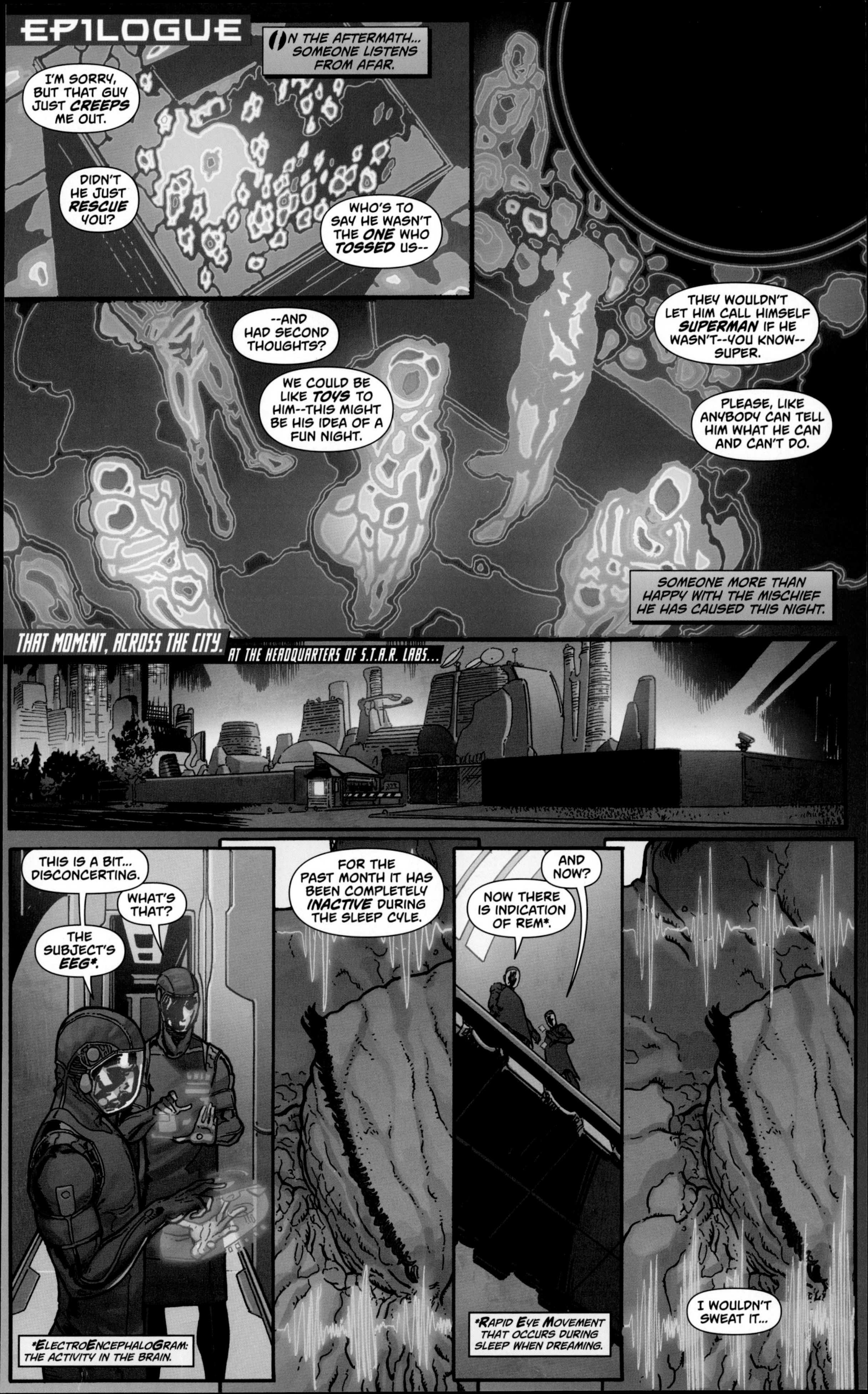
EPILOGUE
IN THE AFTERMATH... SOMEONE LISTENS FROM AFAR.
I'M SORRY, BUT THAT GUY JUST CREEPS ME OUT.
DIDN'T HE JUST RESCUE YOU?
WHO'S TO SAY HE WASN'T THE ONE WHO TOSSED US--
--AND HAD SECOND THOUGHTS?
WE COULD BE LIKE TOYS TO HIM--THIS MIGHT BE HIS IDEA OF A FUN NIGHT.
THEY WOULDN'T LET HIM CALL HIMSELF SUPERMAN IF HE WASN'T--YOU KNOW--SUPER.
PLEASE, LIKE ANYBODY CAN TELL HIM WHAT HE CAN AND CAN'T DO.
SOMEONE MORE THAN HAPPY WITH THE MISCHIEF HE HAS CAUSED THIS NIGHT.
THAT MOMENT, ACROSS THE CITY.
AT THE HEADQUARTERS OF S.T.A.R. LABS...
THIS IS A BIT... DISCONCERTING.
WHAT'S THAT?
THE SUBJECT'S EEG*.
*ELECTROENCEPHALOGRAM: THE ACTIVITY IN THE BRAIN.
FOR THE PAST MONTH IT HAS BEEN COMPLETELY INACTIVE DURING THE SLEEP CYLE.
AND NOW?
NOW THERE IS INDICATION OF REM*.
*RAPID EYE MOVEMENT THAT OCCURS DURING SLEEP WHEN DREAMING.
I WOULDN'T SWEAT IT...

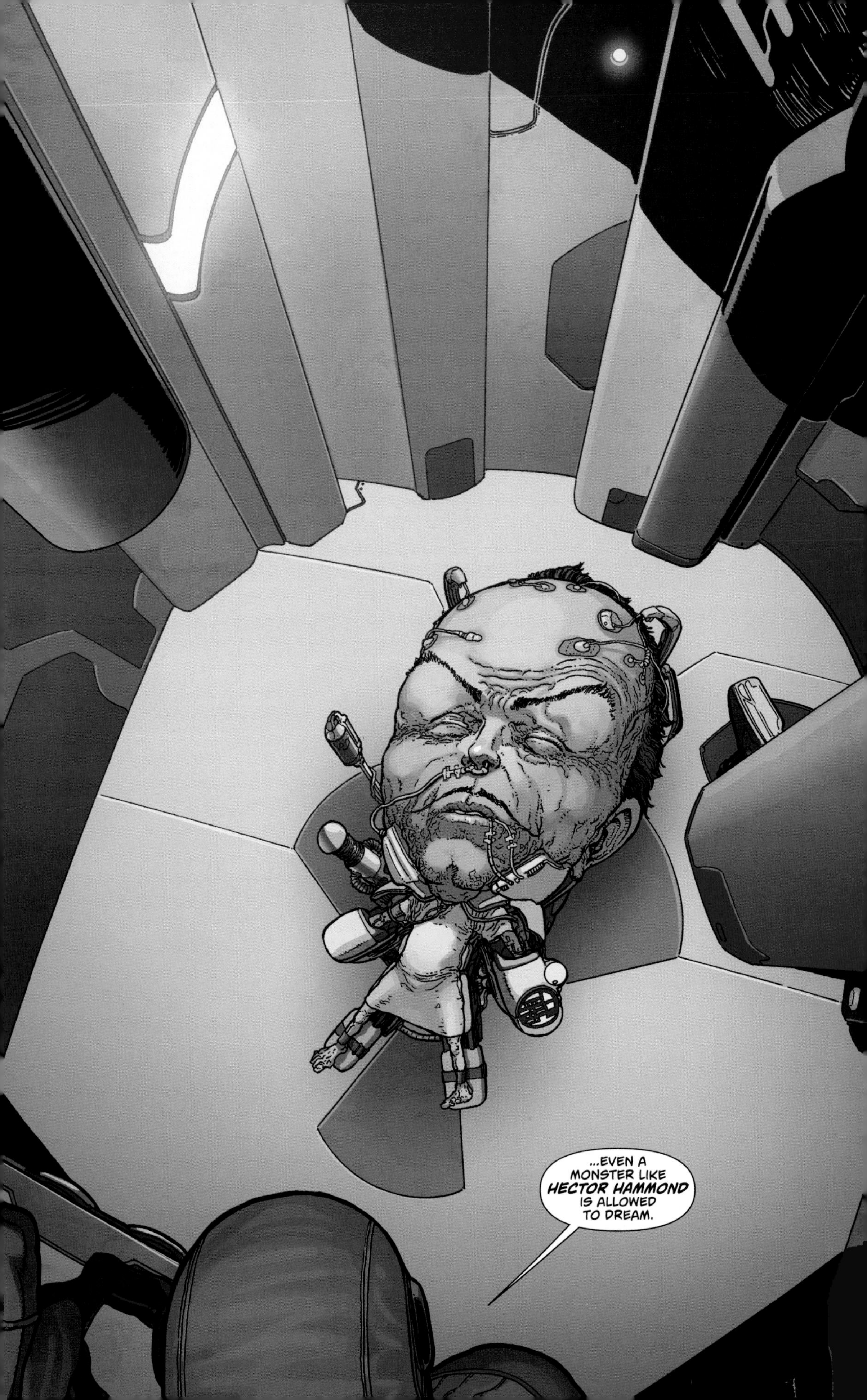
...EVEN A MONSTER LIKE **HECTOR HAMMOND** IS ALLOWED TO DREAM.

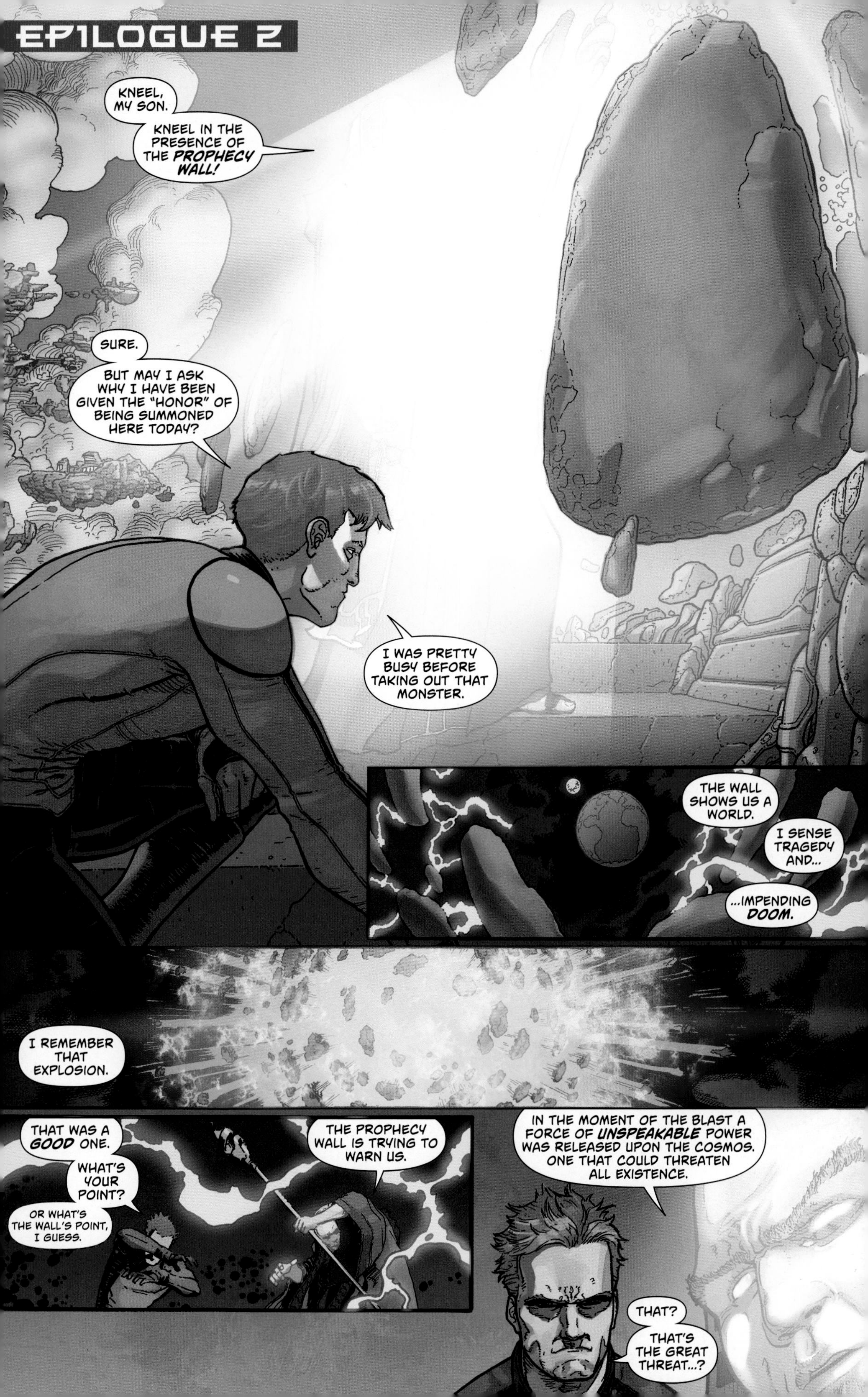
EPILOGUE 2
KNEEL, MY SON.
KNEEL IN THE PRESENCE OF THE PROPHECY WALL!
SURE.
BUT MAY I ASK WHY I HAVE BEEN GIVEN THE "HONOR" OF BEING SUMMONED HERE TODAY?
I WAS PRETTY BUSY BEFORE TAKING OUT THAT MONSTER.
THE WALL SHOWS US A WORLD.
I SENSE TRAGEDY AND...
...IMPENDING DOOM.
I REMEMBER THAT EXPLOSION.
THAT WAS A GOOD ONE.
WHAT'S YOUR POINT?
OR WHAT'S THE WALL'S POINT, I GUESS.
THE PROPHECY WALL IS TRYING TO WARN US.
IN THE MOMENT OF THE BLAST A FORCE OF UNSPEAKABLE POWER WAS RELEASED UPON THE COSMOS. ONE THAT COULD THREATEN ALL EXISTENCE.
THAT?
THAT'S THE GREAT THREAT...?

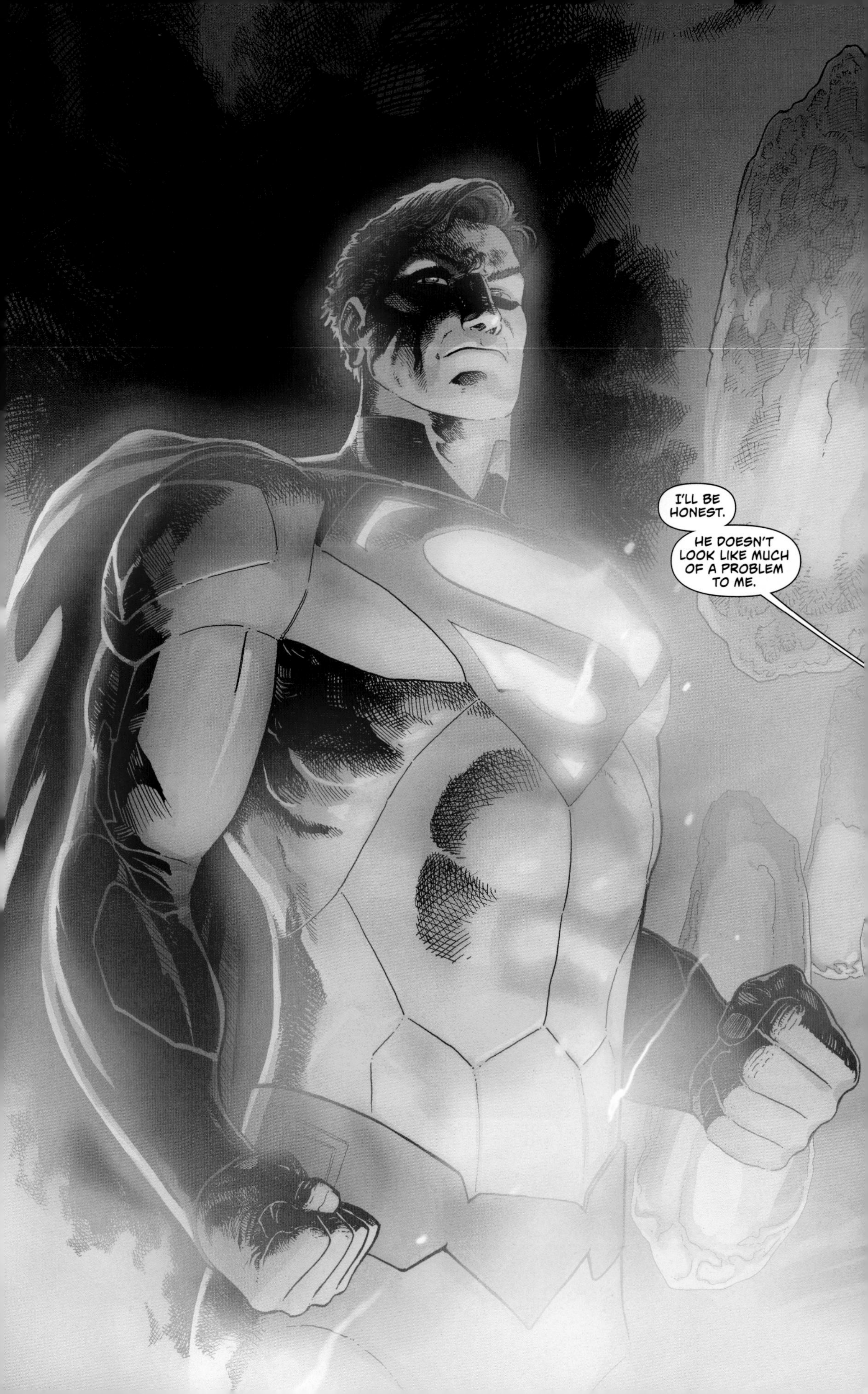
I'LL BE HONEST.
HE DOESN'T LOOK LIKE MUCH OF A PROBLEM TO ME.

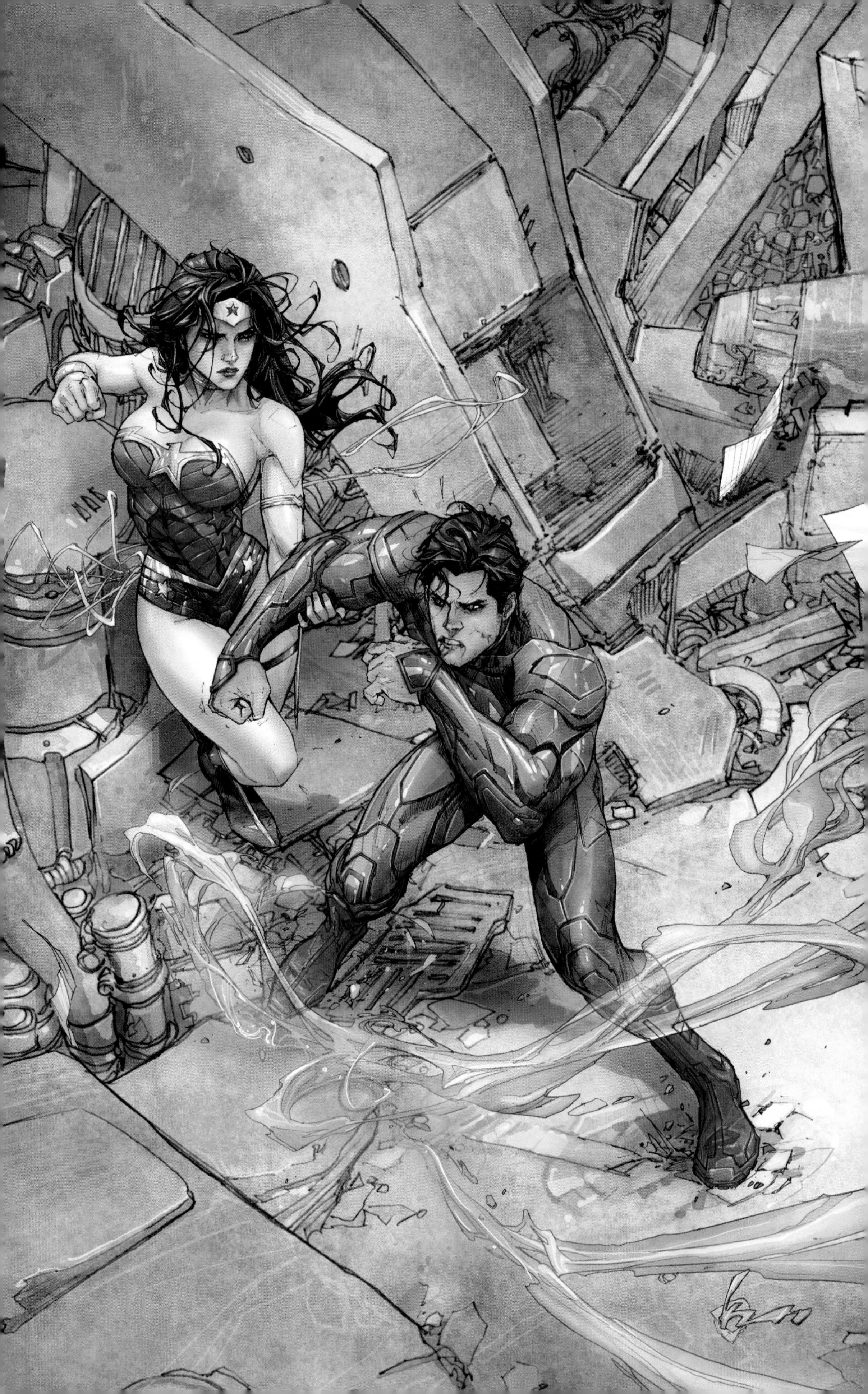

LOOK WHO'S FLYING TO DINNER

SCOTT LOBDELL writer KENNETH ROCAFORT artist cover art by KENNETH ROCAFORT

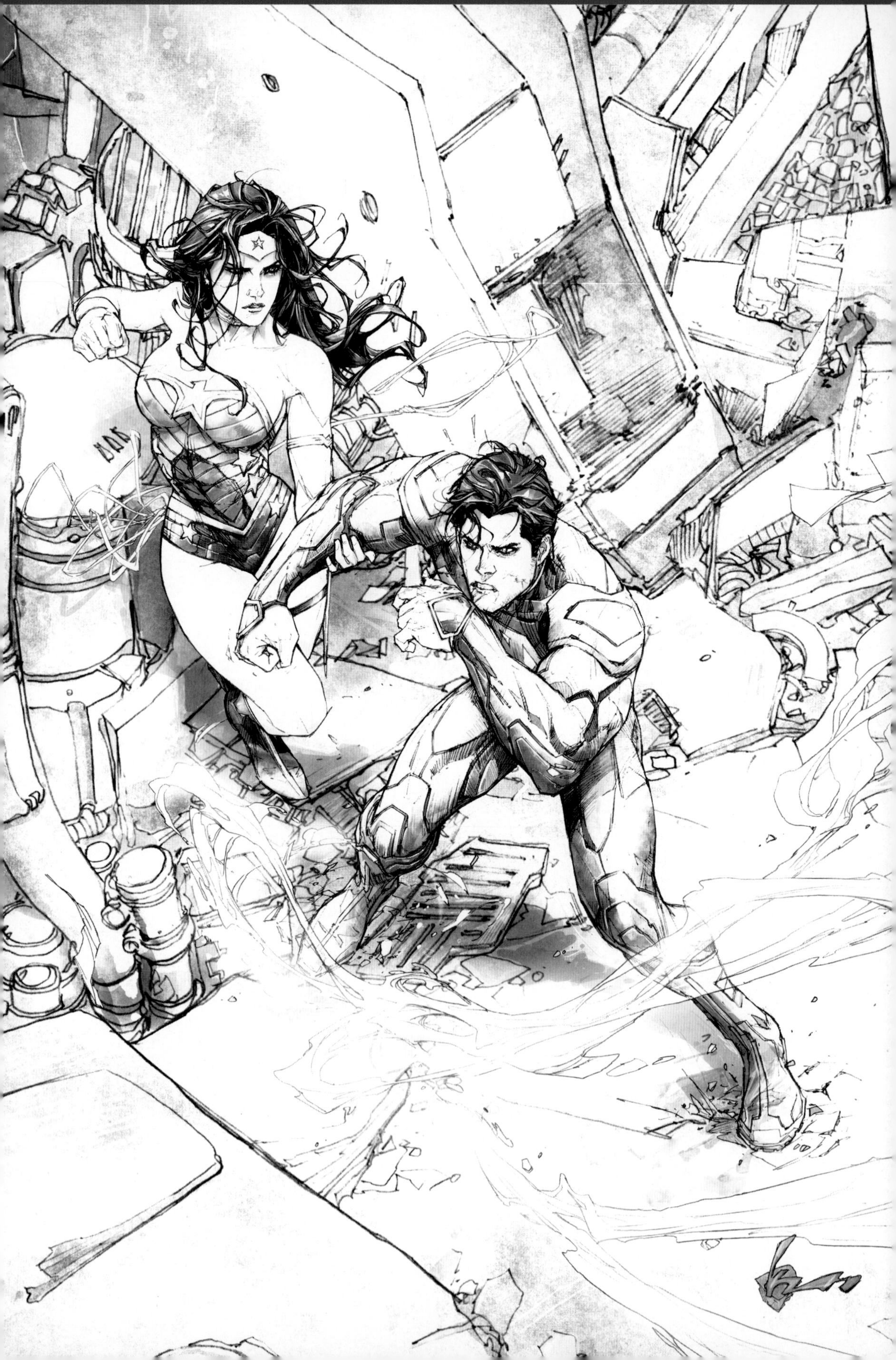

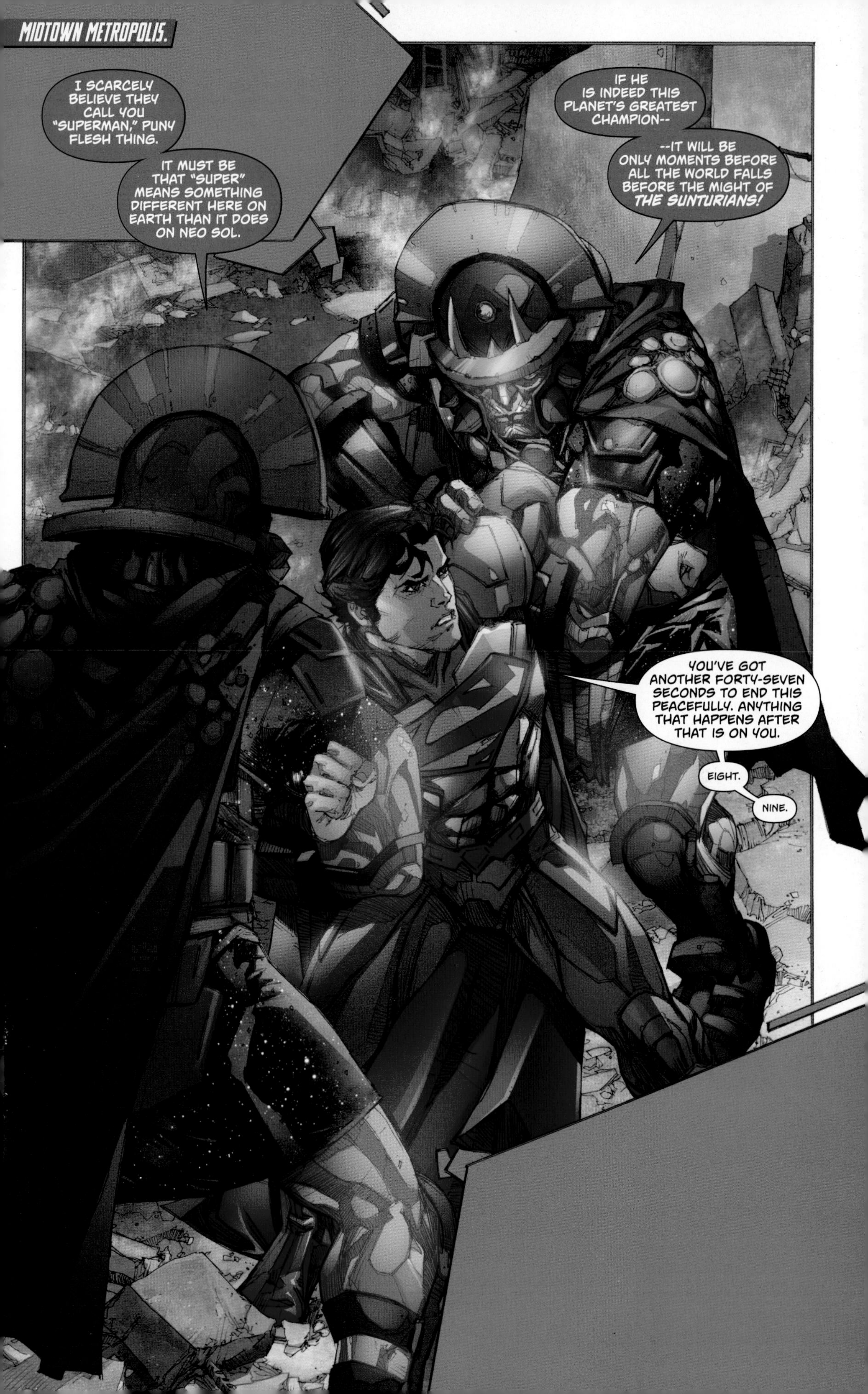
MIDTOWN METROPOLIS.
I SCARCELY BELIEVE THEY CALL YOU "SUPERMAN," PUNY FLESH THING.
IT MUST BE THAT "SUPER" MEANS SOMETHING DIFFERENT HERE ON EARTH THAN IT DOES ON NEO SOL.
IF HE IS INDEED THIS PLANET'S GREATEST CHAMPION--
--IT WILL BE ONLY MOMENTS BEFORE ALL THE WORLD FALLS BEFORE THE MIGHT OF THE SUNTURIANS!
YOU'VE GOT ANOTHER FORTY-SEVEN SECONDS TO END THIS PEACEFULLY. ANYTHING THAT HAPPENS AFTER THAT IS ON YOU.
EIGHT.
NINE.

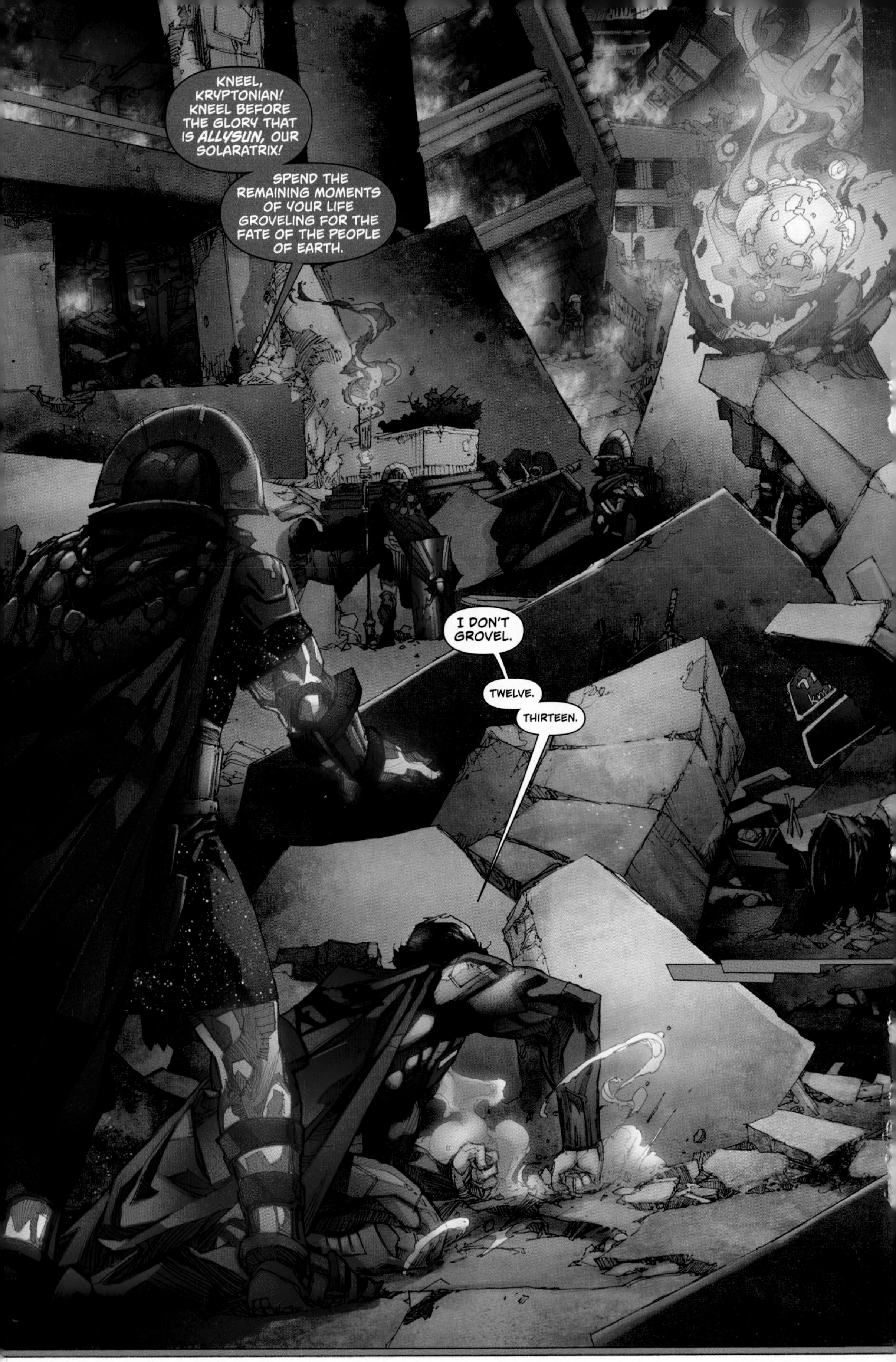
KNEEL, KRYPTONIAN! KNEEL BEFORE THE GLORY THAT IS ALLYSUN, OUR SOLARATRIX!
SPEND THE REMAINING MOMENTS OF YOUR LIFE GROVELING FOR THE FATE OF THE PEOPLE OF EARTH.
I DON'T GROVEL.
TWELVE.
THIRTEEN.

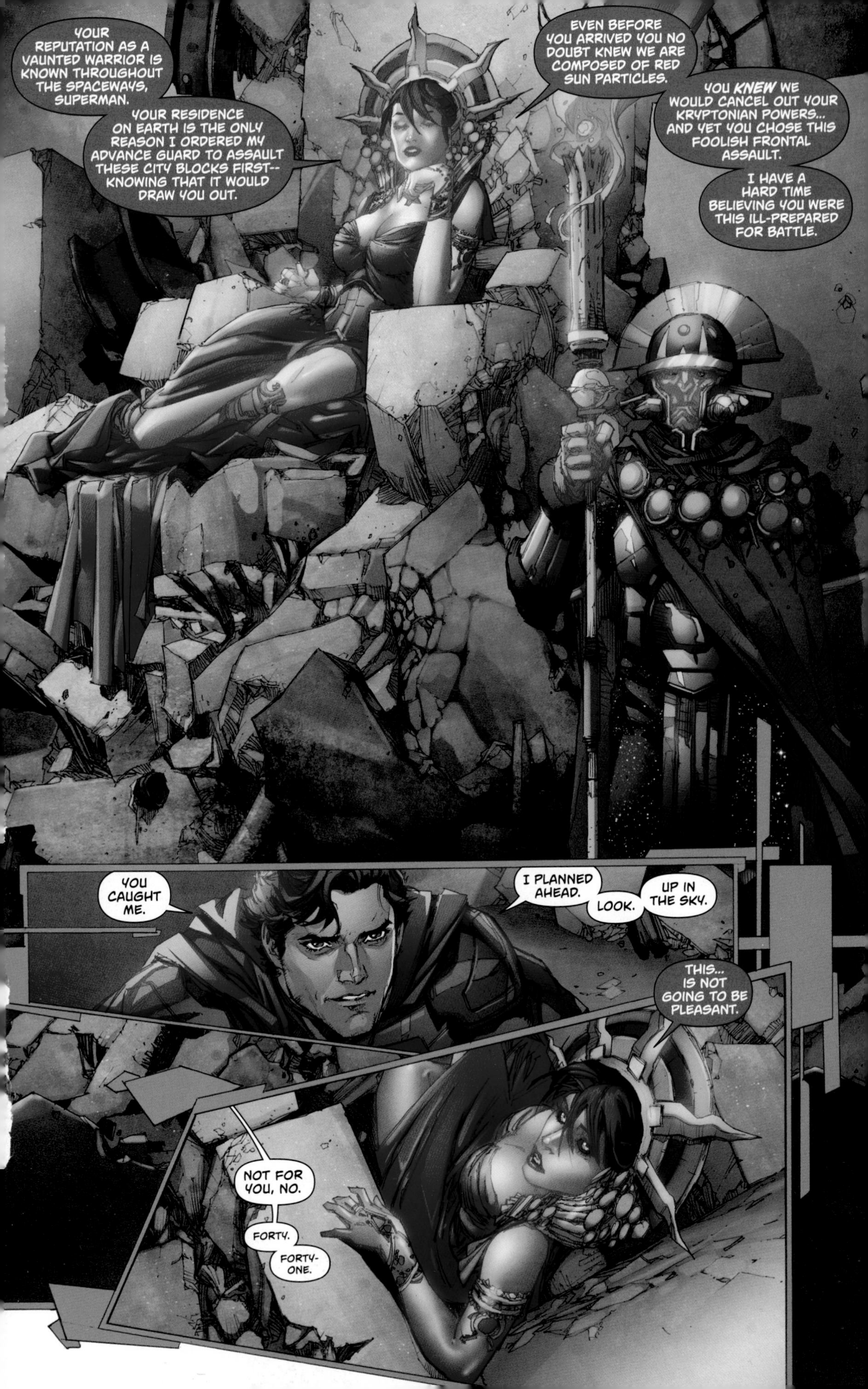
YOUR REPUTATION AS A VAUNTED WARRIOR IS KNOWN THROUGHOUT THE SPACEWAYS, SUPERMAN.
YOUR RESIDENCE ON EARTH IS THE ONLY REASON I ORDERED MY ADVANCE GUARD TO ASSAULT THESE CITY BLOCKS FIRST-- KNOWING THAT IT WOULD DRAW YOU OUT.
EVEN BEFORE YOU ARRIVED YOU NO DOUBT KNEW WE ARE COMPOSED OF RED SUN PARTICLES.
YOU KNEW WE WOULD CANCEL OUT YOUR KRYPTONIAN POWERS... AND YET YOU CHOSE THIS FOOLISH FRONTAL ASSAULT.
I HAVE A HARD TIME BELIEVING YOU WERE THIS ILL-PREPARED FOR BATTLE.
YOU CAUGHT ME.
I PLANNED AHEAD.
LOOK.
UP IN THE SKY.
THIS... IS NOT GOING TO BE PLEASANT.
NOT FOR YOU, NO.
FORTY.
FORTY-ONE.

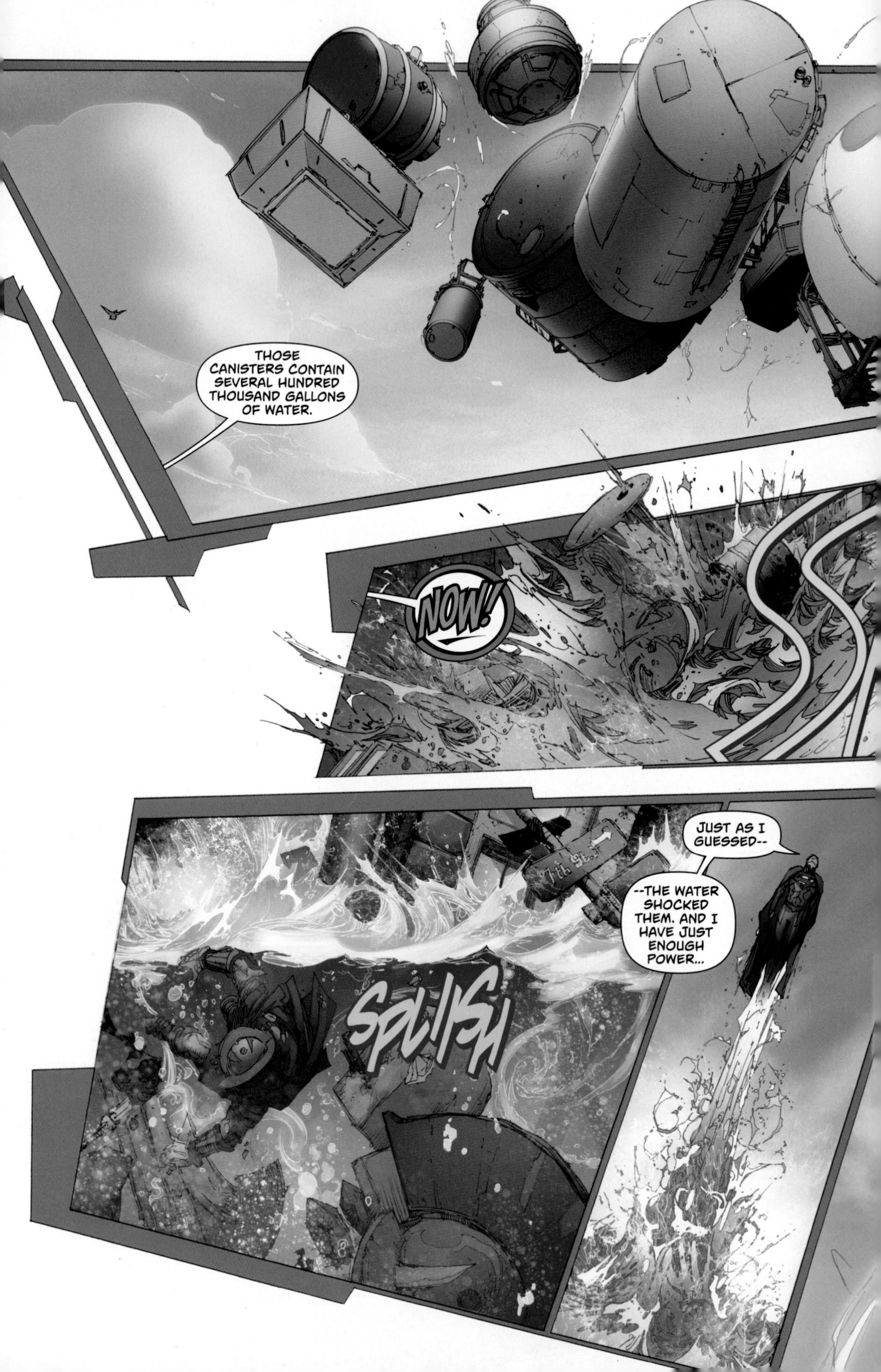
THOSE CANISTERS CONTAIN SEVERAL HUNDRED THOUSAND GALLONS OF WATER.
NOW!
SPLISH
JUST AS I GUESSED--
--THE WATER SHOCKED THEM. AND I HAVE JUST ENOUGH POWER...

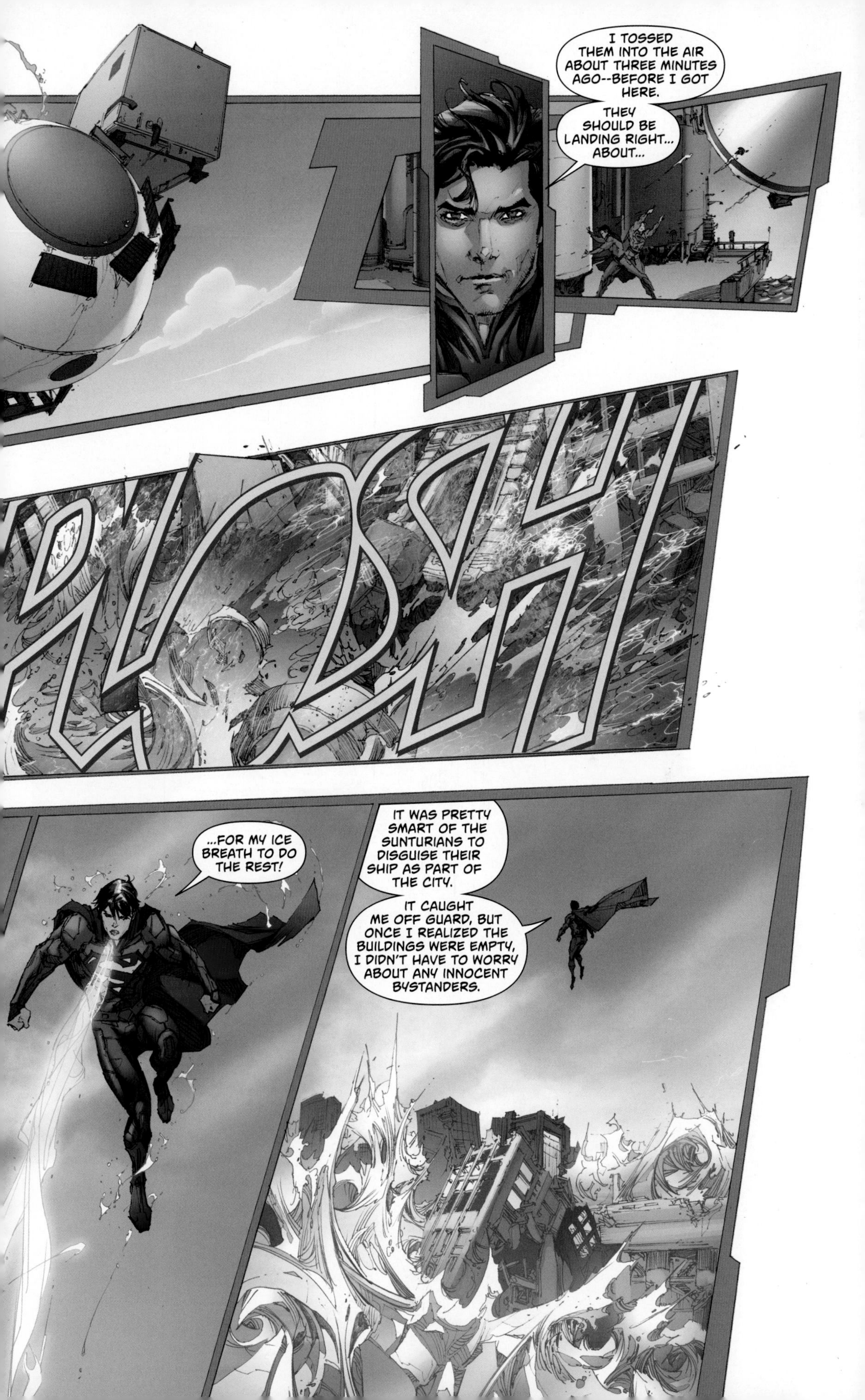
I TOSSED THEM INTO THE AIR ABOUT THREE MINUTES AGO--BEFORE I GOT HERE.
THEY SHOULD BE LANDING RIGHT... ABOUT...
...FOR MY ICE BREATH TO DO THE REST!
IT WAS PRETTY SMART OF THE SUNTURIANS TO DISGUISE THEIR SHIP AS PART OF THE CITY.
IT CAUGHT ME OFF GUARD, BUT ONCE I REALIZED THE BUILDINGS WERE EMPTY, I DIDN'T HAVE TO WORRY ABOUT ANY INNOCENT BYSTANDERS.

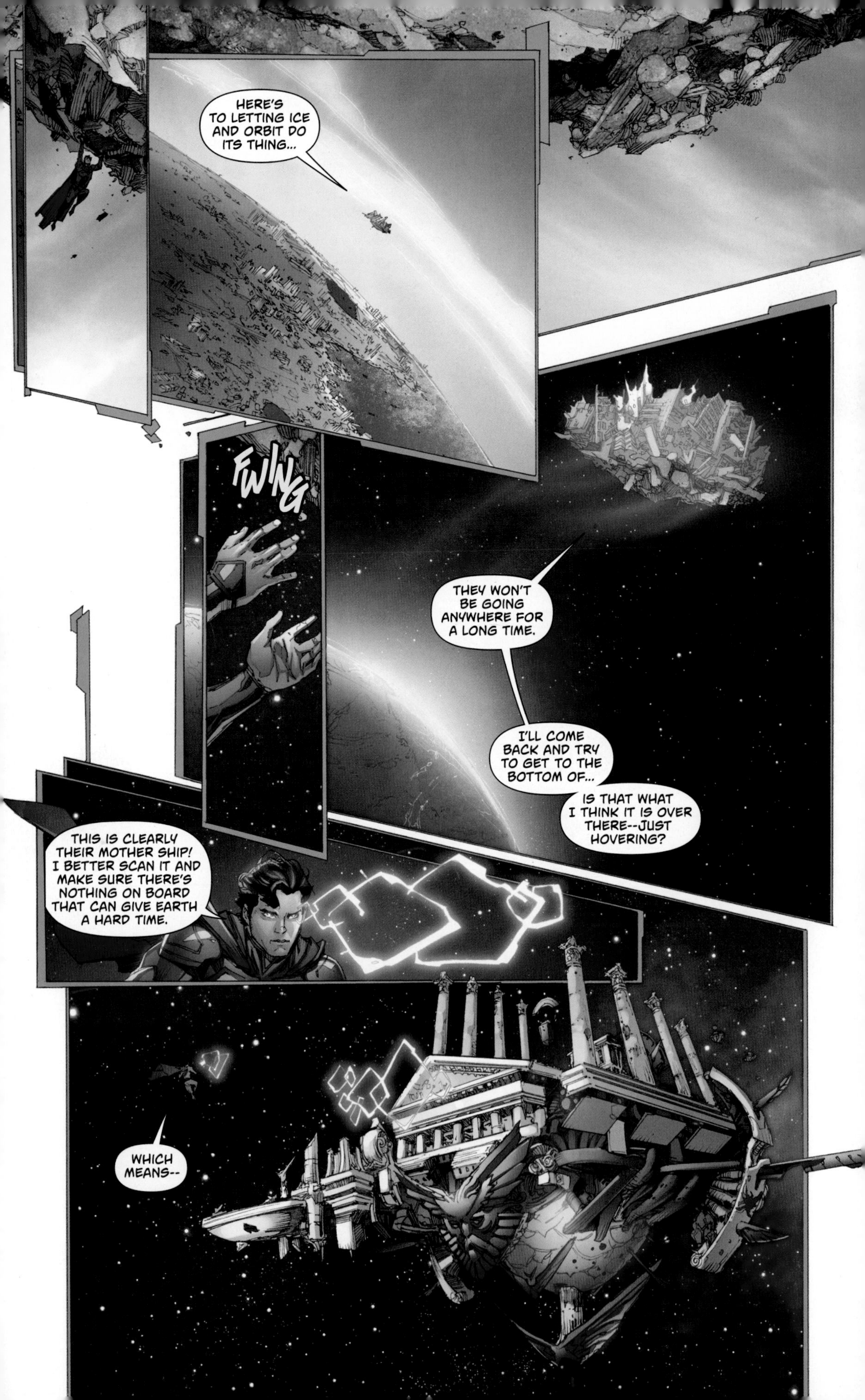
HERE'S TO LETTING ICE AND ORBIT DO ITS THING...
FWING
THEY WON'T BE GOING ANYWHERE FOR A LONG TIME.
I'LL COME BACK AND TRY TO GET TO THE BOTTOM OF...
IS THAT WHAT I THINK IT IS OVER THERE--JUST HOVERING?
THIS IS CLEARLY THEIR MOTHER SHIP! I BETTER SCAN IT AND MAKE SURE THERE'S NOTHING ON BOARD THAT CAN GIVE EARTH A HARD TIME.
WHICH MEANS--

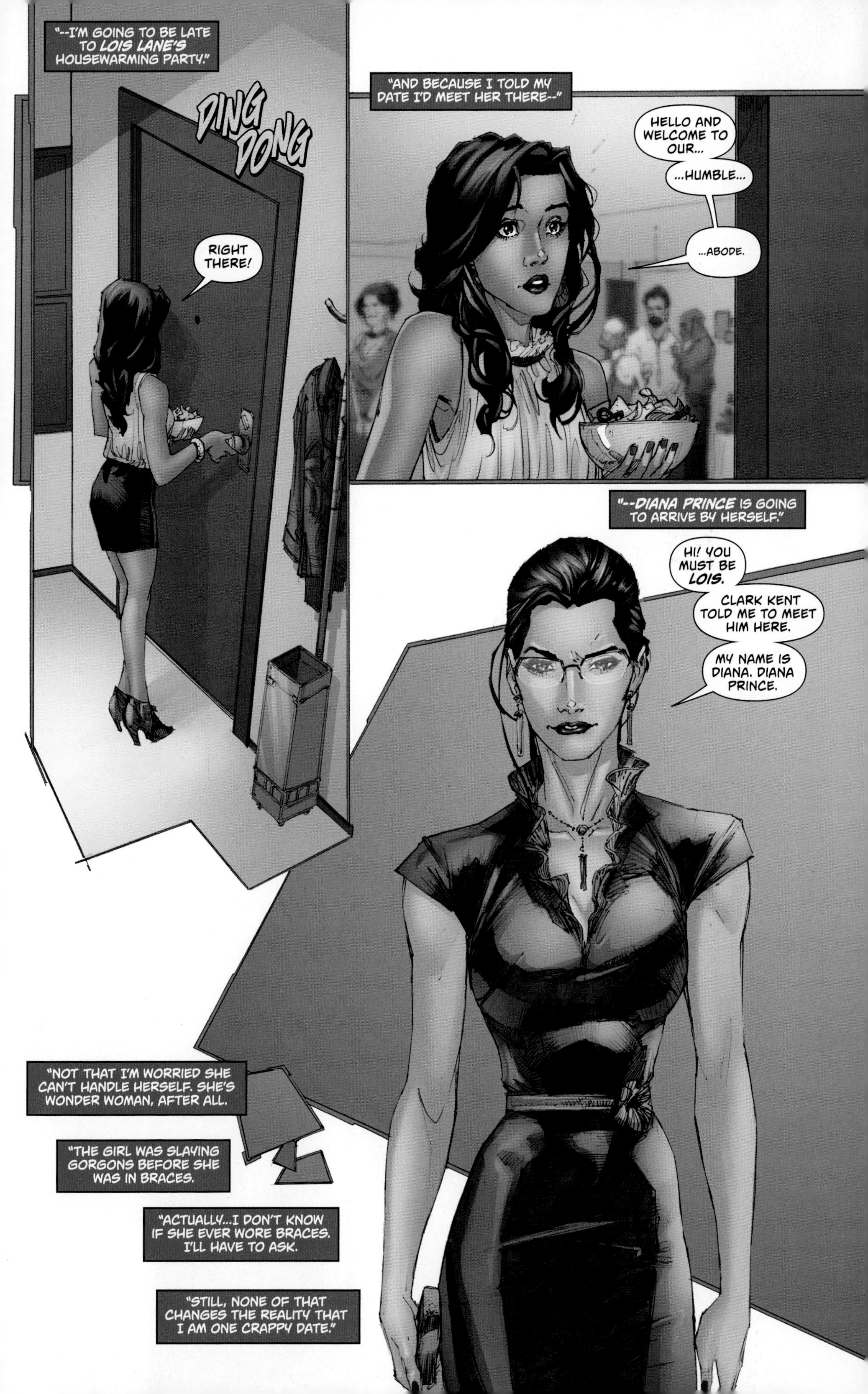
"--I'M GOING TO BE LATE TO LOIS LANE'S HOUSEWARMING PARTY."
DING DONG
RIGHT THERE!
"AND BECAUSE I TOLD MY DATE I'D MEET HER THERE--"
HELLO AND WELCOME TO OUR...
...HUMBLE...
...ABODE.
"--DIANA PRINCE IS GOING TO ARRIVE BY HERSELF."
HI! YOU MUST BE LOIS.
CLARK KENT TOLD ME TO MEET HIM HERE.
MY NAME IS DIANA. DIANA PRINCE.
"NOT THAT I'M WORRIED SHE CAN'T HANDLE HERSELF. SHE'S WONDER WOMAN, AFTER ALL.
"THE GIRL WAS SLAYING GORGONS BEFORE SHE WAS IN BRACES.
"ACTUALLY...I DON'T KNOW IF SHE EVER WORE BRACES. I'LL HAVE TO ASK.
"STILL, NONE OF THAT CHANGES THE REALITY THAT I AM ONE CRAPPY DATE."

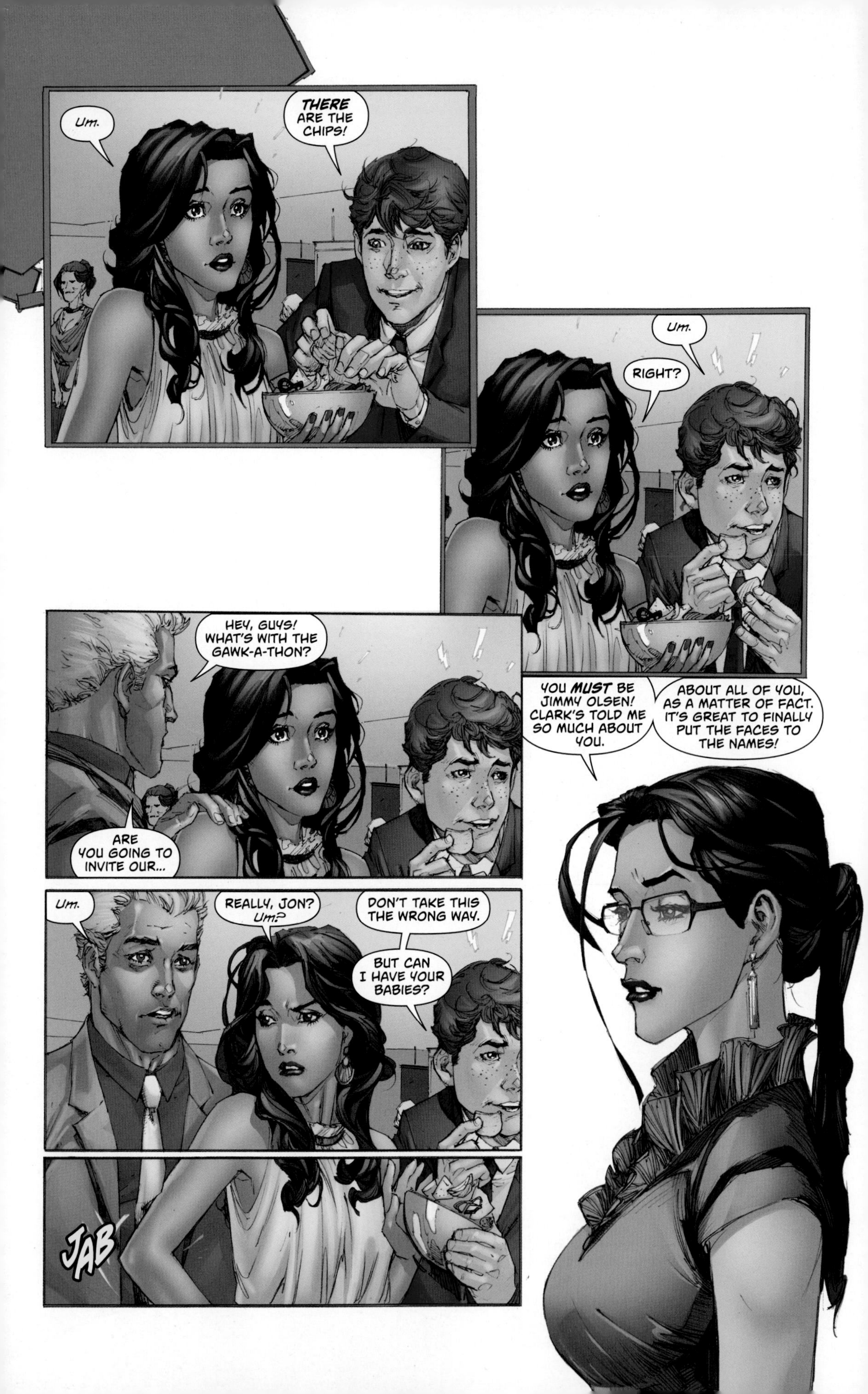
Um.
THERE ARE THE CHIPS!
Um.
RIGHT?
HEY, GUYS! WHAT'S WITH THE GAWK-A-THON?
ARE YOU GOING TO INVITE OUR...
Um.
REALLY, JON? Um?
DON'T TAKE THIS THE WRONG WAY.
BUT CAN I HAVE YOUR BABIES?
JAB
YOU MUST BE JIMMY OLSEN! CLARK'S TOLD ME SO MUCH ABOUT YOU.
ABOUT ALL OF YOU, AS A MATTER OF FACT. IT'S GREAT TO FINALLY PUT THE FACES TO THE NAMES!

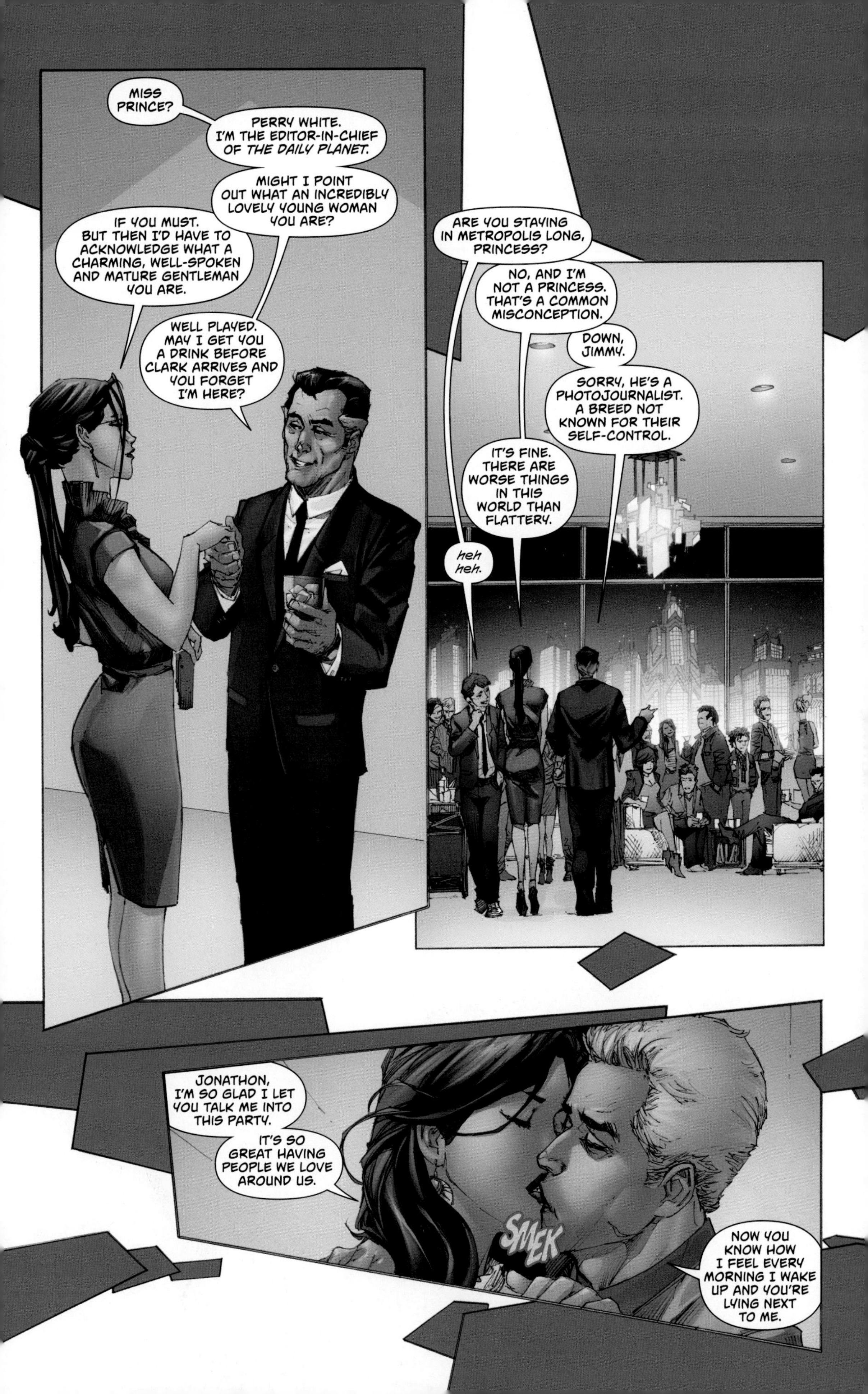
MISS PRINCE?
PERRY WHITE. I'M THE EDITOR-IN-CHIEF OF *THE DAILY PLANET*.
MIGHT I POINT OUT WHAT AN INCREDIBLY LOVELY YOUNG WOMAN YOU ARE?
IF YOU MUST. BUT THEN I'D HAVE TO ACKNOWLEDGE WHAT A CHARMING, WELL-SPOKEN AND MATURE GENTLEMAN YOU ARE.
WELL PLAYED. MAY I GET YOU A DRINK BEFORE CLARK ARRIVES AND YOU FORGET I'M HERE?
ARE YOU STAYING IN METROPOLIS LONG, PRINCESS?
NO, AND I'M NOT A PRINCESS. THAT'S A COMMON MISCONCEPTION.
DOWN, JIMMY.
SORRY, HE'S A PHOTOJOURNALIST. A BREED NOT KNOWN FOR THEIR SELF-CONTROL.
IT'S FINE. THERE ARE WORSE THINGS IN THIS WORLD THAN FLATTERY.
heh heh.
JONATHON, I'M SO GLAD I LET YOU TALK ME INTO THIS PARTY.
IT'S SO GREAT HAVING PEOPLE WE LOVE AROUND US.
SMEK
NOW YOU KNOW HOW I FEEL EVERY MORNING I WAKE UP AND YOU'RE LYING NEXT TO ME.

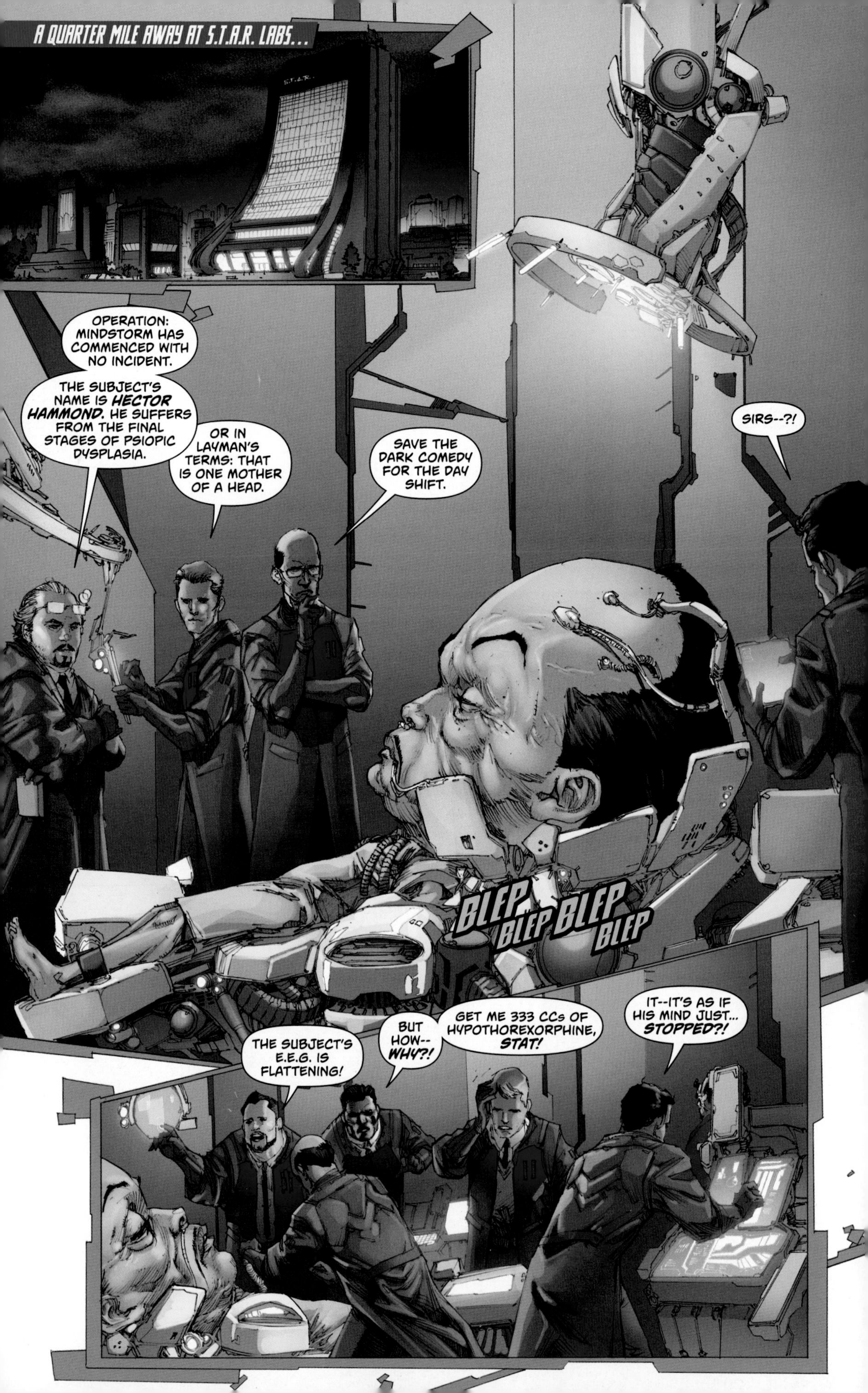
A QUARTER MILE AWAY AT S.T.A.R. LABS...
OPERATION: MINDSTORM HAS COMMENCED WITH NO INCIDENT.
THE SUBJECT'S NAME IS HECTOR HAMMOND. HE SUFFERS FROM THE FINAL STAGES OF PSIOPIC DYSPLASIA.
OR IN LAYMAN'S TERMS: THAT IS ONE MOTHER OF A HEAD.
SAVE THE DARK COMEDY FOR THE DAY SHIFT.
SIRS--?!
BLEP BLEP BLEP BLEP
THE SUBJECT'S E.E.G. IS FLATTENING!
BUT HOW-- WHY?!
GET ME 333 CCs OF HYPOTHOREXORPHINE, STAT!
IT--IT'S AS IF HIS MIND JUST... STOPPED?!

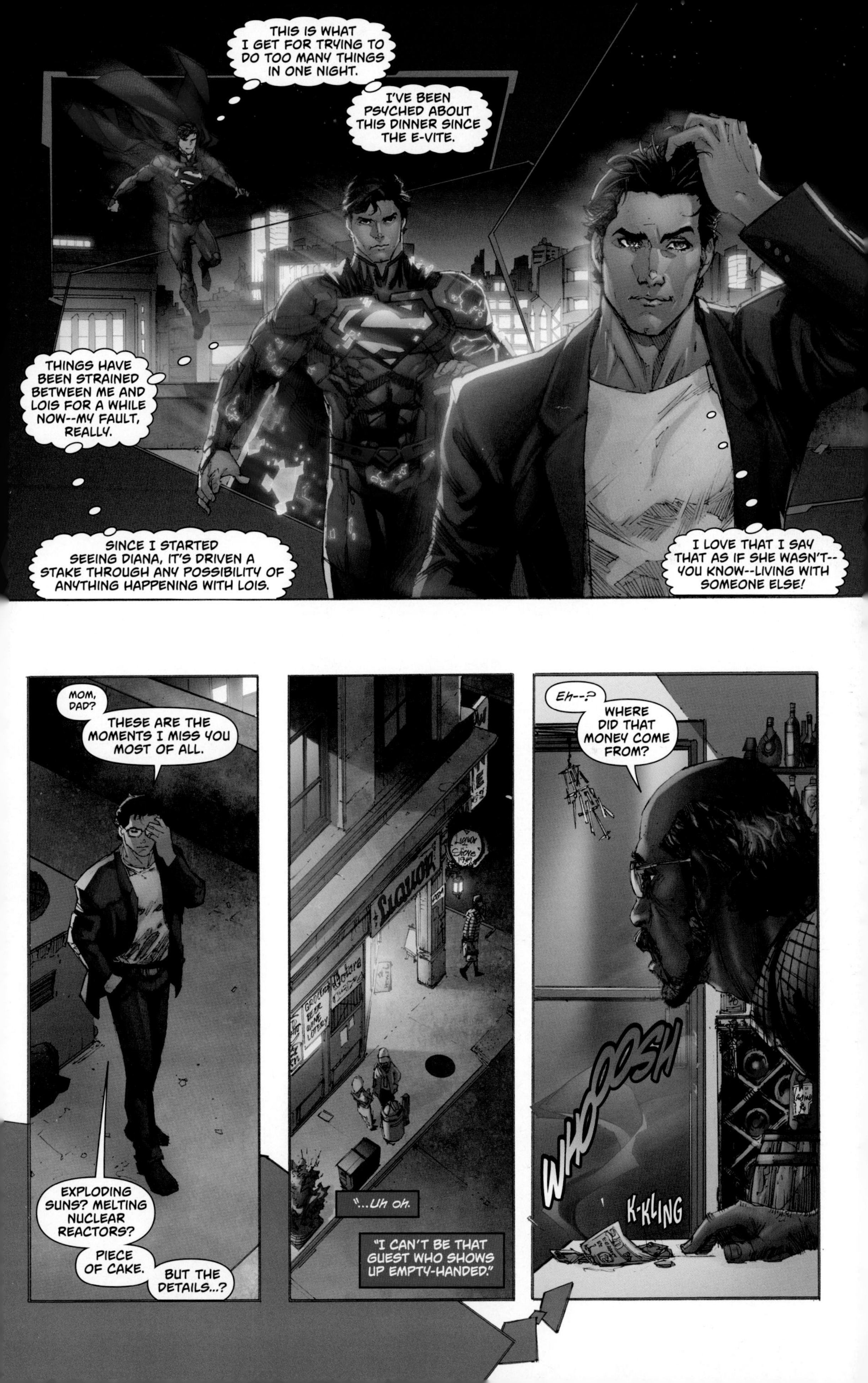
THIS IS WHAT I GET FOR TRYING TO DO TOO MANY THINGS IN ONE NIGHT.
I'VE BEEN PSYCHED ABOUT THIS DINNER SINCE THE E-VITE.
THINGS HAVE BEEN STRAINED BETWEEN ME AND LOIS FOR A WHILE NOW--MY FAULT, REALLY.
SINCE I STARTED SEEING DIANA, IT'S DRIVEN A STAKE THROUGH ANY POSSIBILITY OF ANYTHING HAPPENING WITH LOIS.
I LOVE THAT I SAY THAT AS IF SHE WASN'T--YOU KNOW--LIVING WITH SOMEONE ELSE!
MOM, DAD?
THESE ARE THE MOMENTS I MISS YOU MOST OF ALL.
EXPLODING SUNS? MELTING NUCLEAR REACTORS?
PIECE OF CAKE.
BUT THE DETAILS...?
LIQUOR
"...Uh oh.
"I CAN'T BE THAT GUEST WHO SHOWS UP EMPTY-HANDED."
Eh--?
WHERE DID THAT MONEY COME FROM?
WHOOOSH
K-KLING

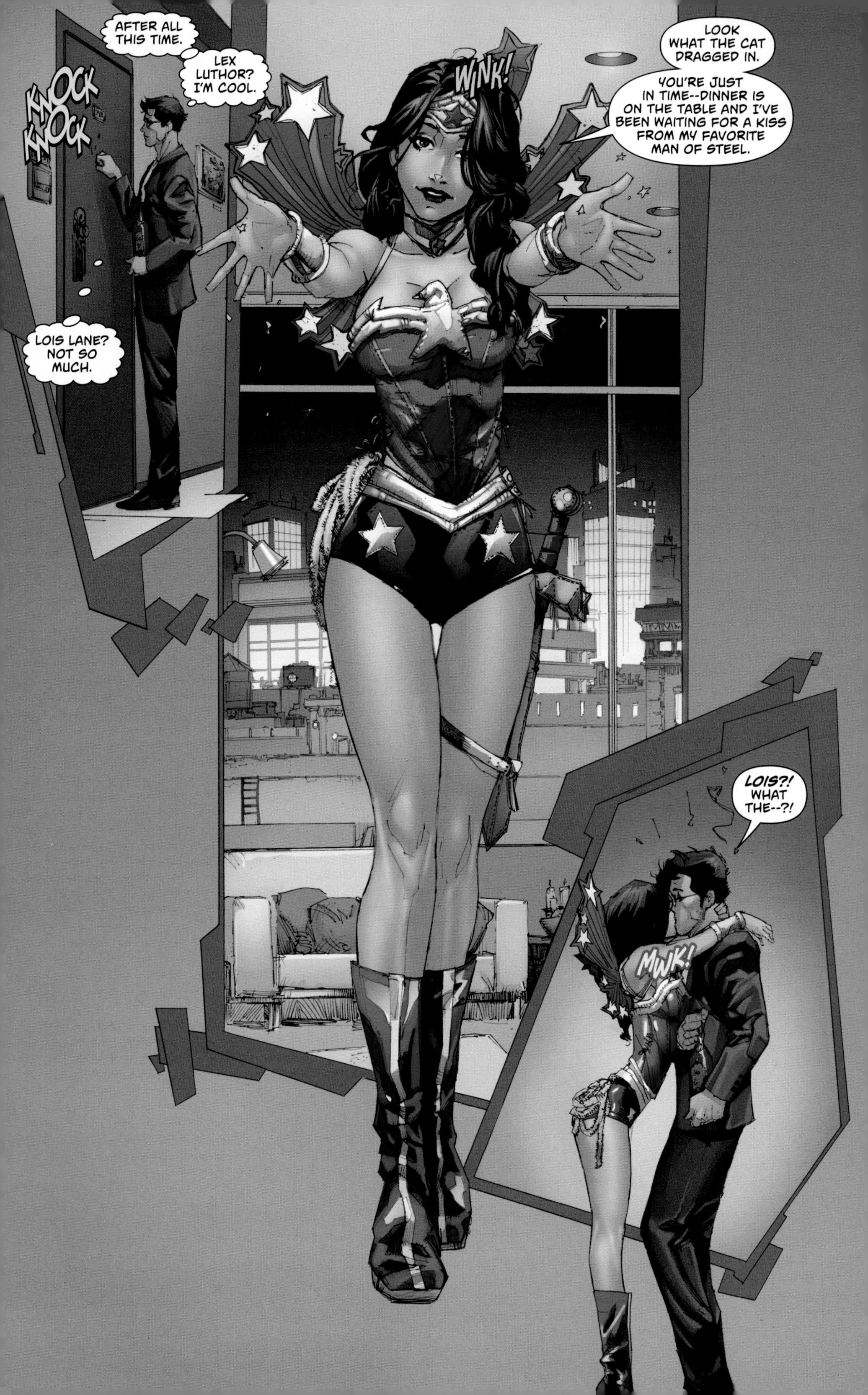
KNOCK KNOCK
AFTER ALL THIS TIME.
LEX LUTHOR? I'M COOL.
LOIS LANE? NOT SO MUCH.
WINK!
LOOK WHAT THE CAT DRAGGED IN.
YOU'RE JUST IN TIME--DINNER IS ON THE TABLE AND I'VE BEEN WAITING FOR A KISS FROM MY FAVORITE MAN OF STEEL.
MWK!
LOIS?! WHAT THE--?!

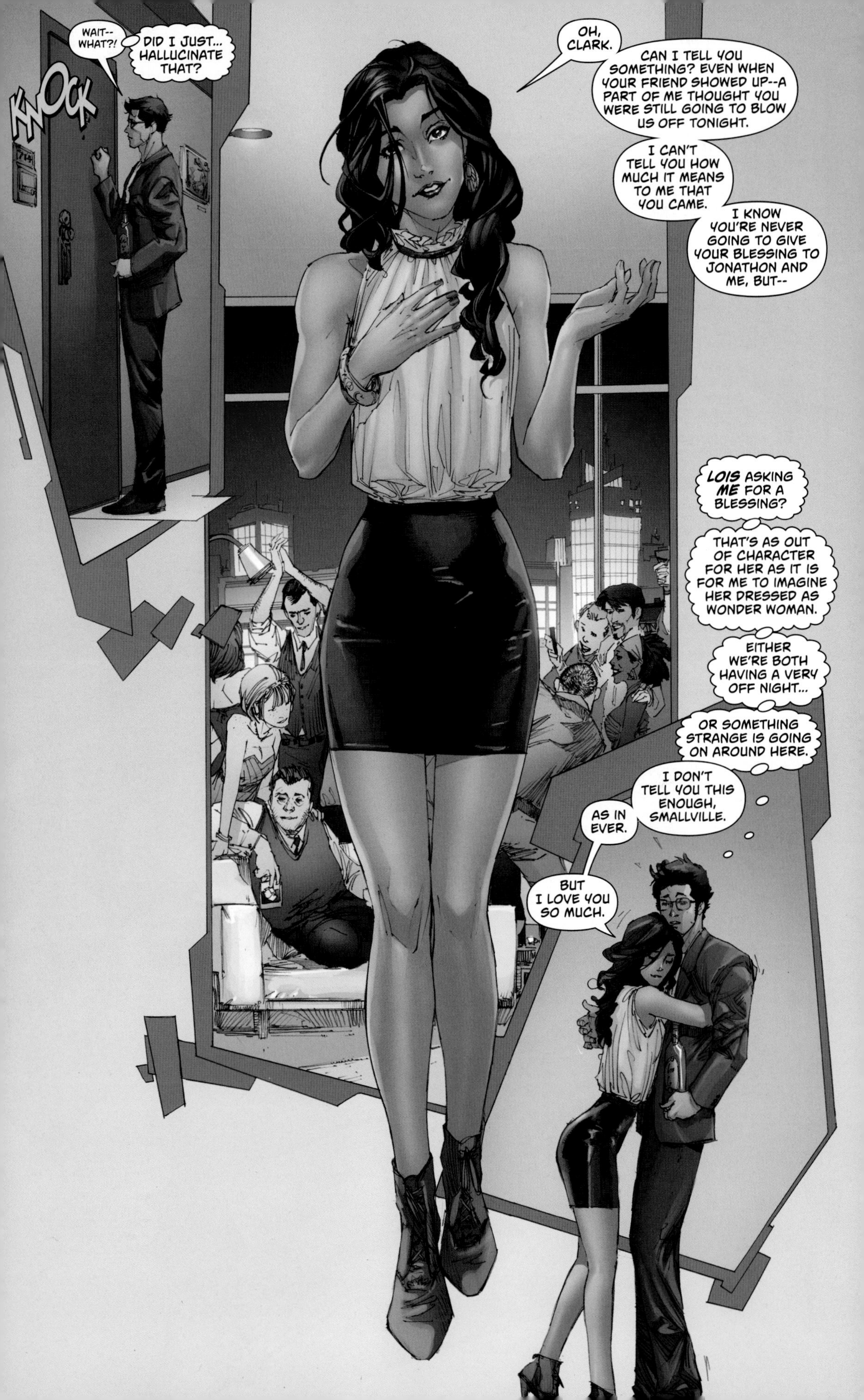
WAIT--
WHAT?!
DID I JUST... HALLUCINATE THAT?
KNOCK
OH, CLARK.
CAN I TELL YOU SOMETHING? EVEN WHEN YOUR FRIEND SHOWED UP--A PART OF ME THOUGHT YOU WERE STILL GOING TO BLOW US OFF TONIGHT.
I CAN'T TELL YOU HOW MUCH IT MEANS TO ME THAT YOU CAME.
I KNOW YOU'RE NEVER GOING TO GIVE YOUR BLESSING TO JONATHON AND ME, BUT--
LOIS ASKING ME FOR A BLESSING?
THAT'S AS OUT OF CHARACTER FOR HER AS IT IS FOR ME TO IMAGINE HER DRESSED AS WONDER WOMAN.
EITHER WE'RE BOTH HAVING A VERY OFF NIGHT...
OR SOMETHING STRANGE IS GOING ON AROUND HERE.
I DON'T TELL YOU THIS ENOUGH, SMALLVILLE.
AS IN EVER.
BUT I LOVE YOU SO MUCH.

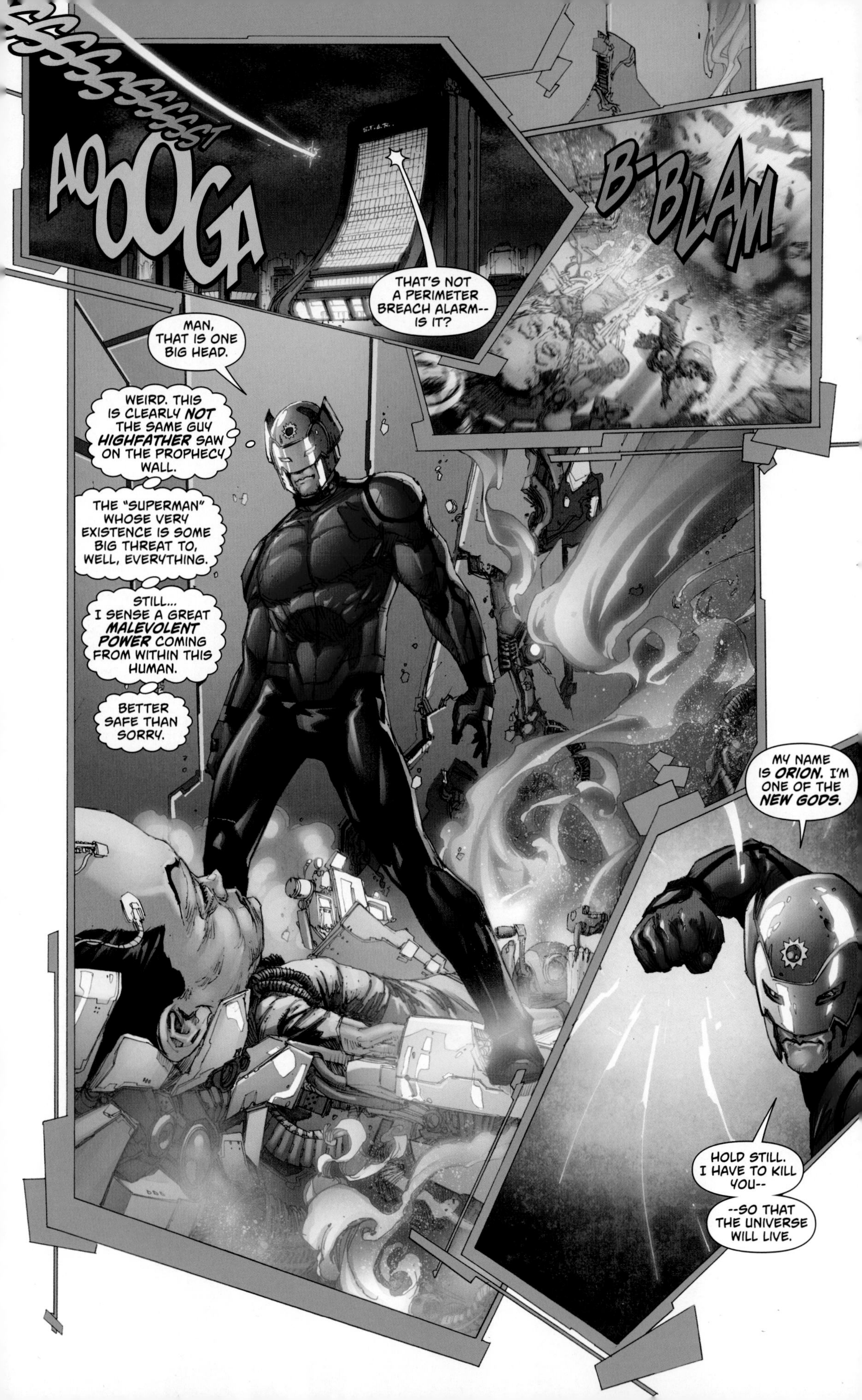
SSSSSSSSST
AOOOGA
S.T.A.R.
THAT'S NOT A PERIMETER BREACH ALARM-- IS IT?
B-BLAM
MAN, THAT IS ONE BIG HEAD.
WEIRD. THIS IS CLEARLY NOT THE SAME GUY HIGHFATHER SAW ON THE PROPHECY WALL.
THE "SUPERMAN" WHOSE VERY EXISTENCE IS SOME BIG THREAT TO, WELL, EVERYTHING.
STILL... I SENSE A GREAT MALEVOLENT POWER COMING FROM WITHIN THIS HUMAN.
BETTER SAFE THAN SORRY.
MY NAME IS ORION. I'M ONE OF THE NEW GODS.
HOLD STILL. I HAVE TO KILL YOU--
--SO THAT THE UNIVERSE WILL LIVE.

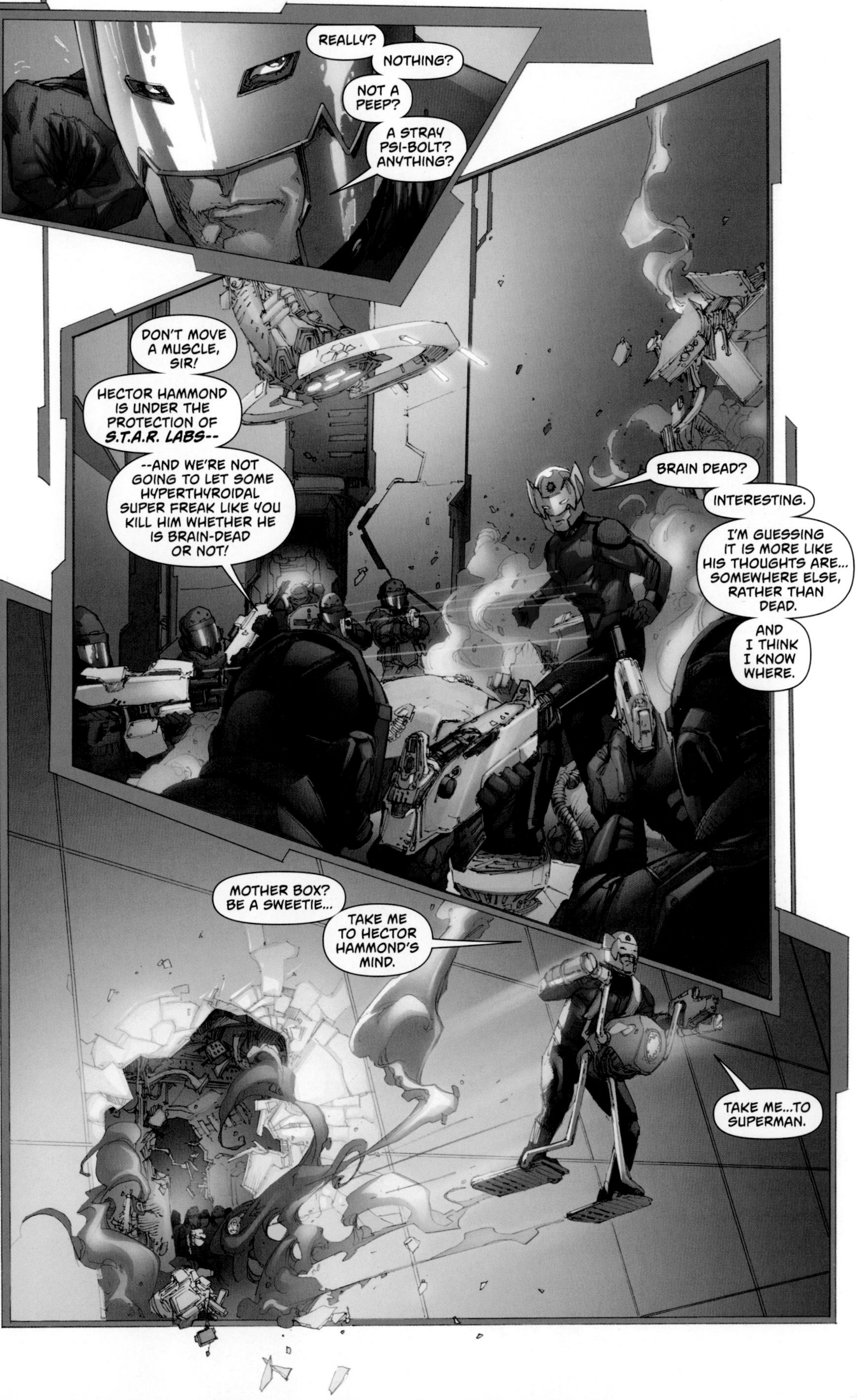
REALLY?
NOTHING?
NOT A PEEP?
A STRAY PSI-BOLT? ANYTHING?
DON'T MOVE A MUSCLE, SIR!
HECTOR HAMMOND IS UNDER THE PROTECTION OF S.T.A.R. LABS--
--AND WE'RE NOT GOING TO LET SOME HYPERTHYROIDAL SUPER FREAK LIKE YOU KILL HIM WHETHER HE IS BRAIN-DEAD OR NOT!
BRAIN DEAD?
INTERESTING.
I'M GUESSING IT IS MORE LIKE HIS THOUGHTS ARE... SOMEWHERE ELSE, RATHER THAN DEAD.
AND I THINK I KNOW WHERE.
MOTHER BOX? BE A SWEETIE...
TAKE ME TO HECTOR HAMMOND'S MIND.
TAKE ME...TO SUPERMAN.

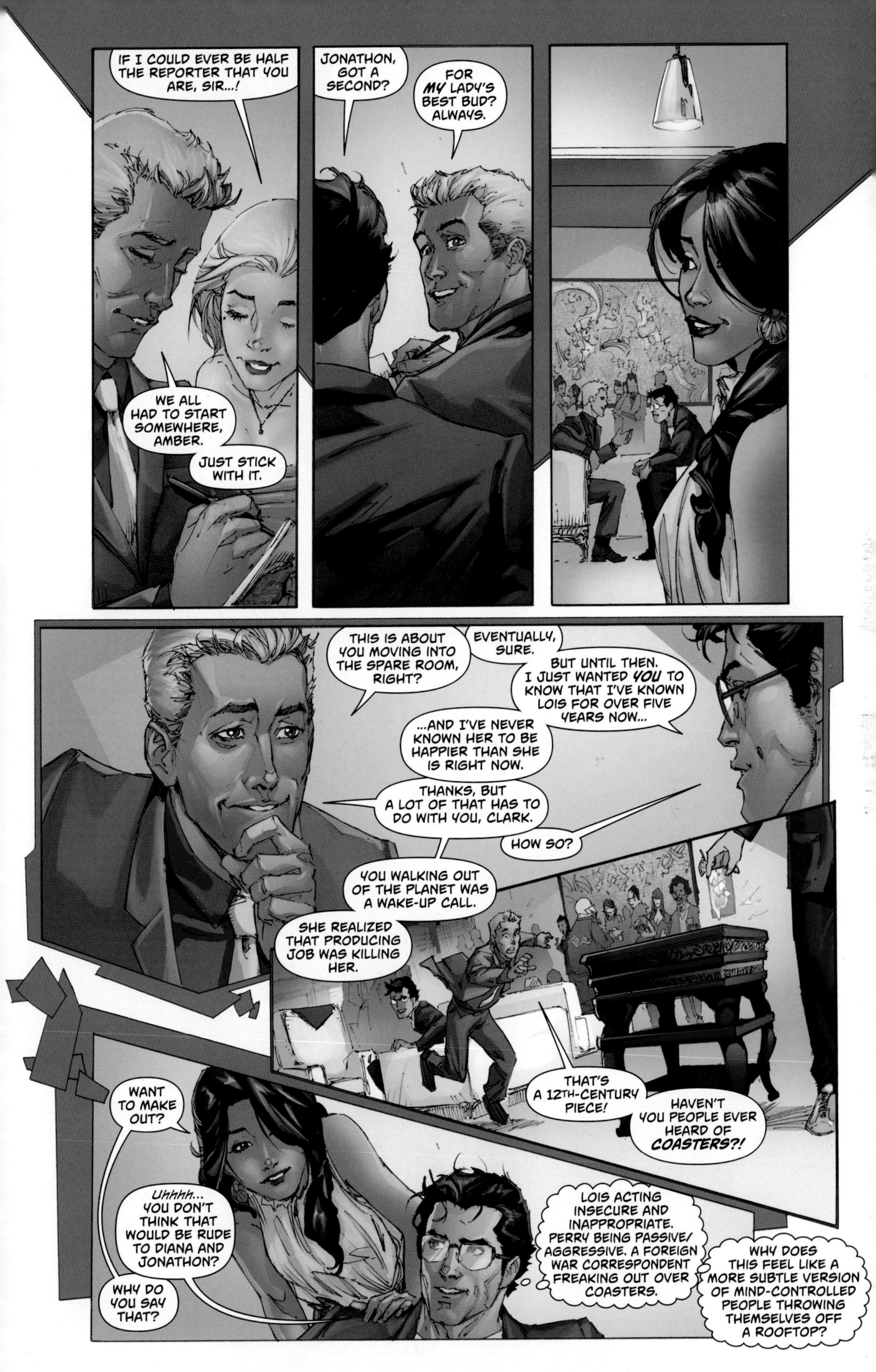
IF I COULD EVER BE HALF THE REPORTER THAT YOU ARE, SIR...!
WE ALL HAD TO START SOMEWHERE, AMBER.
JUST STICK WITH IT.
JONATHON, GOT A SECOND?
FOR *MY* LADY'S BEST BUD? ALWAYS.
THIS IS ABOUT YOU MOVING INTO THE SPARE ROOM, RIGHT?
EVENTUALLY, SURE.
BUT UNTIL THEN. I JUST WANTED *YOU* TO KNOW THAT I'VE KNOWN LOIS FOR OVER FIVE YEARS NOW...
...AND I'VE NEVER KNOWN HER TO BE HAPPIER THAN SHE IS RIGHT NOW.
THANKS, BUT A LOT OF THAT HAS TO DO WITH YOU, CLARK.
HOW SO?
YOU WALKING OUT OF THE PLANET WAS A WAKE-UP CALL.
SHE REALIZED THAT PRODUCING JOB WAS KILLING HER.
THAT'S A 12TH-CENTURY PIECE!
HAVEN'T YOU PEOPLE EVER HEARD OF *COASTERS?!*
WANT TO MAKE OUT?
Uhhhh... YOU DON'T THINK THAT WOULD BE RUDE TO DIANA AND JONATHON?
WHY DO YOU SAY THAT?
LOIS ACTING INSECURE AND INAPPROPRIATE. PERRY BEING PASSIVE/ AGGRESSIVE. A FOREIGN WAR CORRESPONDENT FREAKING OUT OVER COASTERS.
WHY DOES THIS FEEL LIKE A MORE SUBTLE VERSION OF MIND-CONTROLLED PEOPLE THROWING THEMSELVES OFF A ROOFTOP?

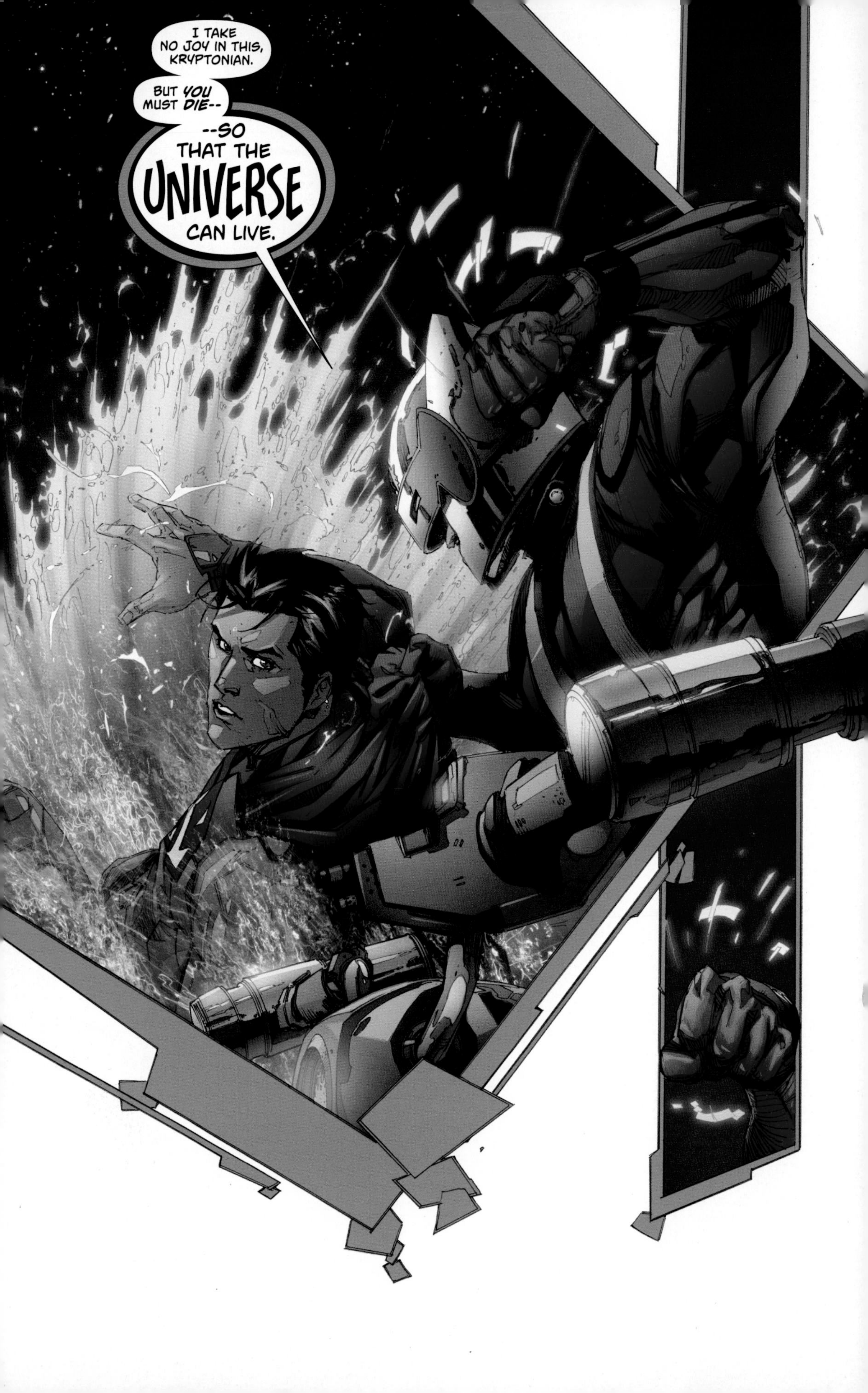
I TAKE NO JOY IN THIS, KRYPTONIAN.
BUT *YOU* MUST *DIE*--
--SO THAT THE UNIVERSE CAN LIVE.

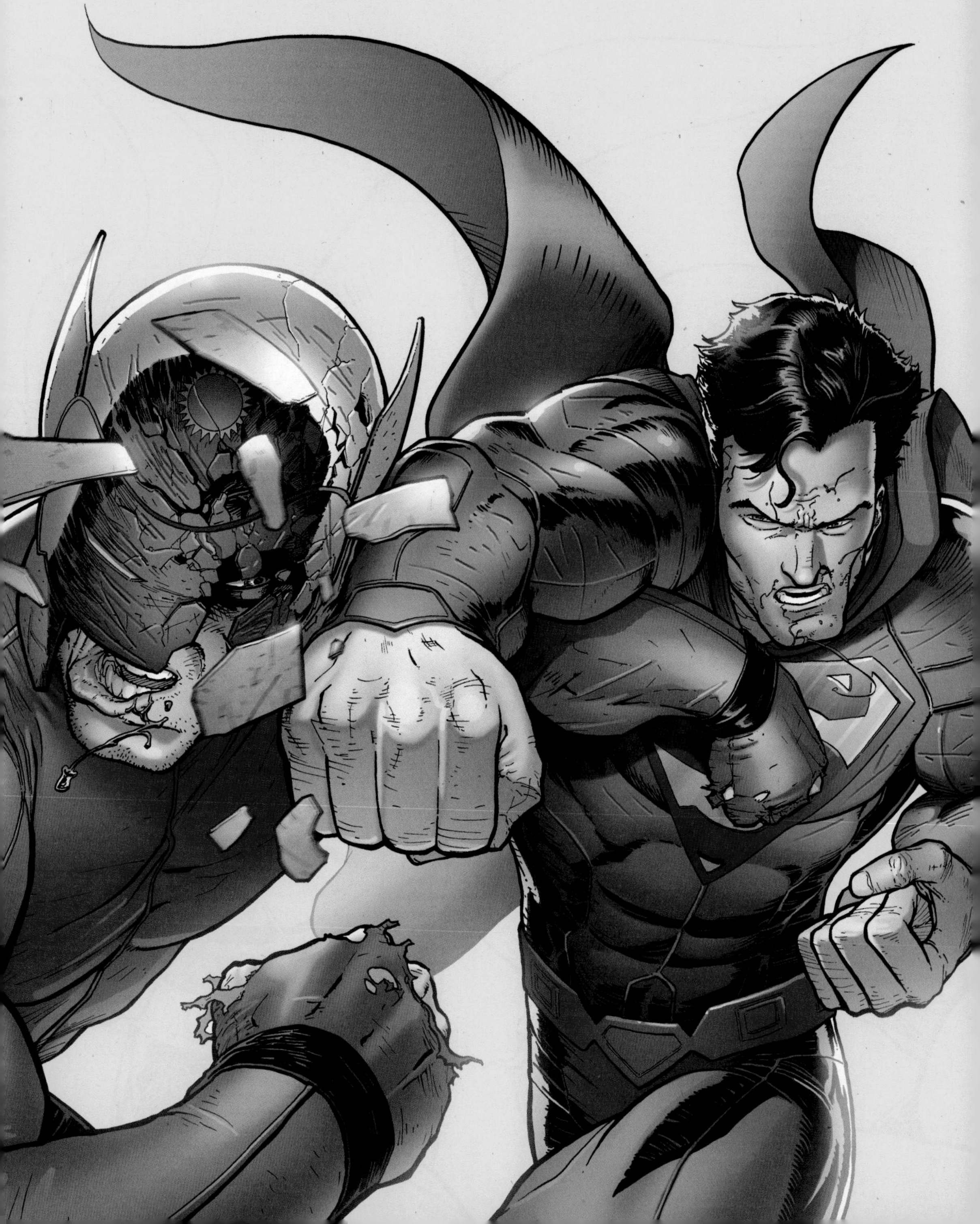

WHAM!

SCOTT LOBDELL writer AARON KUDER artist cover art by AARON KUDER & QUINTANA

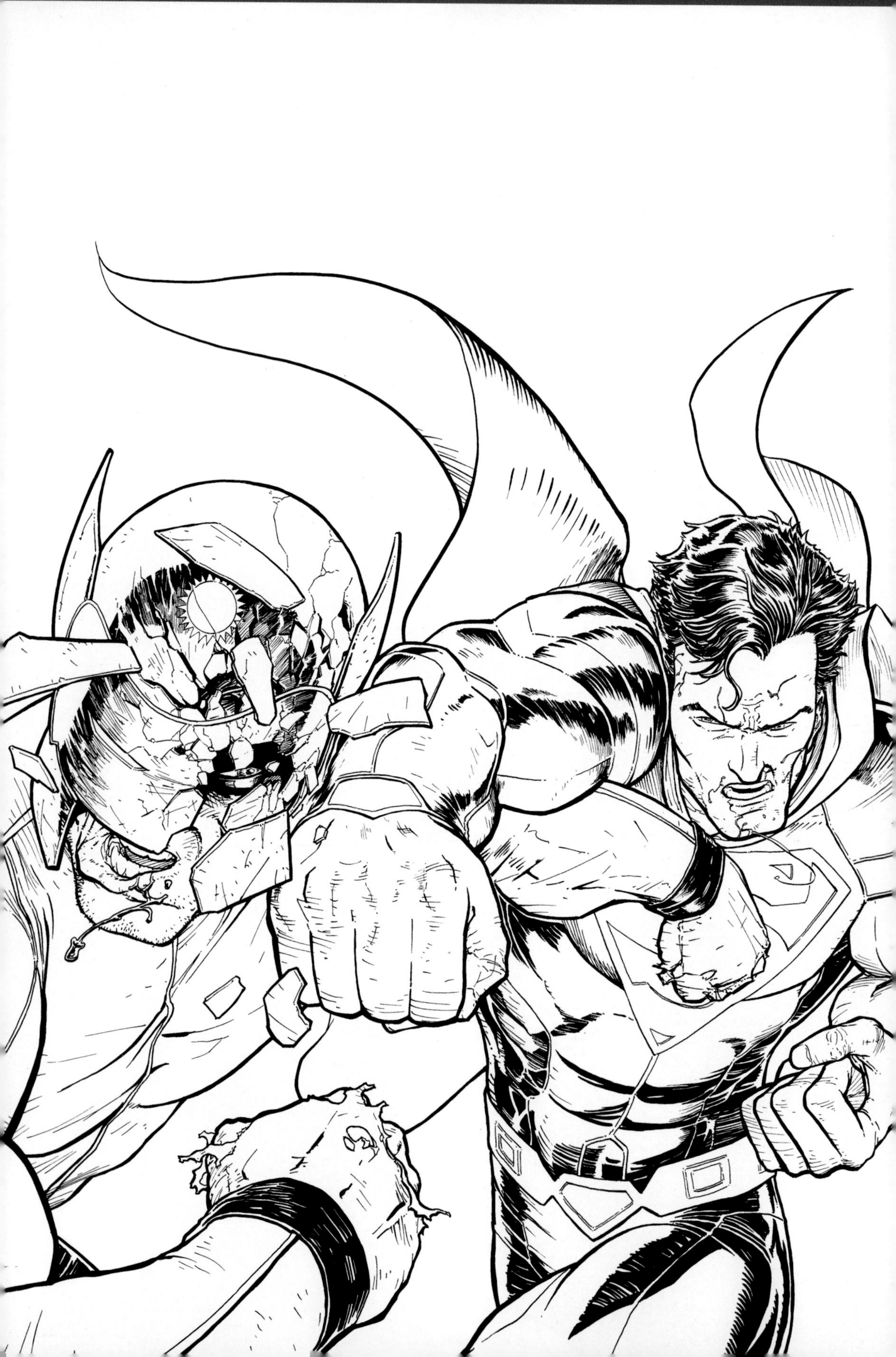

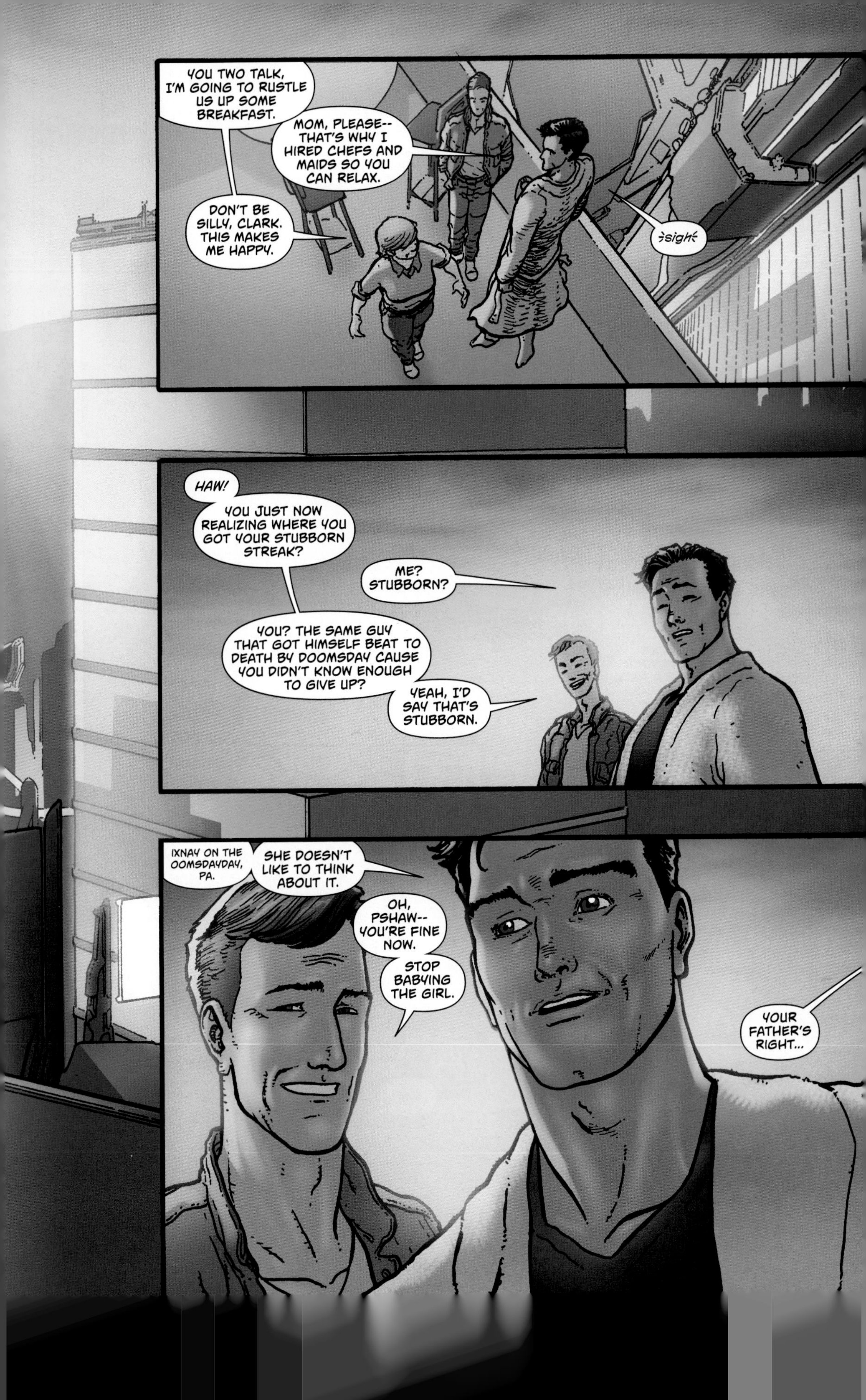
YOU TWO TALK, I'M GOING TO RUSTLE US UP SOME BREAKFAST.
MOM, PLEASE-- THAT'S WHY I HIRED CHEFS AND MAIDS SO YOU CAN RELAX.
DON'T BE SILLY, CLARK. THIS MAKES ME HAPPY.
sigh
HAW!
YOU JUST NOW REALIZING WHERE YOU GOT YOUR STUBBORN STREAK?
ME? STUBBORN?
YOU? THE SAME GUY THAT GOT HIMSELF BEAT TO DEATH BY DOOMSDAY CAUSE YOU DIDN'T KNOW ENOUGH TO GIVE UP?
YEAH, I'D SAY THAT'S STUBBORN.
IXNAY ON THE OOMSDAYDAY, PA.
SHE DOESN'T LIKE TO THINK ABOUT IT.
OH, PSHAW-- YOU'RE FINE NOW.
STOP BABYING THE GIRL.
YOUR FATHER'S RIGHT...

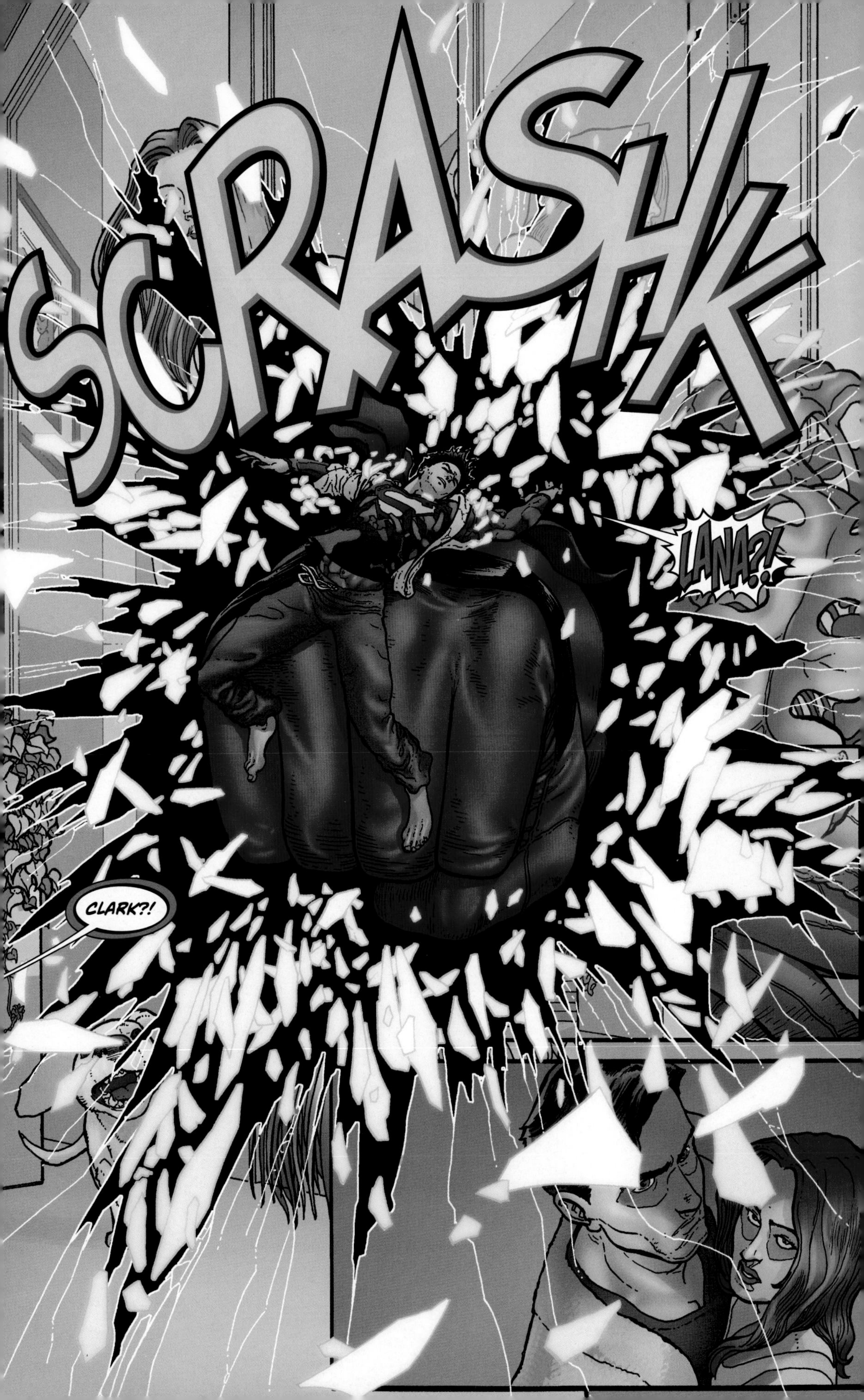
SCRASHK
LANA?!
CLARK?!

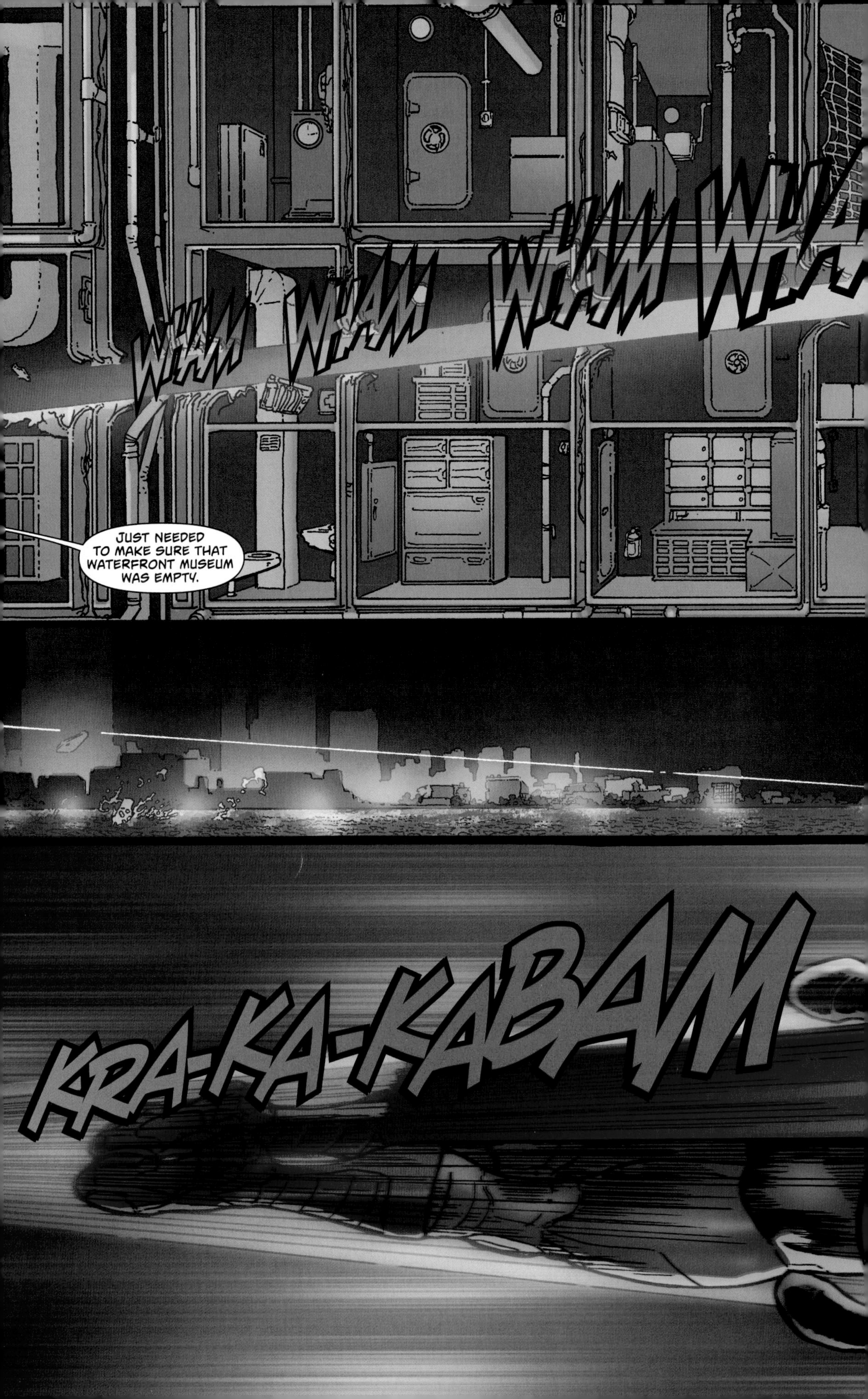
WHAM WHAM WHAM WHAM
JUST NEEDED TO MAKE SURE THAT WATERFRONT MUSEUM WAS EMPTY.
KRA-KA-KABAM

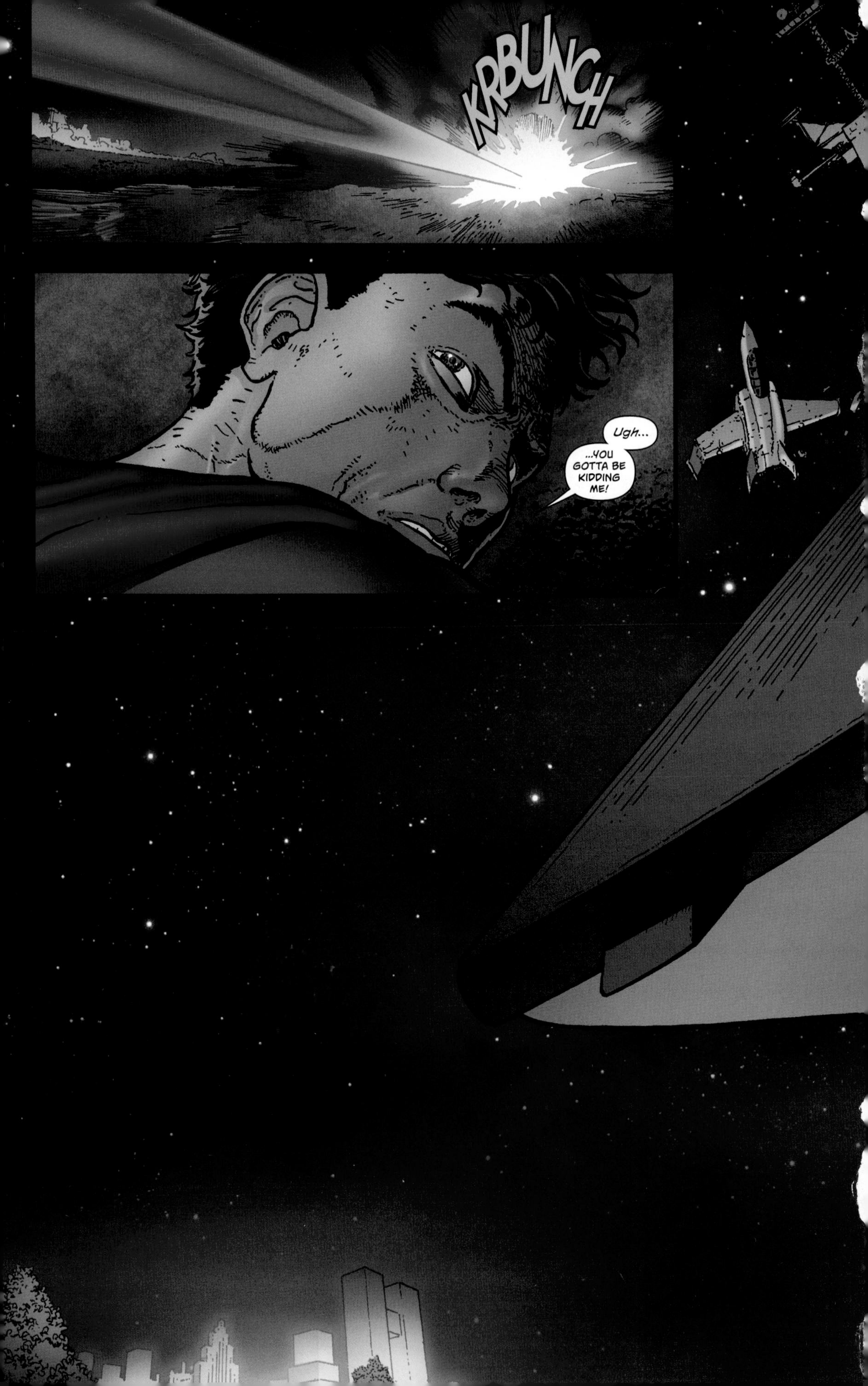
KRBUNCH
Ugh...
...YOU GOTTA BE KIDDING ME!

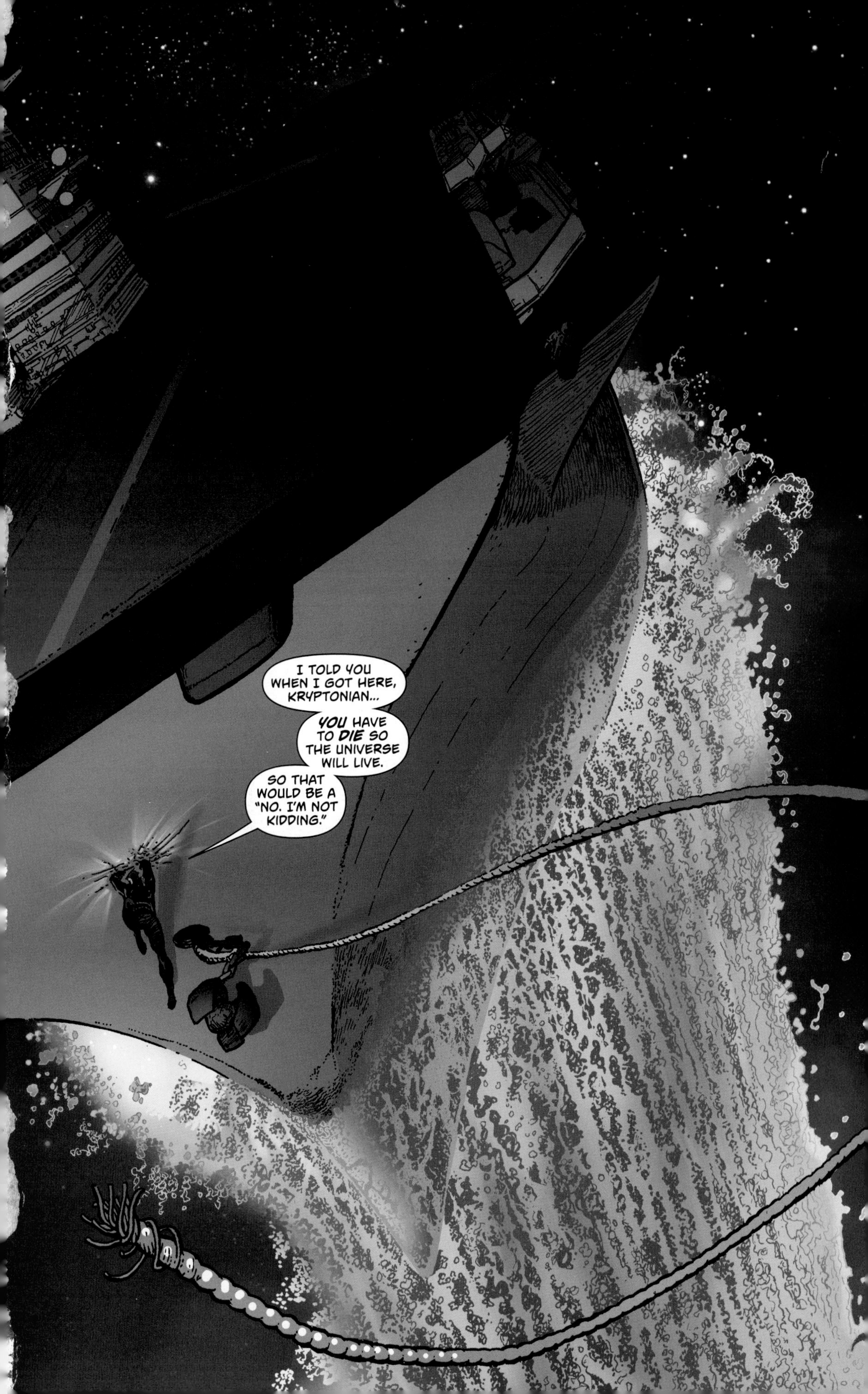
I TOLD YOU WHEN I GOT HERE, KRYPTONIAN...
YOU HAVE TO DIE SO THE UNIVERSE WILL LIVE.
SO THAT WOULD BE A "NO. I'M NOT KIDDING."

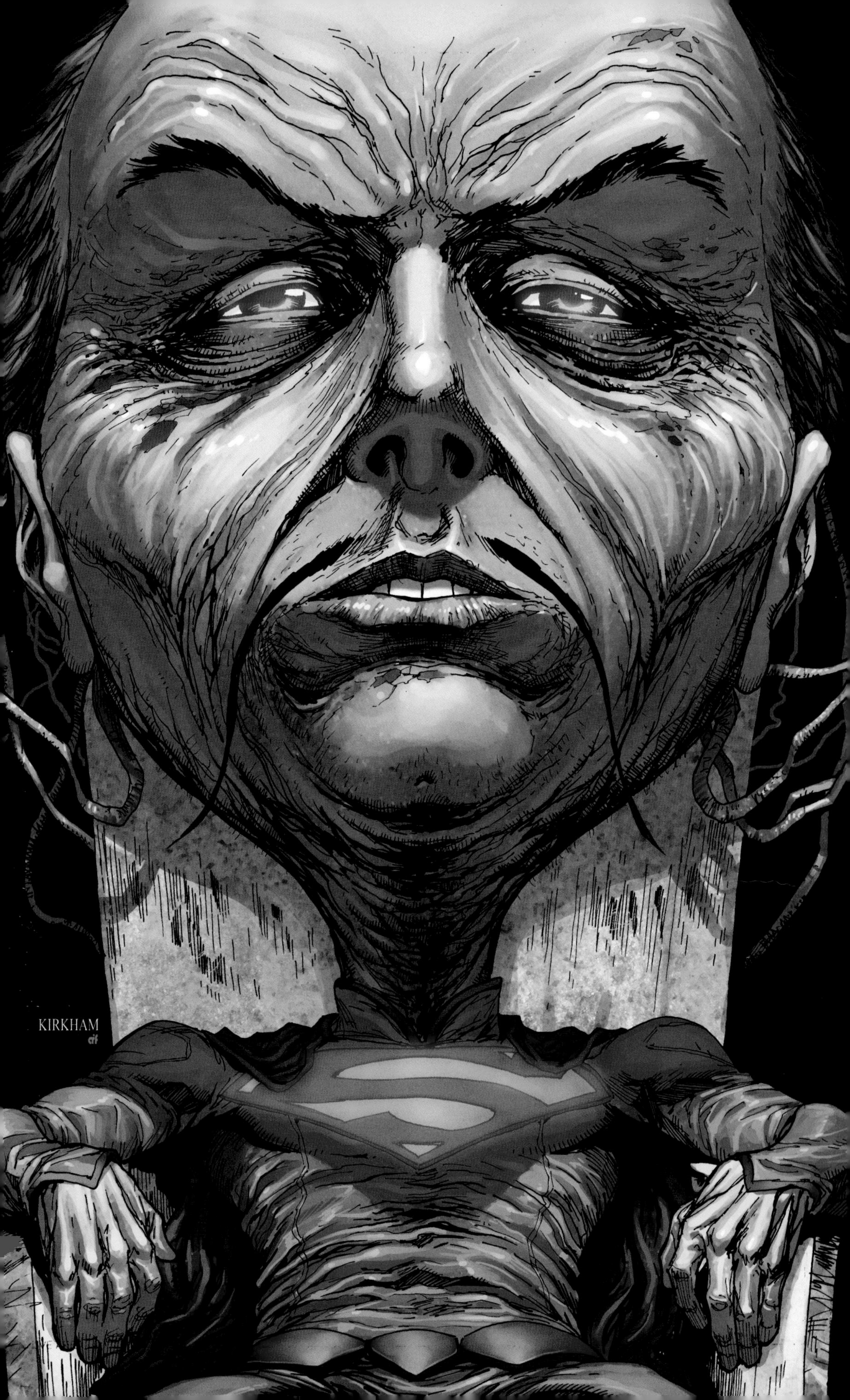
KIRKHAM

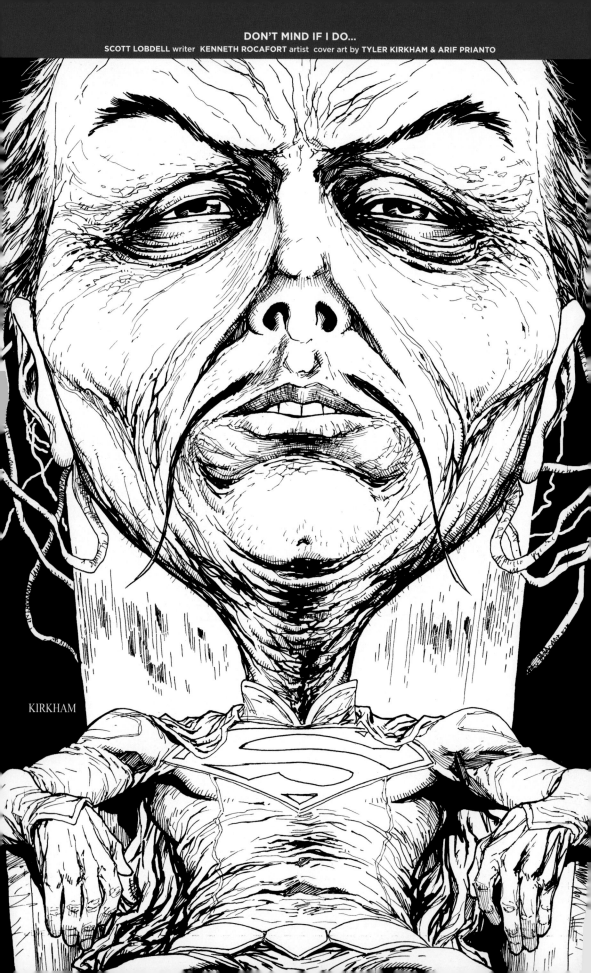

KIRKHAM

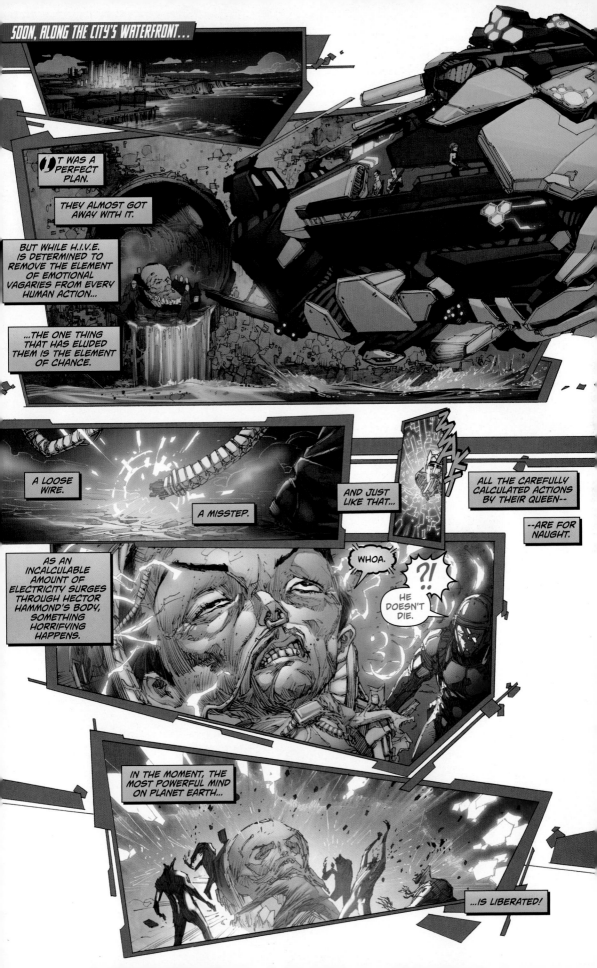

SOON, ALONG THE CITY'S WATERFRONT...

IT WAS A PERFECT PLAN.

THEY ALMOST GOT AWAY WITH IT.

BUT WHILE H.I.V.E. IS DETERMINED TO REMOVE THE ELEMENT OF EMOTIONAL VAGARIES FROM EVERY HUMAN ACTION...

...THE ONE THING THAT HAS ELUDED THEM IS THE ELEMENT OF CHANCE.

A LOOSE WIRE.

A MISSTEP.

AND JUST LIKE THAT...

ALL THE CAREFULLY CALCULATED ACTIONS BY THEIR QUEEN--

--ARE FOR NAUGHT.

AS AN INCALCULABLE AMOUNT OF ELECTRICITY SURGES THROUGH HECTOR HAMMOND'S BODY, SOMETHING HORRIFYING HAPPENS.

WHOA.

?!

HE DOESN'T DIE.

IN THE MOMENT, THE MOST POWERFUL MIND ON PLANET EARTH...

...IS LIBERATED!

MEANWHILE... ...IN THE UNDERGROUND COMPLEX THAT HOUSES H.I.V.E....
...
WHAT DO YOU MEAN YOU LOST CONTACT?! THAT'S IMPOSSIBLE.
EVERY MEMBER OF H.I.V.E. IS MINE TO CONTROL AS I SEE FIT.
WHAT HAPPENED OUT THERE?! WHAT HAPPENED TO MY PRIZE?
...
YES, I SEE HIM!
Phew!
AT LAST.
WITH A WEAPON LIKE HAMMOND, I'LL BE UNSTOPPABLE.
...
...
RIGHT?

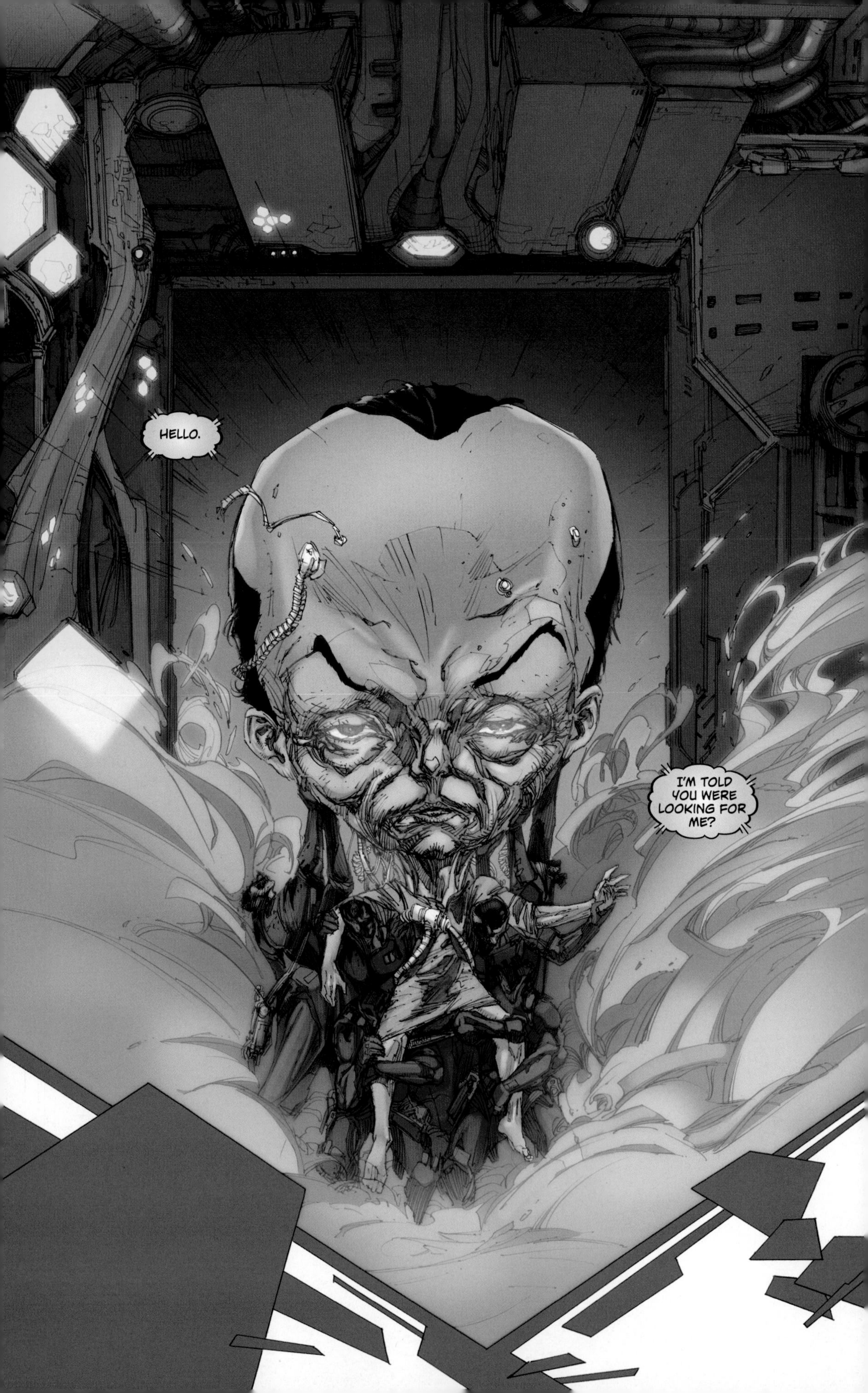
HELLO.
I'M TOLD YOU WERE LOOKING FOR ME?

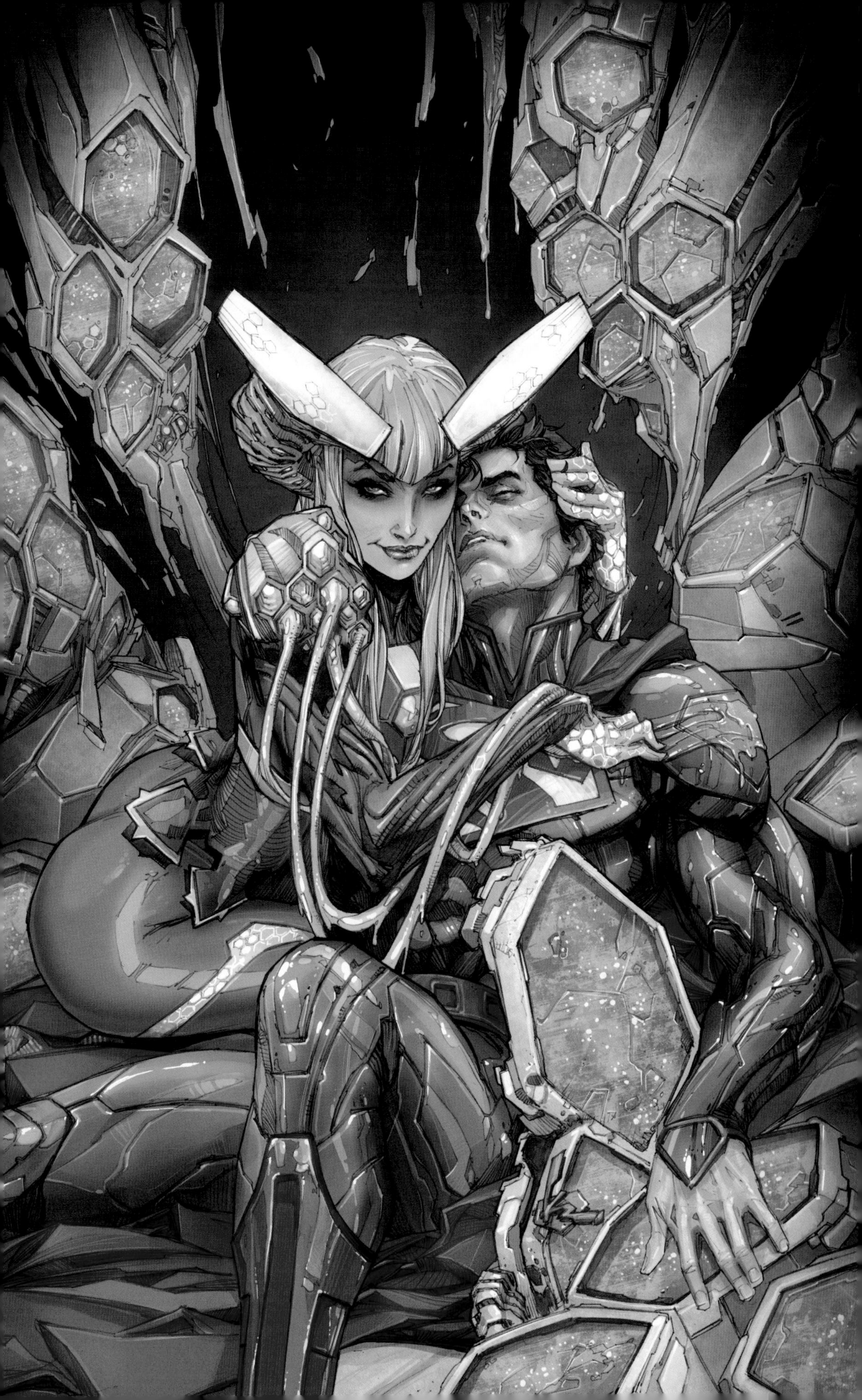

HEADACHES

SCOTT LOBDELL writer EDDY BARROWS DANIEL HDR GERALDO BORGES pencillers
EBER FERREIRA DANIEL HDR GERALDO BORGES inkers cover art by KENNETH ROCAFORT

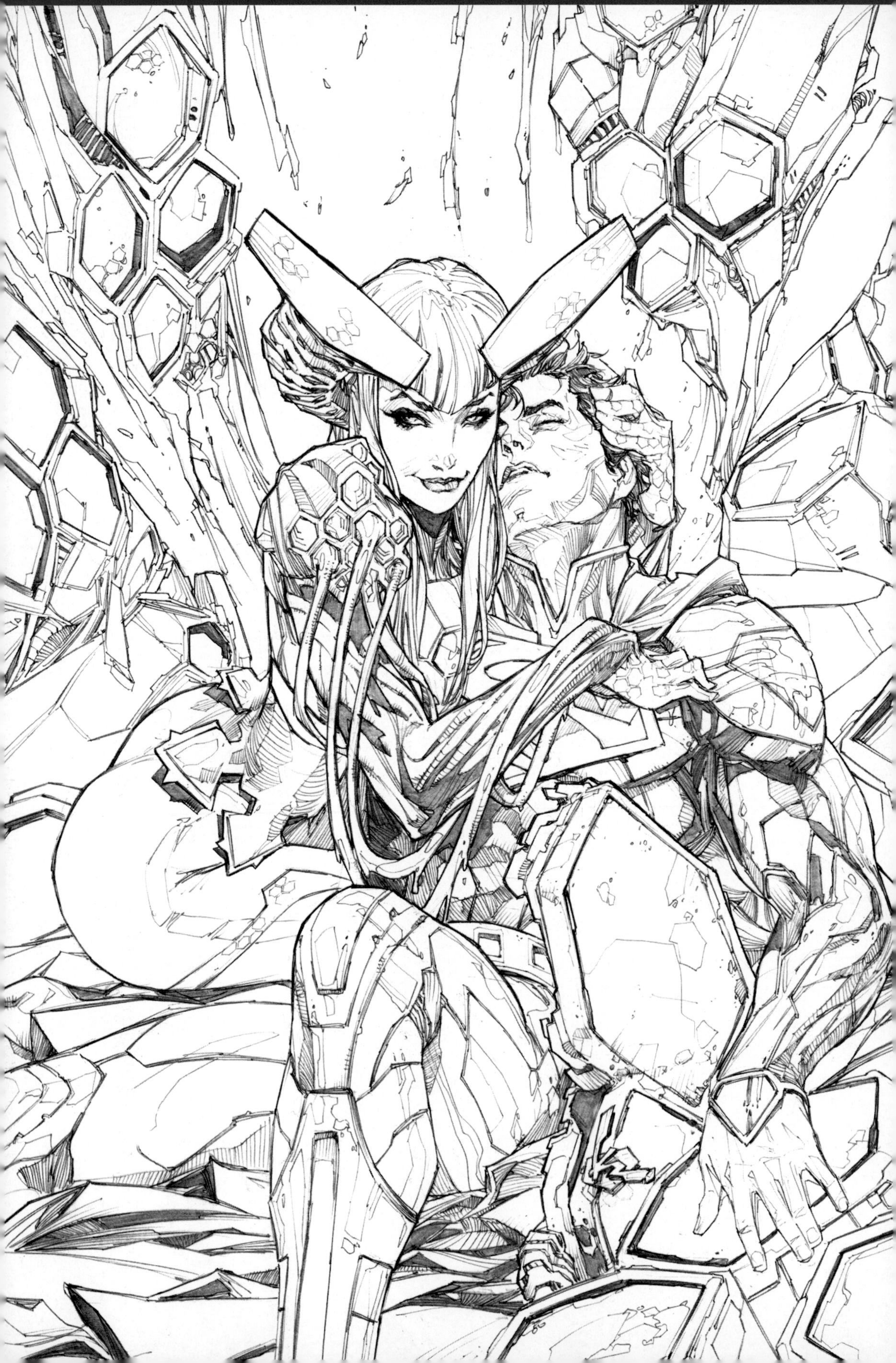

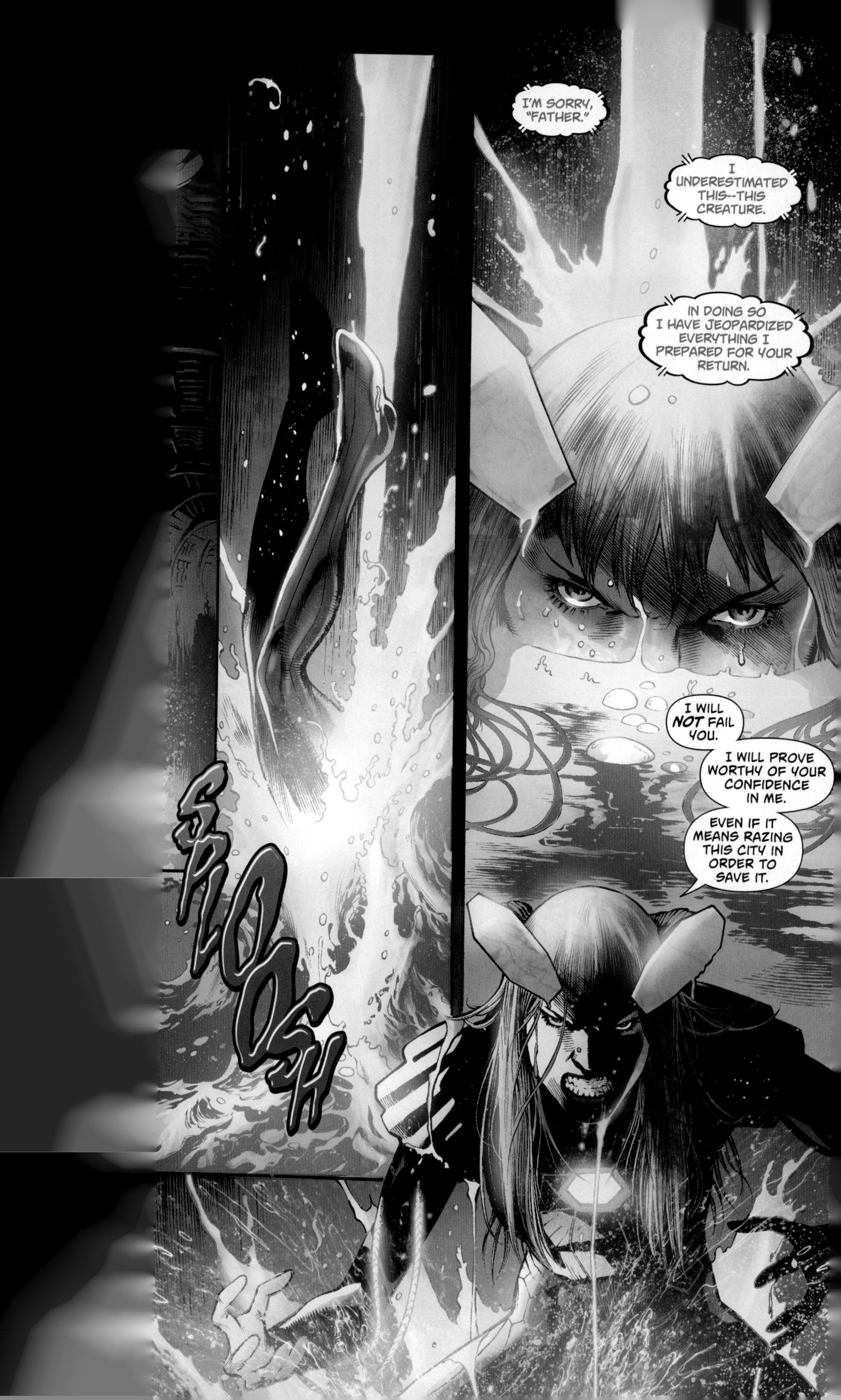

I'M SORRY, "FATHER."
I UNDERESTIMATED THIS--THIS CREATURE.
IN DOING SO I HAVE JEOPARDIZED EVERYTHING I PREPARED FOR YOUR RETURN.
SPLOOSH
I WILL **NOT** FAIL YOU.
I WILL PROVE WORTHY OF YOUR CONFIDENCE IN ME.
EVEN IF IT MEANS RAZING THIS CITY IN ORDER TO SAVE IT.

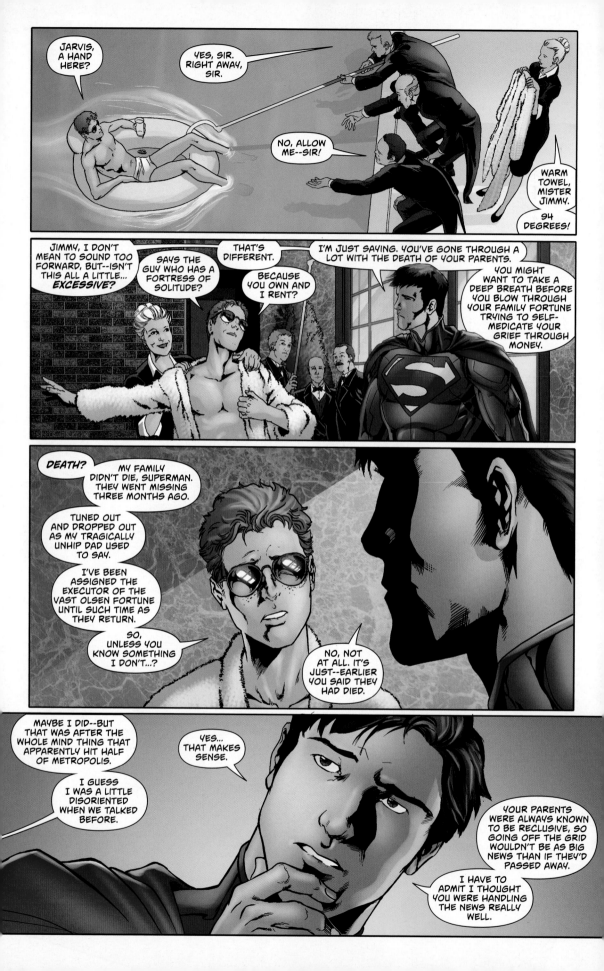

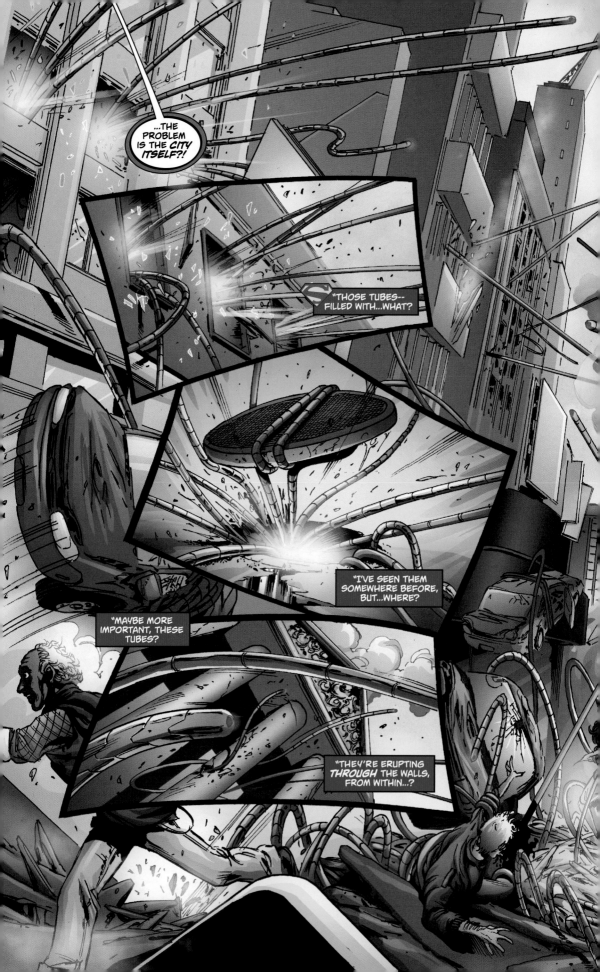

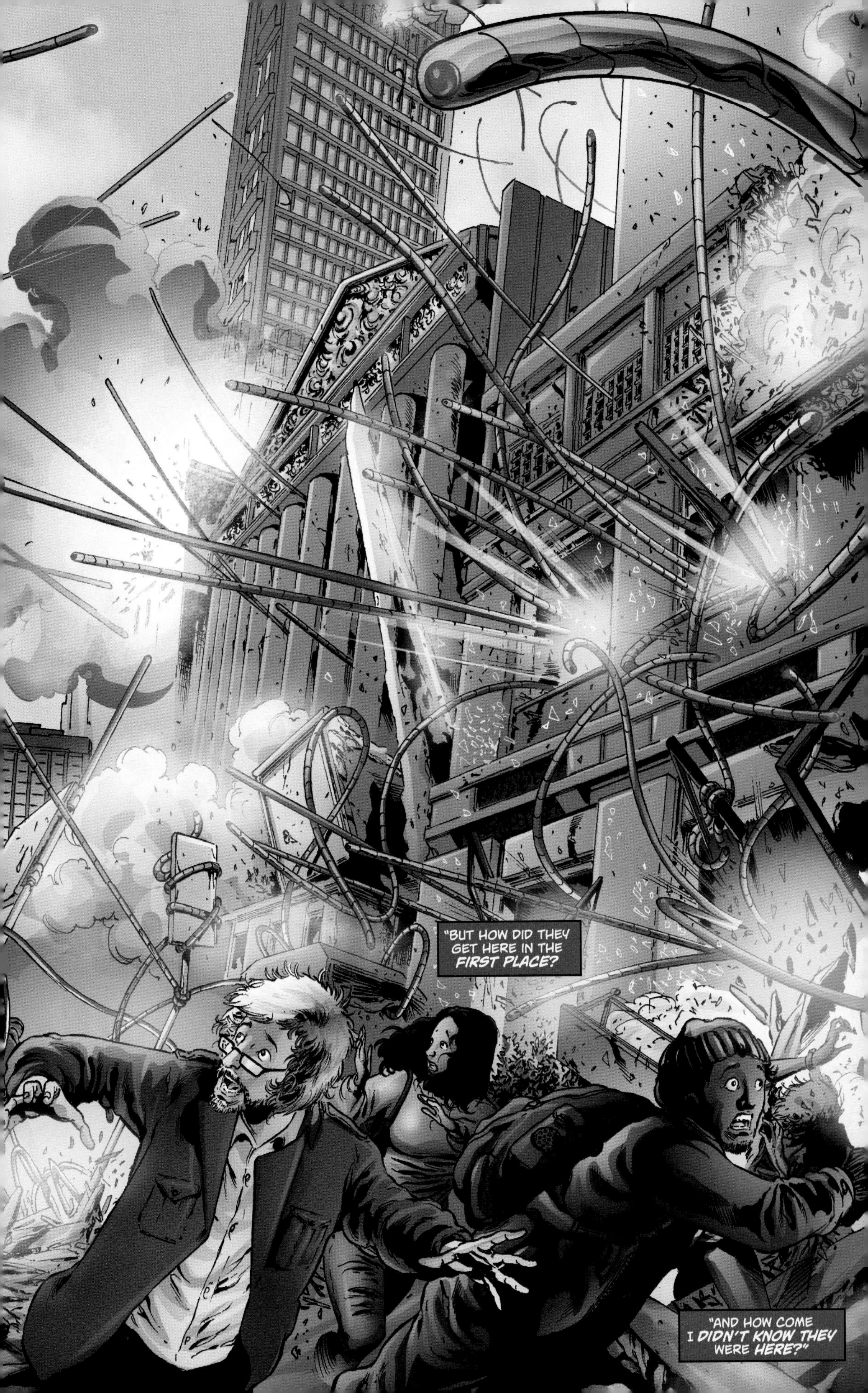
"BUT HOW DID THEY GET HERE IN THE FIRST PLACE?
"AND HOW COME I DIDN'T KNOW THEY WERE HERE?"

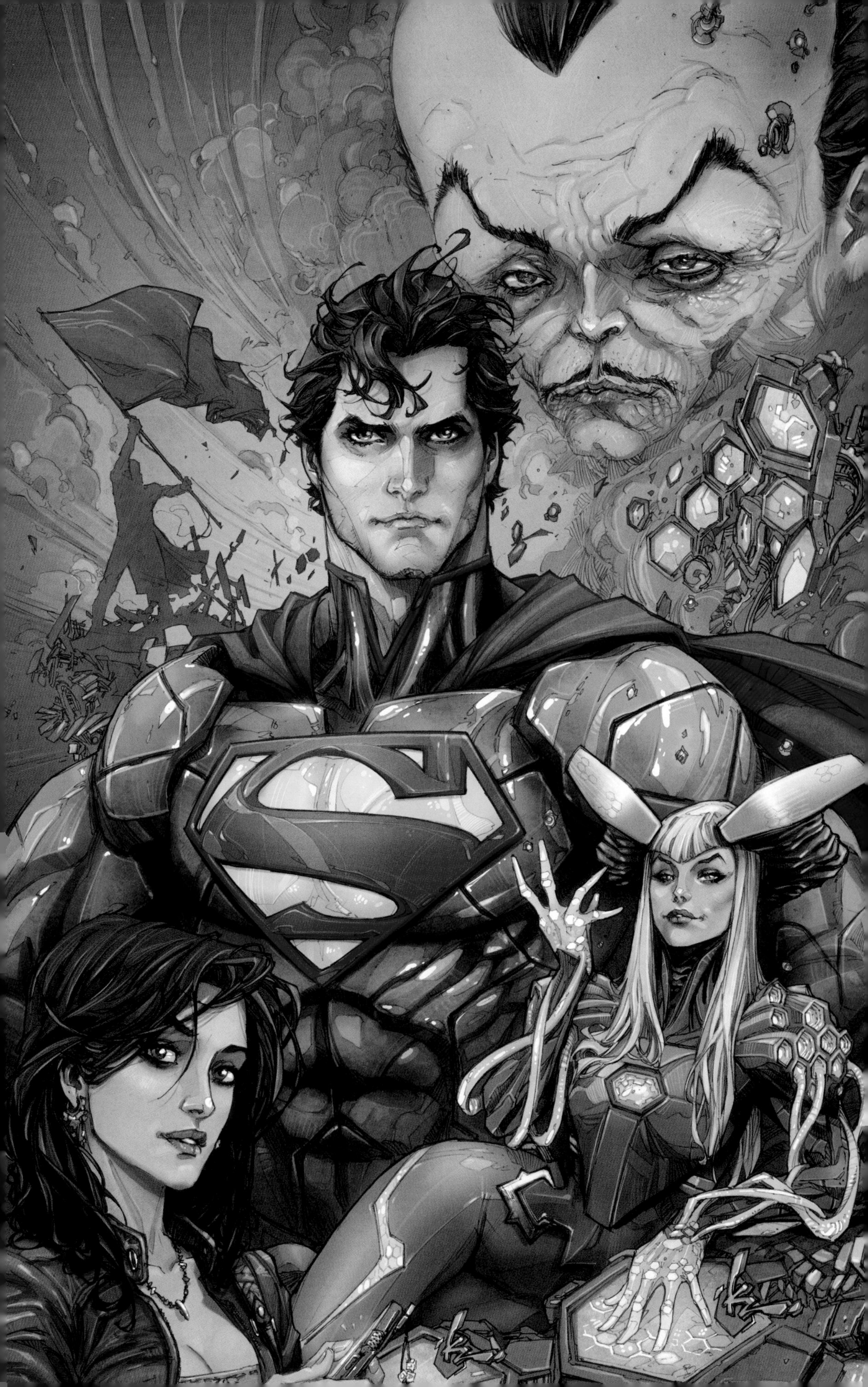

PSI WAR: PART ONE

MIKE JOHNSON writer **EDDY BARROWS** thumbnails **JESUS MERINO** artist cover art by **KENNETH ROCAFORT**

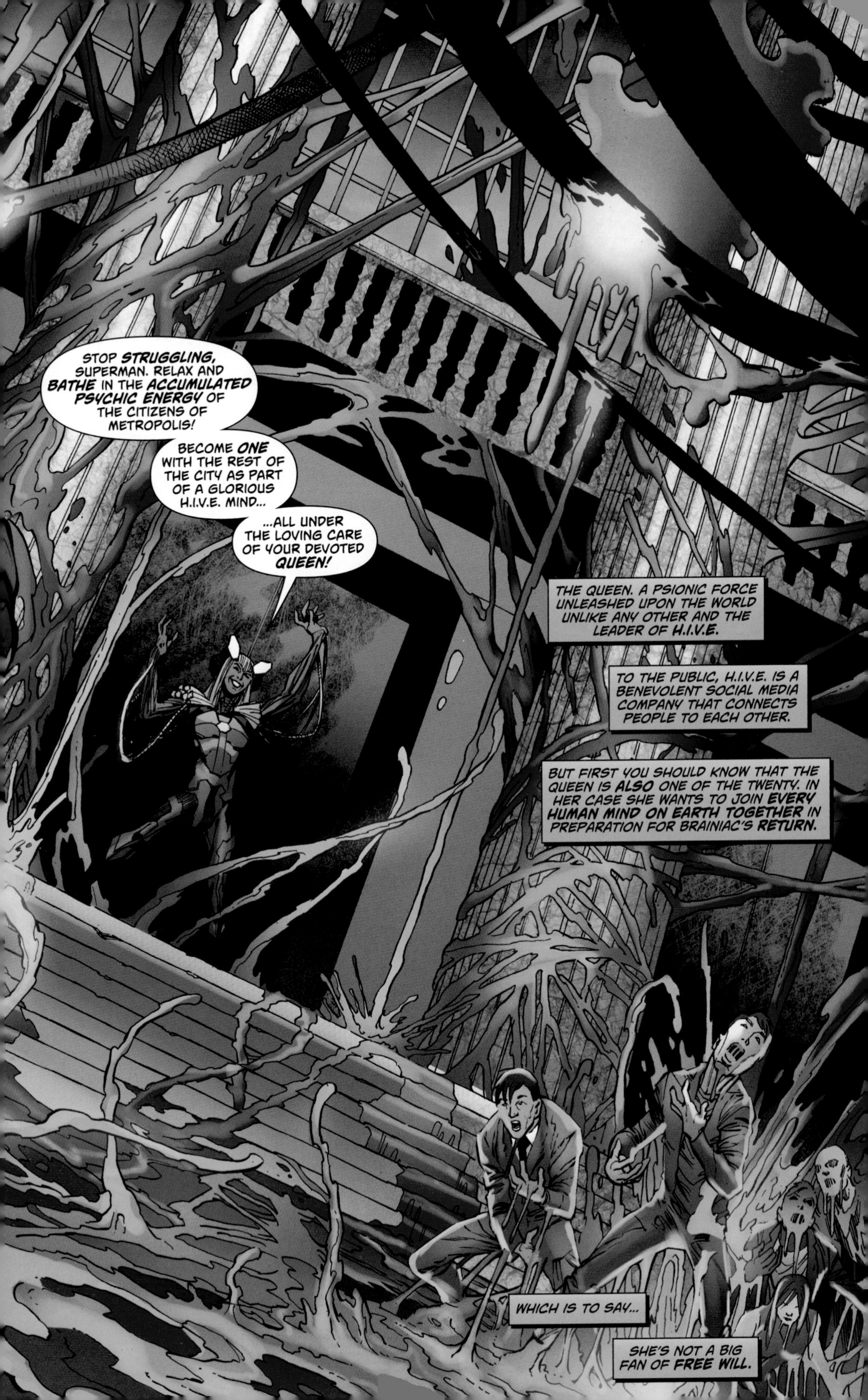
STOP STRUGGLING, SUPERMAN. RELAX AND BATHE IN THE ACCUMULATED PSYCHIC ENERGY OF THE CITIZENS OF METROPOLIS!
BECOME ONE WITH THE REST OF THE CITY AS PART OF A GLORIOUS H.I.V.E. MIND...
...ALL UNDER THE LOVING CARE OF YOUR DEVOTED QUEEN!
THE QUEEN. A PSIONIC FORCE UNLEASHED UPON THE WORLD UNLIKE ANY OTHER AND THE LEADER OF H.I.V.E.
TO THE PUBLIC, H.I.V.E. IS A BENEVOLENT SOCIAL MEDIA COMPANY THAT CONNECTS PEOPLE TO EACH OTHER.
BUT FIRST YOU SHOULD KNOW THAT THE QUEEN IS ALSO ONE OF THE TWENTY. IN HER CASE SHE WANTS TO JOIN EVERY HUMAN MIND ON EARTH TOGETHER IN PREPARATION FOR BRAINIAC'S RETURN.
WHICH IS TO SAY...
SHE'S NOT A BIG FAN OF FREE WILL.

LANE, L.

LOIS LANE. WORLD FAMOUS AND AWARD WINNING REPORTER FOR THE DAILY PLANET.

JONATHON CAROL. WAR CORRESPONDENT AND BOYFRIEND OF LOIS LANE.

HE HASN'T LEFT LOIS'S SIDE SINCE SHE FELL INTO A COMA.*

HE HOLDS HER HAND IN HIS SLEEP. WAITING, HOPING TO FEEL ANY SORT OF MOVEMENT TO LET HIM KNOW THAT THE WOMAN HE LOVES IS OKAY.

JON IS AS GALLANT A FELLOW AS ANY I'VE EVER MET. HE IS NOT WHY WE'RE HERE THOUGH.

*AS SEEN IN SUPERMAN ANNUAL #2! --Eddie.

KEEP YOUR EYES ON LOIS.

WAIT FOR IT...

NOW.

FWASHH

AAAAH!!

LOIS!!

IT'S OKAY, HONEY! I'M HERE!

...SUHH...

...SUUUUP...

...SUPERMANNN...

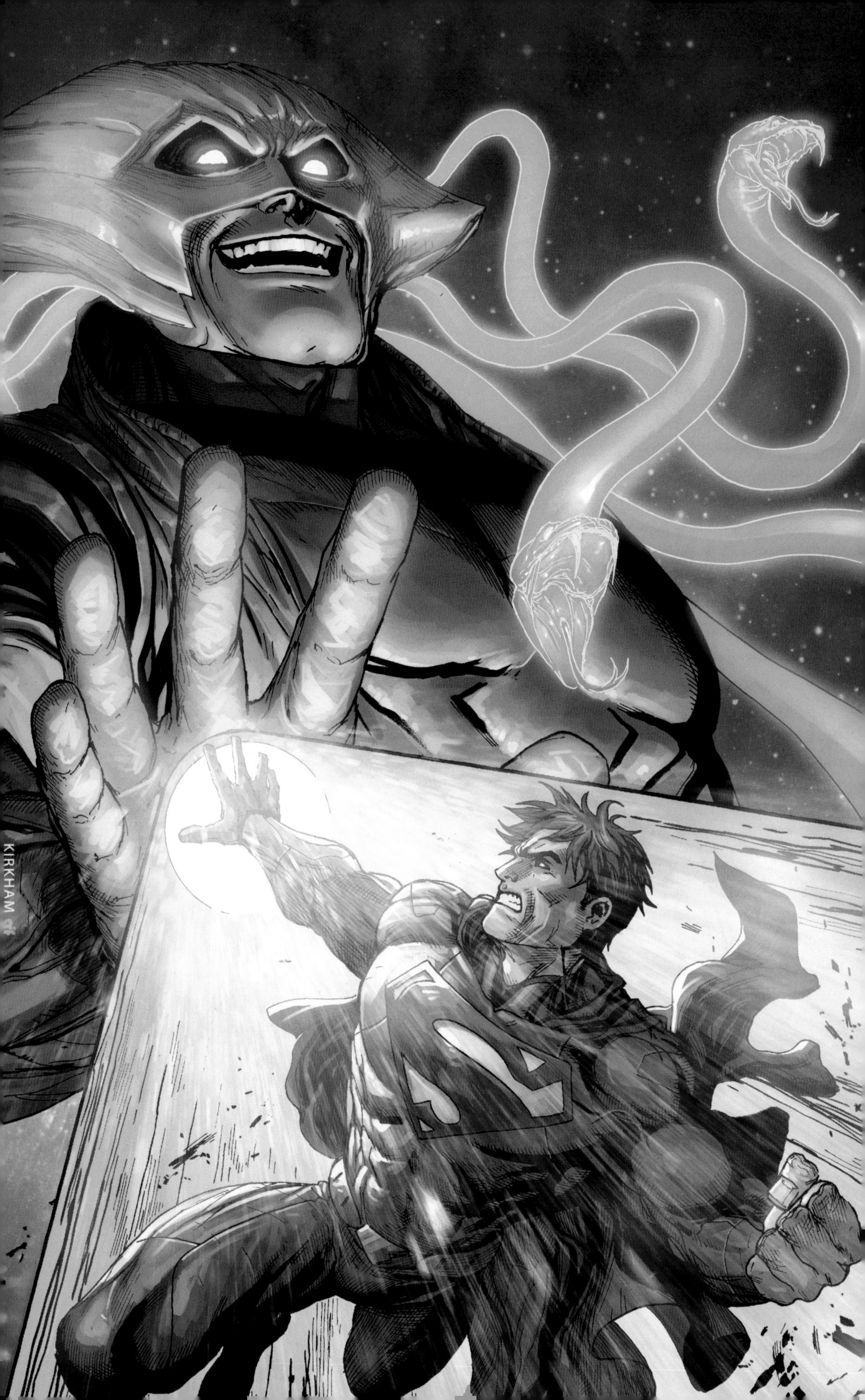
KIRKHAM

METROPOLIS GENERAL HOSPITAL.
PATIENT #61938.
NAME: LANE, L.

THERE WAS THIS--THIS *BURST* OF ENERGY AROUND HER, LIKE *FIREWORKS*--AND SHE SAID *ONE WORD*--

"*SUPERMAN*"!

MR. CAROL, MAY I SPEAK TO YOU OUTSIDE FOR A MOMENT?

I'M TELLING YOU, SHE WAS AWAKE ONE MINUTE *AGO*!

I KNOW IT SOUNDS *CRAZY*--

NOTHING ON THE MONITORS INDICATES ANY CHANGE IN HER CONDITION, MR. CAROL. SHE'S STILL *COMATOSE*.

YOU, ON THE OTHER HAND, HAVE BEEN KEEPING WATCH AT HER SIDE FOR *DAYS*...

EXACTLY--!

YOU *MISUNDERSTAND* ME. YOU'VE BEEN GOING WITHOUT SLEEP FOR *TOO LONG*.

THE MOST LIKELY EXPLANATION FOR WHAT YOU SAW IS THAT YOUR *MIND* WAS PLAYING *TRICKS* ON YOU.

YOU'RE WRONG, DOCTOR! I KNOW WHAT I *SAW*!

SHE'S COMING OUT OF HER COMA!

LOIS! *LOIS*, WAKE--

...UP...?

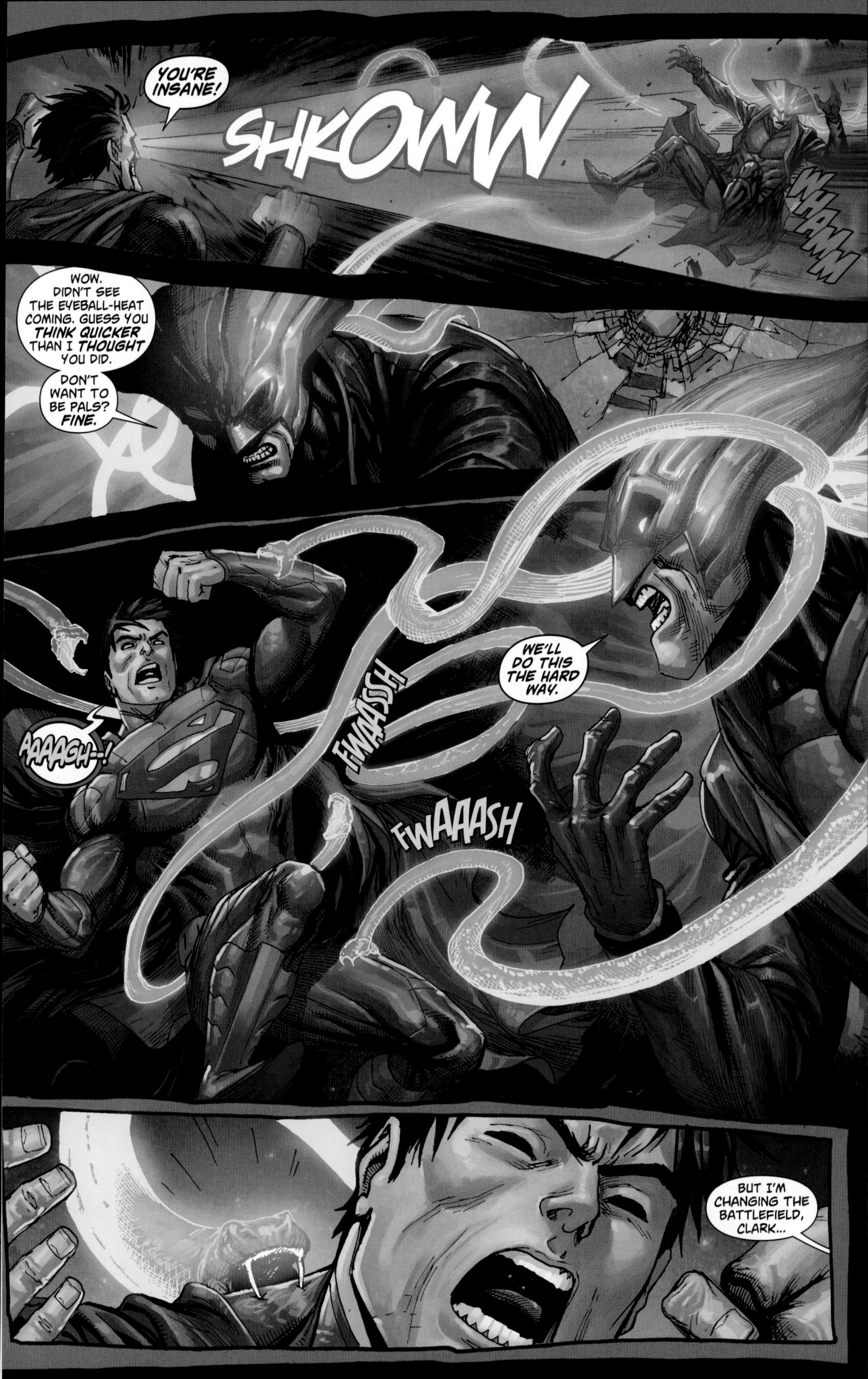
YOU'RE INSANE!
SHKOWW
WHAMM
WOW. DIDN'T SEE THE EYEBALL-HEAT COMING. GUESS YOU THINK QUICKER THAN I THOUGHT YOU DID.
DON'T WANT TO BE PALS? FINE.
WE'LL DO THIS THE HARD WAY.
AAAAGH--!
FWAASSH
FWAAASH
BUT I'M CHANGING THE BATTLEFIELD, CLARK...

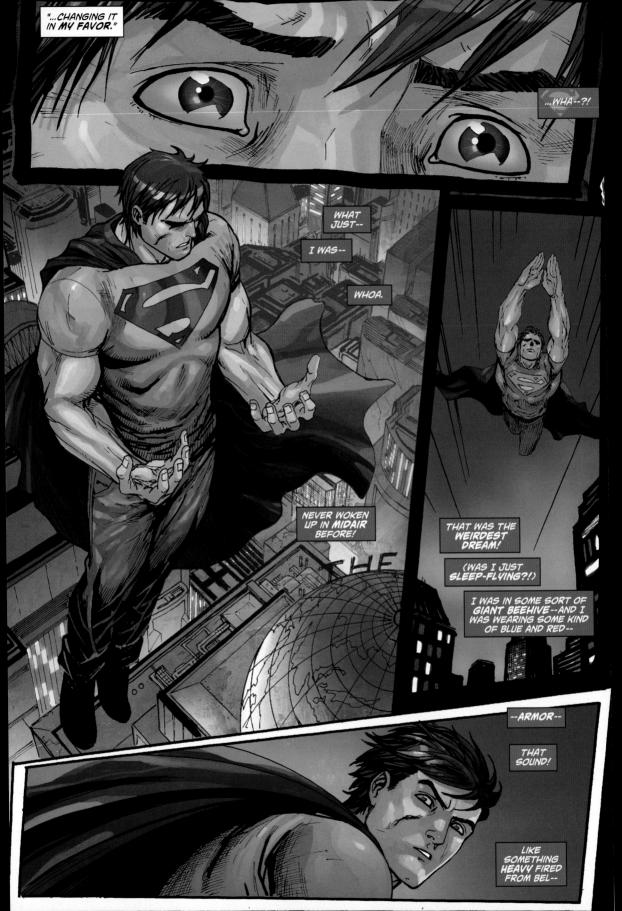

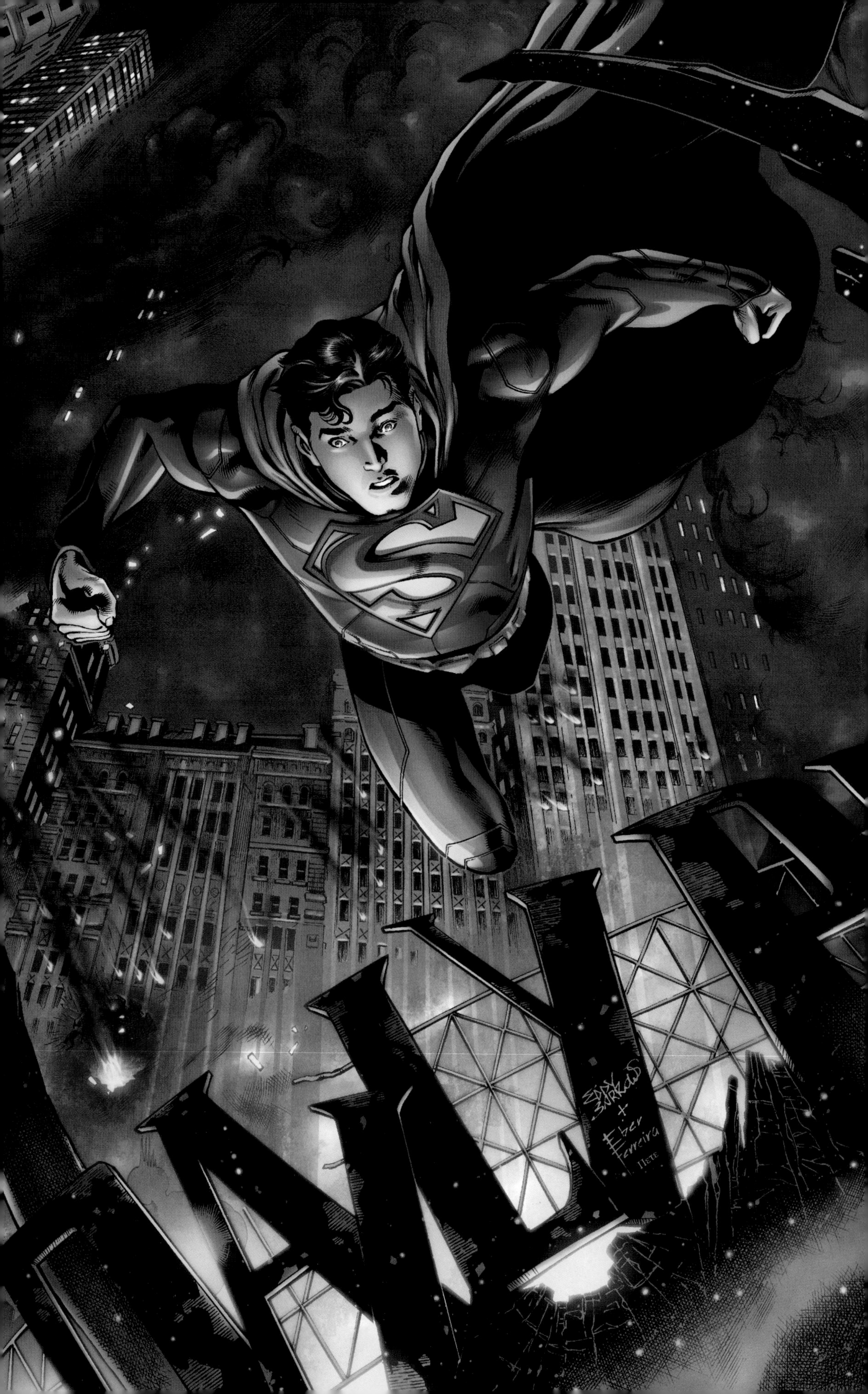
EDDY BARROWS
+
Eber Ferreira

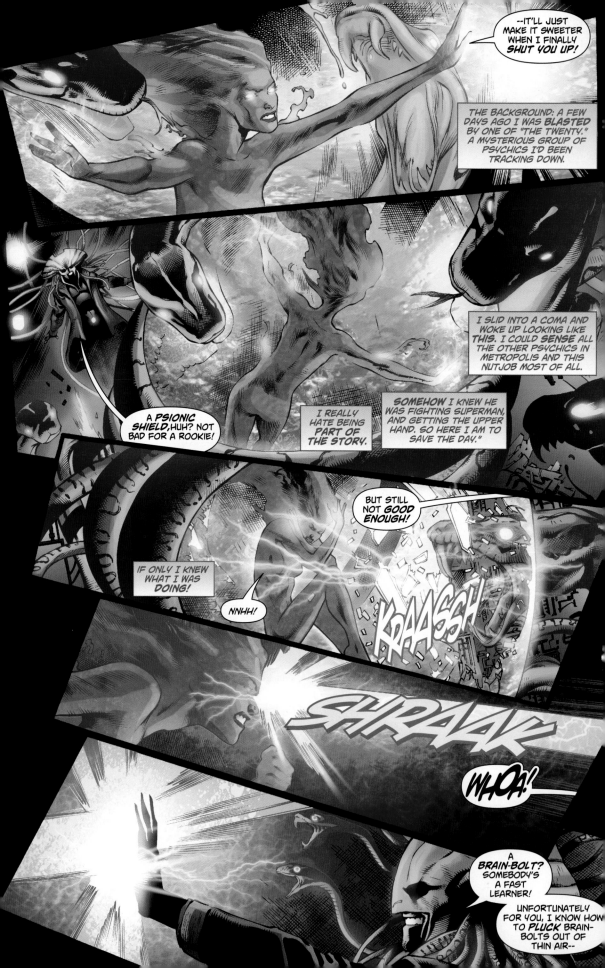

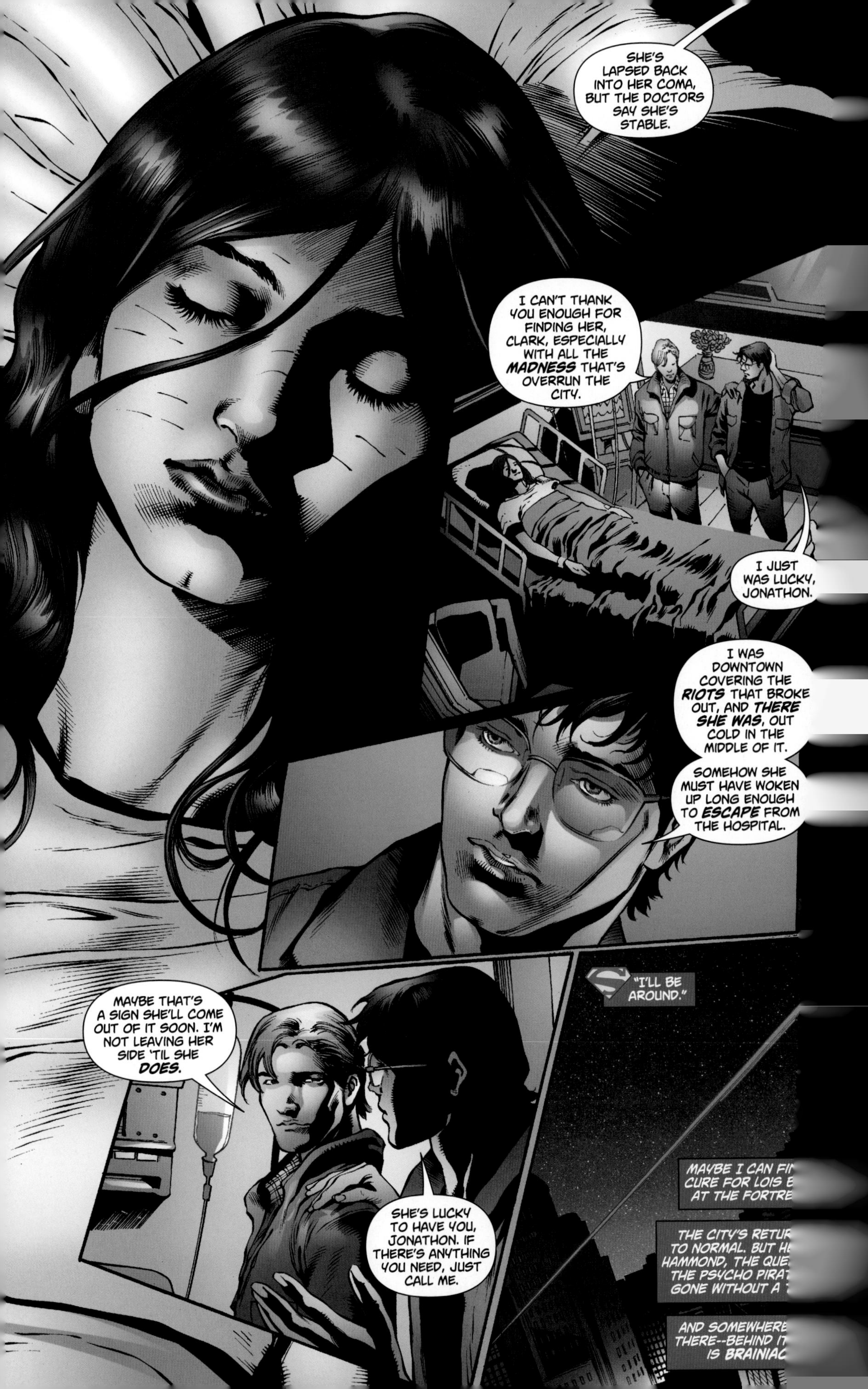
SHE'S LAPSED BACK INTO HER COMA, BUT THE DOCTORS SAY SHE'S STABLE.
I CAN'T THANK YOU ENOUGH FOR FINDING HER, CLARK, ESPECIALLY WITH ALL THE MADNESS THAT'S OVERRUN THE CITY.
I JUST WAS LUCKY, JONATHON.
I WAS DOWNTOWN COVERING THE RIOTS THAT BROKE OUT, AND THERE SHE WAS, OUT COLD IN THE MIDDLE OF IT.
SOMEHOW SHE MUST HAVE WOKEN UP LONG ENOUGH TO ESCAPE FROM THE HOSPITAL.
MAYBE THAT'S A SIGN SHE'LL COME OUT OF IT SOON. I'M NOT LEAVING HER SIDE 'TIL SHE DOES.
SHE'S LUCKY TO HAVE YOU, JONATHON. IF THERE'S ANYTHING YOU NEED, JUST CALL ME.
"I'LL BE AROUND."
MAYBE I CAN FI
CURE FOR LOIS
AT THE FORTRE
THE CITY'S RETUR
TO NORMAL. BUT H
HAMMOND, THE QUE
THE PSYCHO PIRAT
GONE WITHOUT A
AND SOMEWHERE
THERE--BEHIND IT
IS BRAINIAC

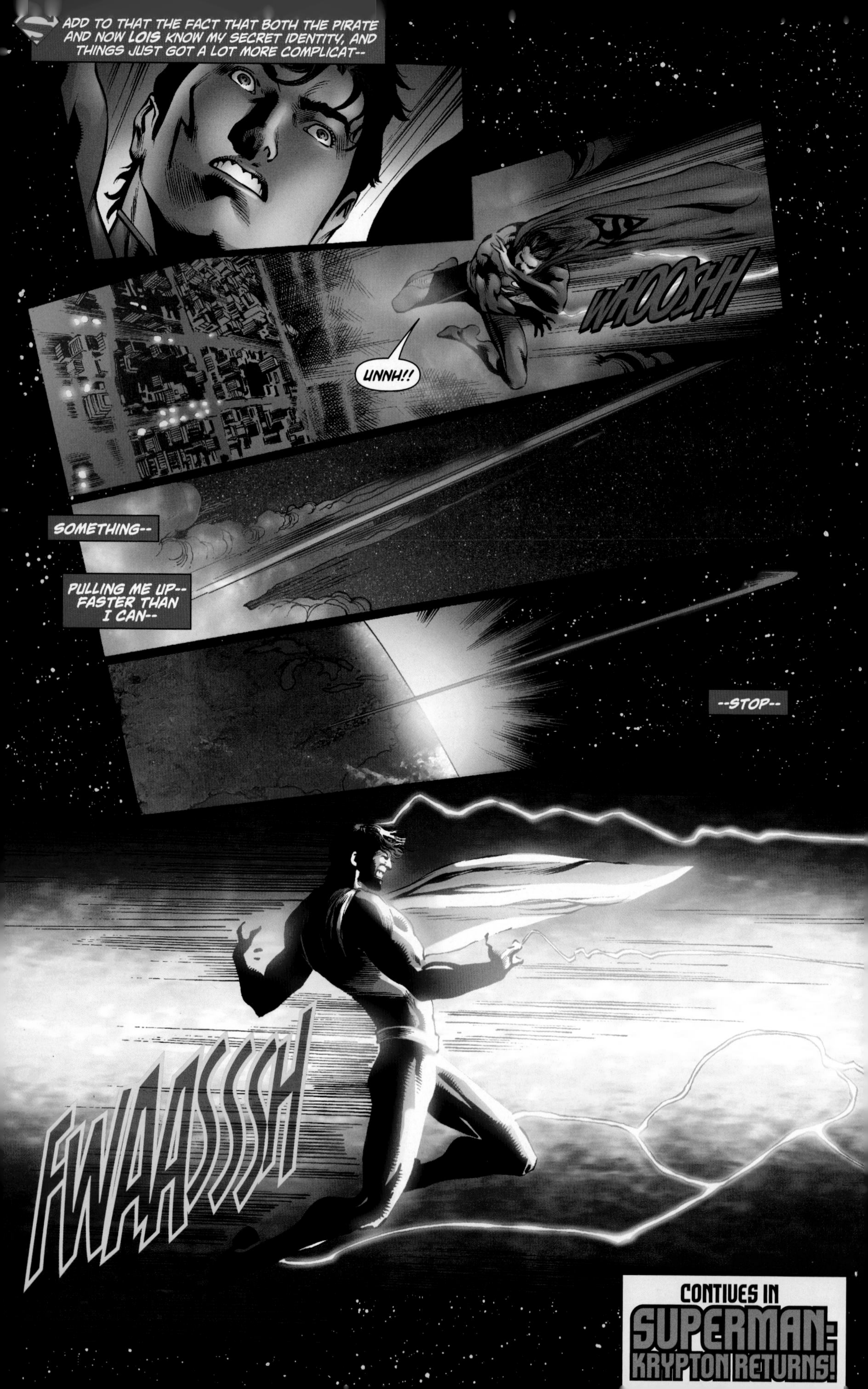
ADD TO THAT THE FACT THAT BOTH THE PIRATE AND NOW LOIS KNOW MY SECRET IDENTITY, AND THINGS JUST GOT A LOT MORE COMPLICAT--
WHOOSHH
UNNH!!
SOMETHING--
PULLING ME UP-- FASTER THAN I CAN--
--STOP--
FWAASSSH
CONTIVES IN SUPERMAN: KRYPTON RETURNS!

MAD variant cover for SUPERMAN #19
by John Caldwell & Carrie Strachan

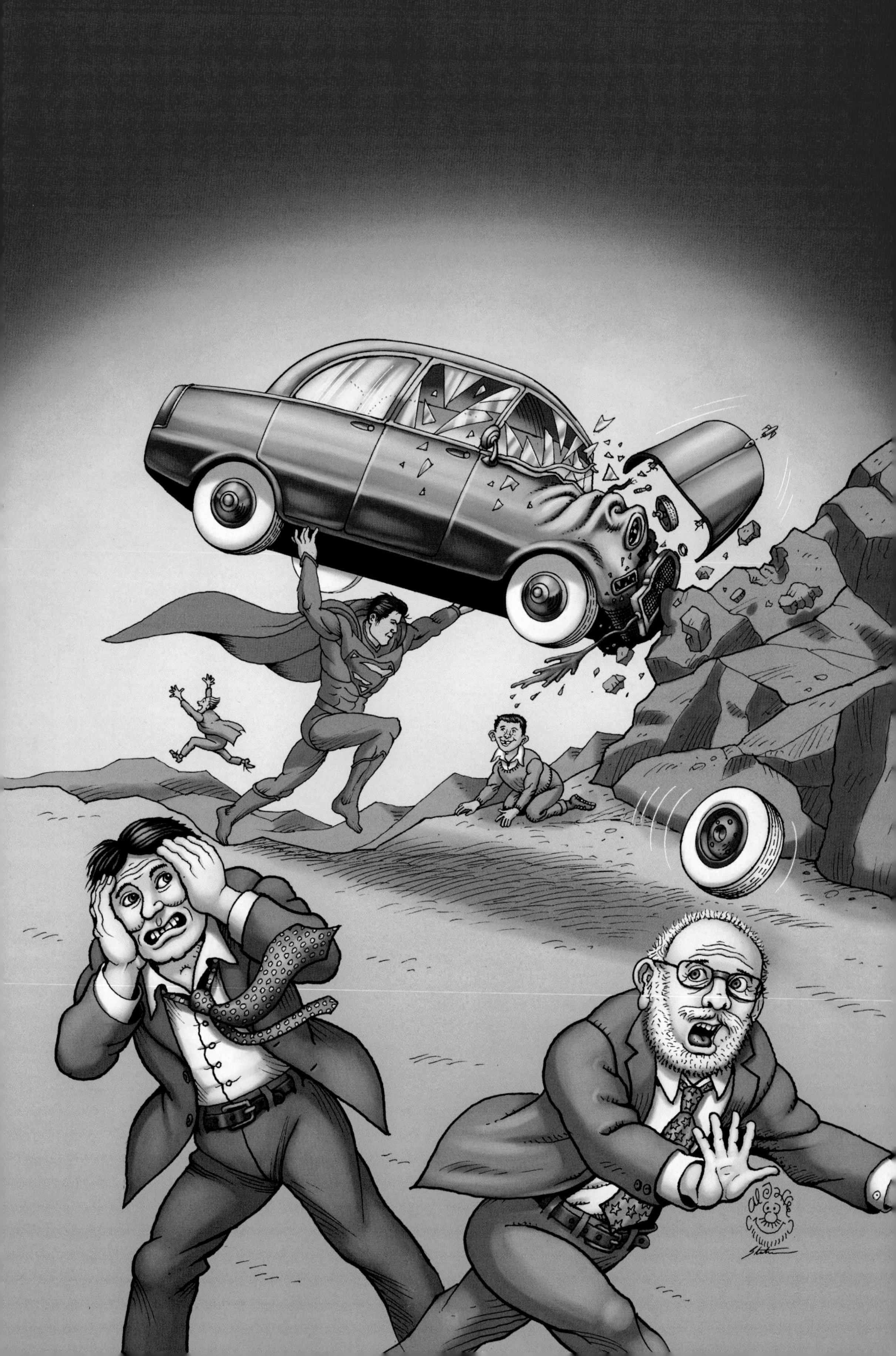

Full spread cover for SUPERMAN #19
by Kenneth Rocafort

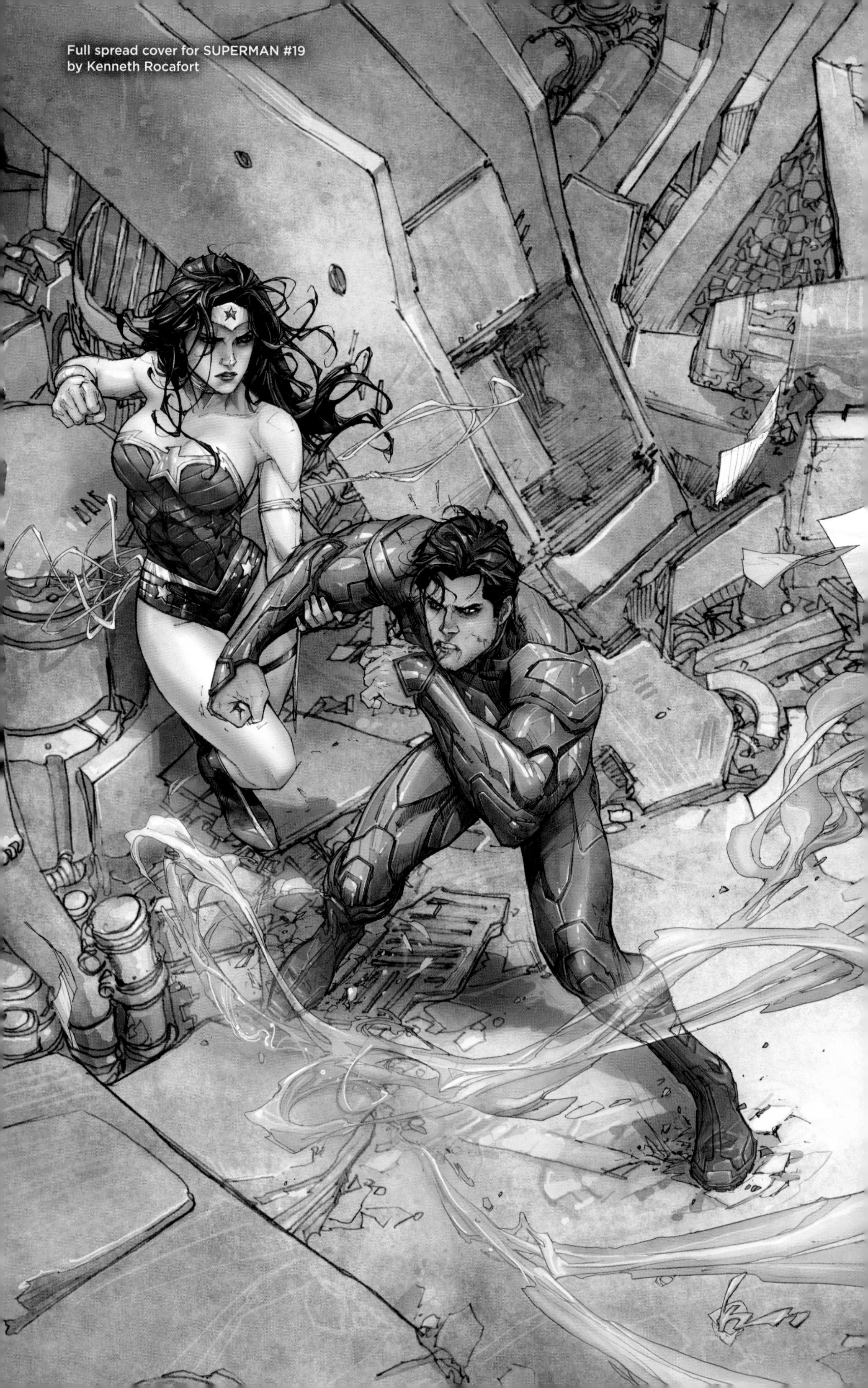

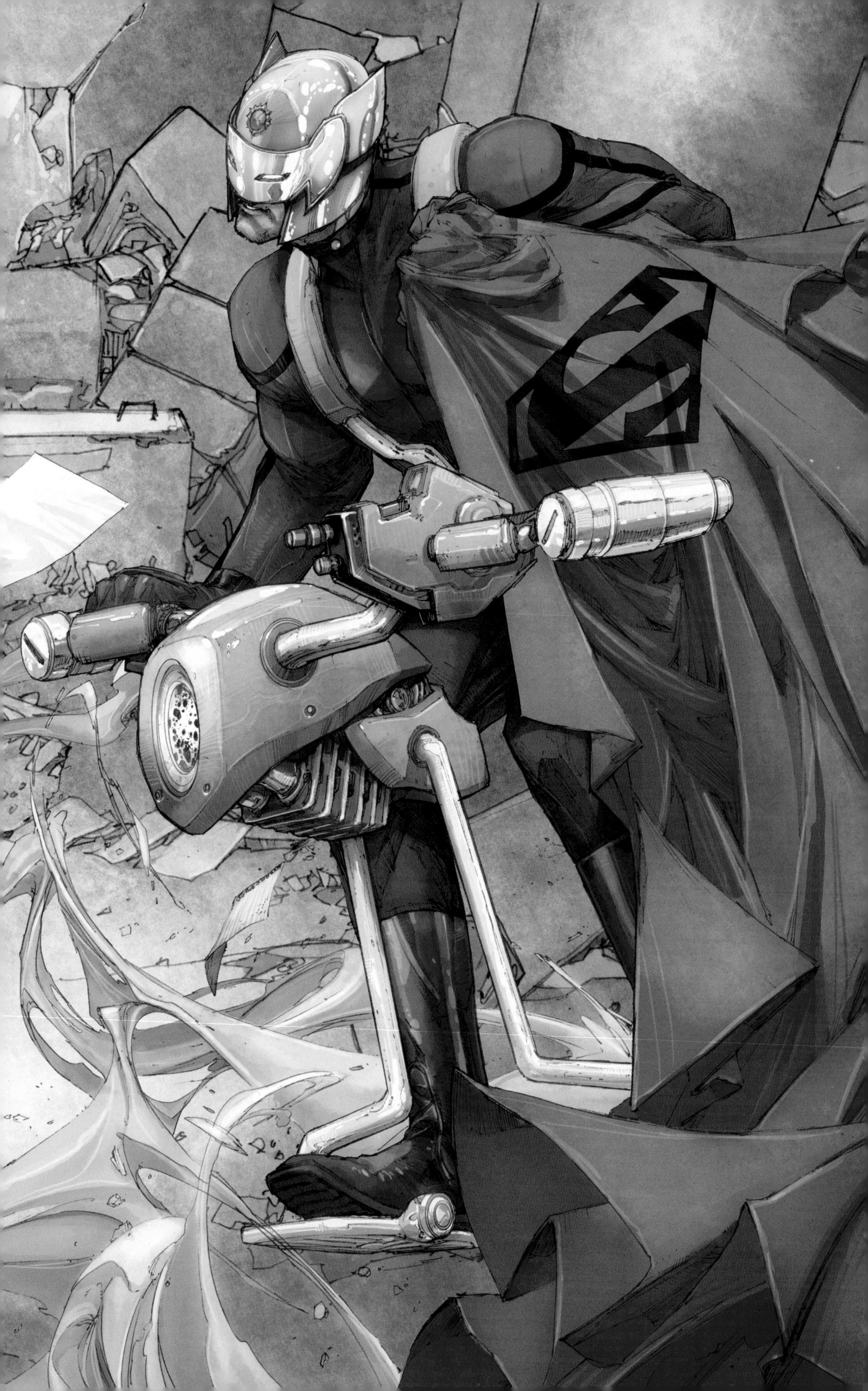

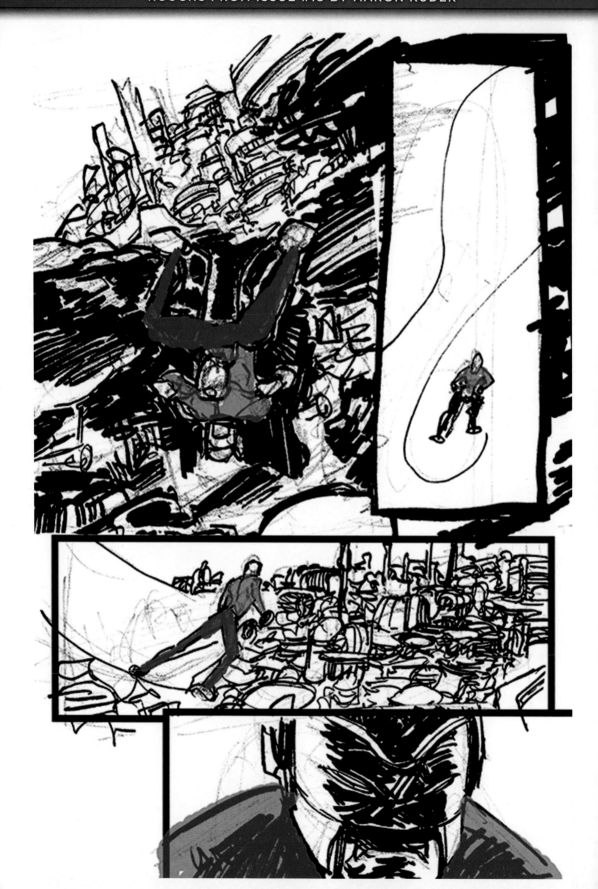

DC COMICS™

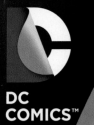

"Superman is still super."
—WALL STREET JOURNAL

"The SUPERMAN world is also one now where fans new and old, young and not-so-young, can come to a common ground to talk about the superhero that started it all."
—CRAVE ONLINE

START AT THE BEGINNING!

SUPERMAN VOLUME 1: WHAT PRICE TOMORROW?

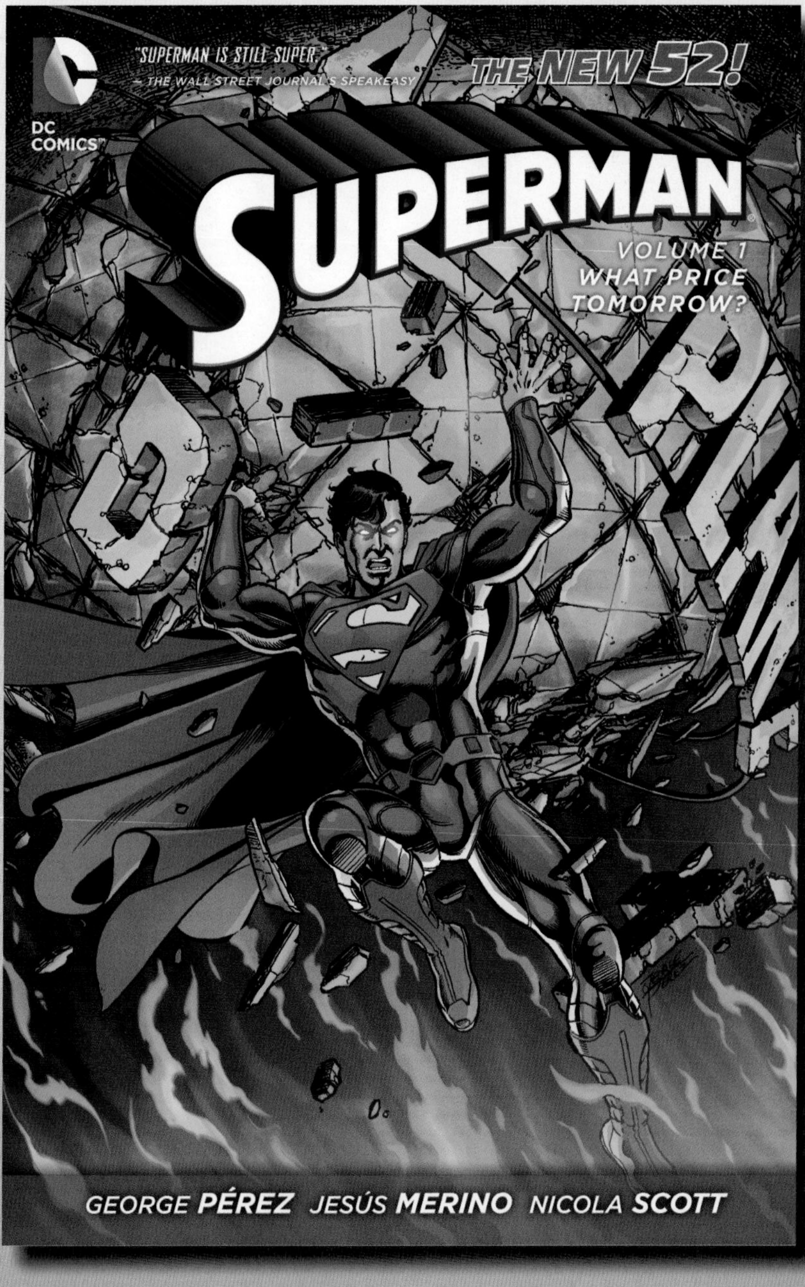
DC COMICS
"SUPERMAN IS STILL SUPER."
— THE WALL STREET JOURNAL'S SPEAKEASY
THE NEW 52!
SUPERMAN
VOLUME 1
WHAT PRICE TOMORROW?
GEORGE PÉREZ JESÚS MERINO NICOLA SCOTT

SUPERMAN VOL. 2:
SECRETS & LIES

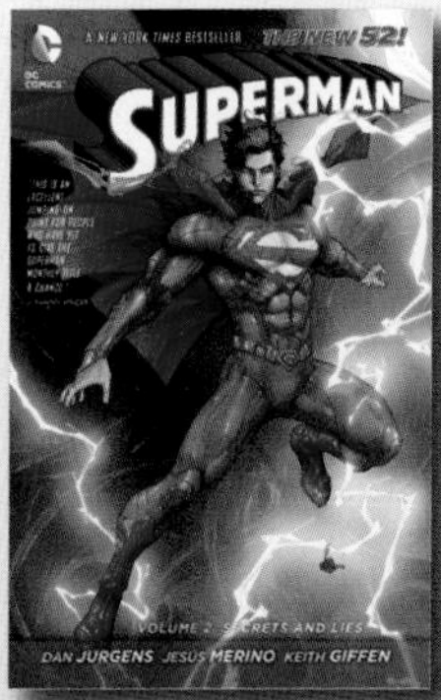
THE NEW 52!
SUPERMAN
VOLUME 2: SECRETS AND LIES
DAN JURGENS JESÚS MERINO KEITH GIFFEN

SUPERMAN VOL. 3:
FURY AT WORLD'S END

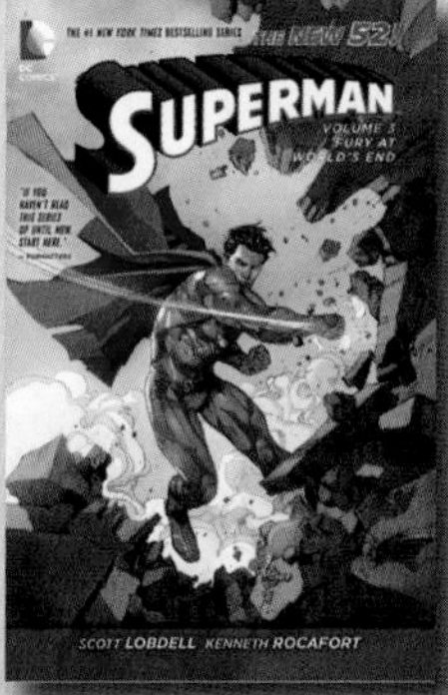
THE NEW 52!
SUPERMAN
VOLUME 3
FURY AT WORLD'S END
SCOTT LOBDELL KENNETH ROCAFORT

SUPERMAN:
H'EL ON EARTH

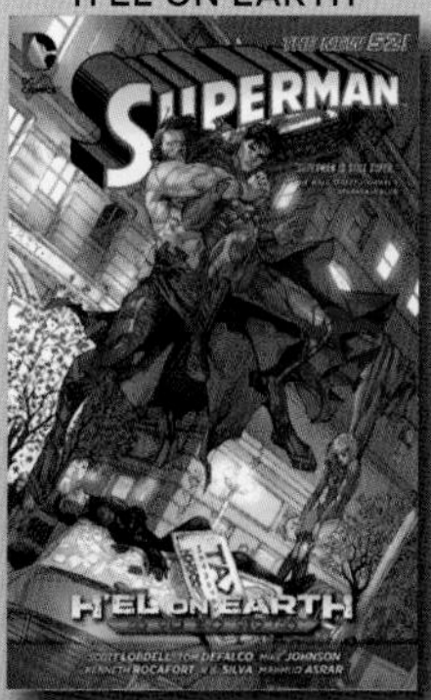
THE NEW 52!
SUPERMAN
H'EL ON EARTH

"ACTION COMICS has successfully carved its own territory and continued exploring Morrison's familiar themes about heroism and ideas."—IGN

"Casts the character in a new light, opens up fresh storytelling possibilities, and pushes it all forward with dynamic Rags Morales art. I loved it."—THE ONION/AV CLUB

START AT THE BEGINNING!

SUPERMAN: ACTION COMICS VOLUME 1:
SUPERMAN AND THE MEN OF STEEL

SUPERMAN:
ACTION COMICS
VOL. 2: BULLETPROOF

with GRANT
MORRISON and RAGS
MORALES

SUPERMAN: ACTION
COMICS VOL. 3: AT
THE END OF DAYS

with GRANT
MORRISON and RAGS
MORALES

SUPERBOY VOL. 1:
INCUBATION

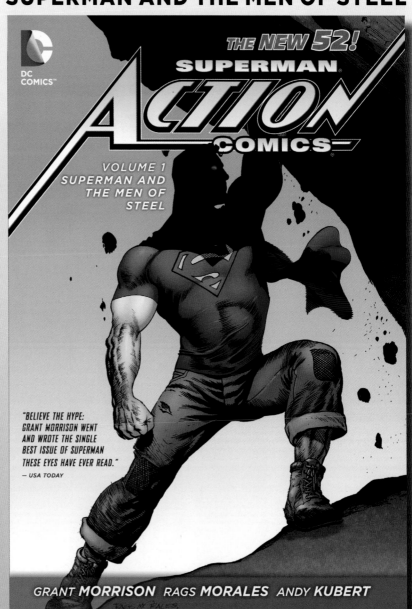

THE NEW 52!
DC COMICS™
SUPERMAN®
ACTION COMICS®

VOLUME 1
SUPERMAN AND
THE MEN OF
STEEL

*"BELIEVE THE HYPE:
GRANT MORRISON WENT
AND WROTE THE SINGLE
BEST ISSUE OF SUPERMAN
THESE EYES HAVE EVER READ."*
— USA TODAY

GRANT **MORRISON** RAGS **MORALES** ANDY **KUBERT**

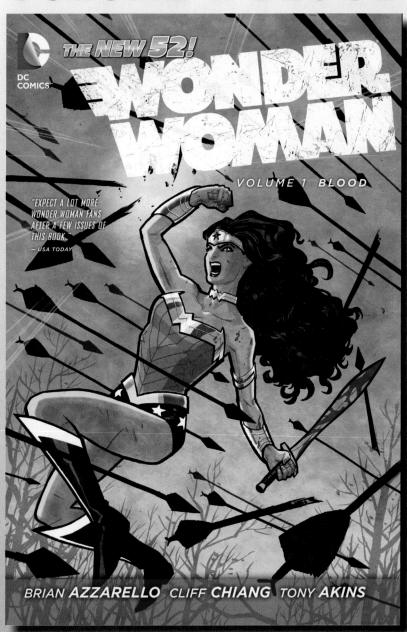

DC COMICS™

START AT THE BEGINNING!

WONDER WOMAN VOLUME 1: BLOOD

WONDER WOMAN
VOL. 2: GUTS

by BRIAN
AZZARELLO and
CLIFF CHIANG

WONDER WOMAN
VOL. 3: IRON

by BRIAN
AZZARELLO and
CLIFF CHIANG

SUPERGIRL VOL. 1:
LAST DAUGHTER OF
KRYPTON

"EXPECT A LOT MORE WONDER WOMAN FANS AFTER A FEW ISSUES OF THIS BOOK."
— USA TODAY

BRIAN **AZZARELLO** CLIFF **CHIANG** TONY **AKINS**

DC COMICS™

"Welcoming to new fans looking to get into superhero comics for the first time and old fans who gave up on the funny-books long ago."
—SCRIPPS HOWARD NEWS SERVICE

START AT THE BEGINNING!

JUSTICE LEAGUE VOLUME 1: ORIGIN

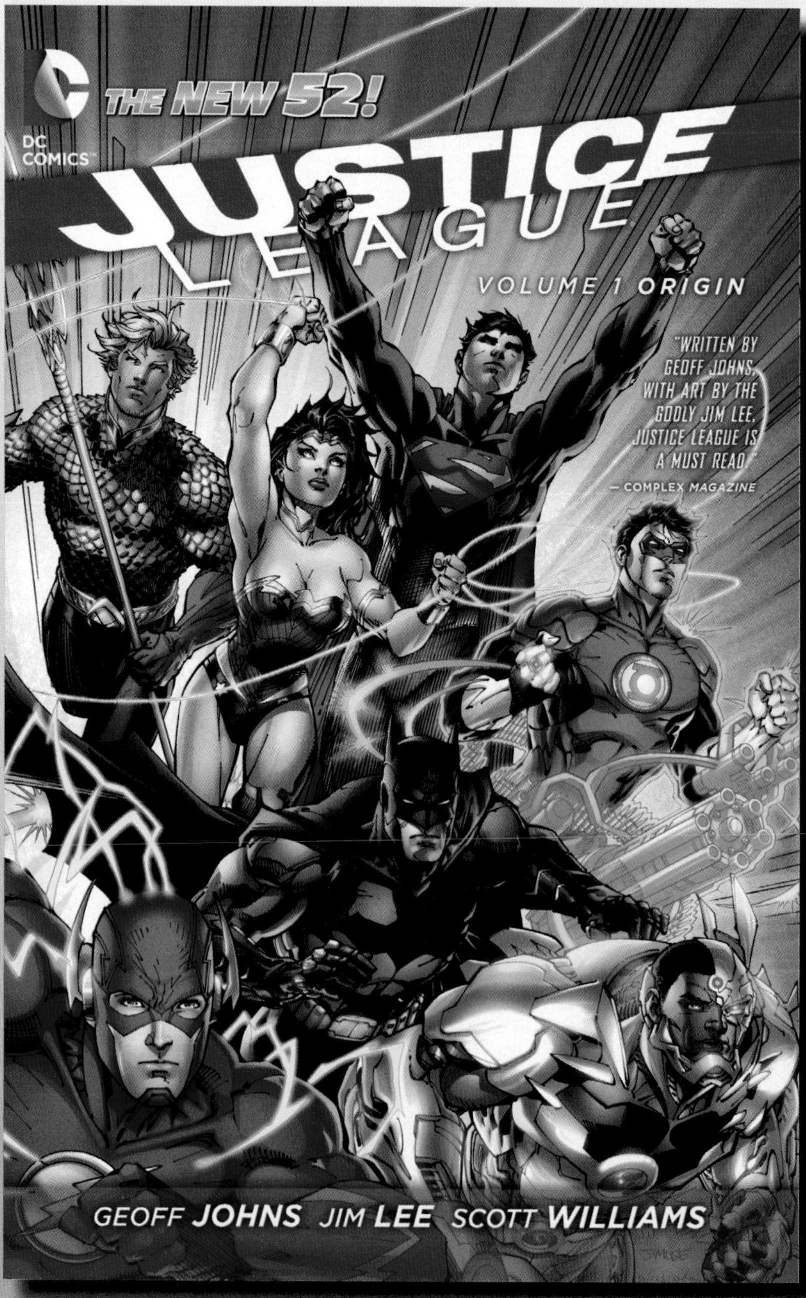
THE NEW 52!
DC COMICS
JUSTICE LEAGUE
VOLUME 1 ORIGIN
"WRITTEN BY GEOFF JOHNS, WITH ART BY THE GODLY JIM LEE, JUSTICE LEAGUE IS A MUST READ."
— COMPLEX MAGAZINE
GEOFF JOHNS JIM LEE SCOTT WILLIAMS

AQUAMAN VOLUME 1: THE TRENCH

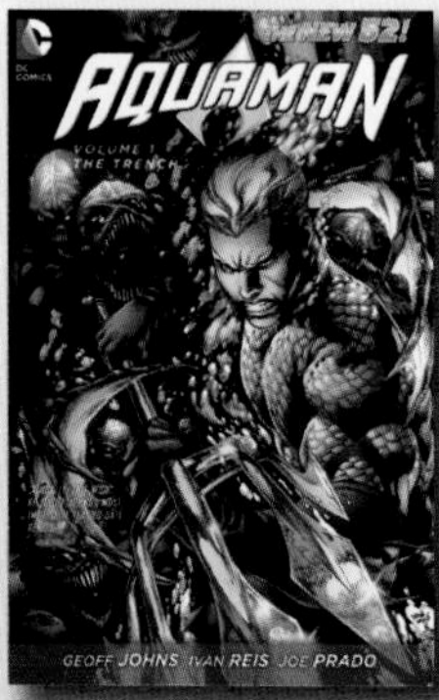
THE NEW 52!
AQUAMAN
VOLUME 1 THE TRENCH
GEOFF JOHNS IVAN REIS JOE PRADO

THE SAVAGE HAWKMAN VOLUME 1: DARKNESS RISING

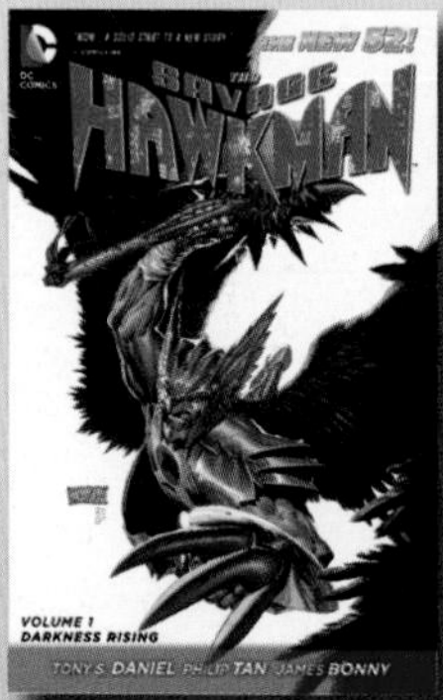
THE NEW 52!
THE SAVAGE HAWKMAN
VOLUME 1 DARKNESS RISING
TONY S. DANIEL PHILIP TAN JAMES BONNY

GREEN ARROW VOLUME 1: THE MIDAS TOUCH

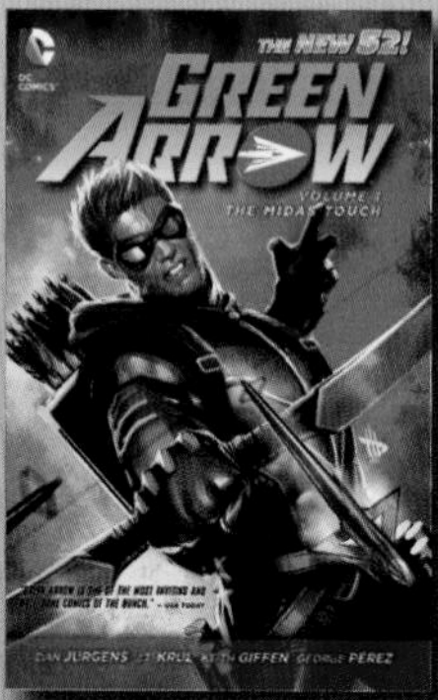
THE NEW 52!
GREEN ARROW
VOLUME 1 THE MIDAS TOUCH